# THE RISE AND FALL OF THE TEA PARTY

## AND HOW IT ELECTED DONALD TRUMP

# THE RISE AND FALL OF THE TEA PARTY

## AND HOW IT ELECTED DONALD TRUMP

MICHAEL SWARTZ

Gadsden flag image on front cover is public domain.
ISBN-13: 978-1-0937-6604-2

Dedicated to freedom fighters.

Matthew 5:14

# TABLE OF CONTENTS

# THANKLIST

It's well understood that an undertaking such as this doesn't happen in a vacuum, so there are a number of people to whom I want to express my gratitude for helping along the way. This is after I thank my Lord and Savior Jesus Christ, for as Rush Limbaugh often mentions our talent is "on loan from God."

The first pair to thank are my long-suffering wife Kimberley and her daughter Kassie, who watched me toil at my laptop for many nights and allowed me to complete this work. Now I hope they reap the rewards.

As far as the writing of the book goes, I need to thank those early TEA Party leaders who gave of their time and expertise to share their thoughts and experiences. A fair number of them were bloggers like myself who have (or had) kept their sites up as a historical reference, such as Keri Carender, Sandra Crosnoe, the late Shelli Dawdy (who passed away as I was writing this book), Erika Franzi, Michael Patrick Leahy, Eric Odom, and Phil Russo. However, I'm truly indebted to those from whom I received more direct input: that latter group includes Gary Aminoff, Eric Eisenhammer, Joan Fabiano, Michael Johns, Ralph Reagan, and Mark Williams. All of them aren't just great leaders, but great people in their own right.

There are two other inspiring people I need to thank before I close. One is Bob Densic, a longtime friend of mine who introduced me to the aforementioned Limbaugh's radio show in a workplace we shared which he dubbed the "Rebeldome." We only said it was called that because it was on the south side of the building, but we were the true rebels plotting against the excesses of government. In 2017 Bob finally got to enter the belly of the beast, as he was elected to the city council in his small Ohio town. Governing is the hard part, isn't it?

The second is Chris Lewis, the lead organizer of our Salisbury Tax Day TEA Party that got me started in the movement. He was just someone who found a way to make a difference – little did he realize his effort would bear fruit in this most unusual way. Despite my vote the last time he tried, Chris couldn't bring his philosophy to government.

In a collective sense, my final thanks is to all those who have supported my writing endeavors over the years from blogger to columnist to author for the second time, including those of you who bought this book. (I would be remiss in that writing realm to exclude the Eastern Shore Writers Association and The Writer's Allies social media group for their input and advice. They made this a better book than I could have.)

My hope is that you receive some large portion of the education I received about the TEA Party, the political process, and life in general in completing this book. Thank you, the reader, for coming along on this journey.

# INTRODUCTION

*I believe this movement, the Tea Party movement, has the opportunity to break the boom-and-bust cycle (of fiscal and political conservatism) and restore a constitutionally limited government and bring fiscal sanity to Washington.* - Dick Armey and Matt Libbe, *Give Us Liberty: A Tea Party Manifesto* (2010)

There was a day in my life that I recall as a cloudy, late-summer Saturday afternoon. But it was an afternoon spent in the company of thousands of wonderful people who came from every state in the union; a gathering of those who had the shared belief that the vague promises of change promised by the Presidential candidate who had won the election just ten scant months before weren't turning out to be the changes they were interested in making.

The number of people who descended upon the Mall in Washington, D.C. on September 12, 2009 has been subject to debate ever since the 9/12 Rally (also known as the Taxpayer March on Washington)[1] took place. Those who supported the TEA Party and its aims tended to state the number was over one million,[2] while naysayers pushed the number into the low six digits[3] – or even less.[4] But as one who was there, allow me to just say that it was more people than I had ever encountered in one place, before or since.

On that day, my journey to the 9/12 event was on a chartered bus that began its route near Ocean City, Maryland, stopping in the city of Salisbury where I live before working its way up Maryland's Eastern Shore toward our nation's capital. The Eastern Shore was ripe territory for a movement such as the TEA Party – as one of the few conservative bastions of the reliably Democratic state of Maryland, we on the Eastern Shore knew onetime Maryland Governor William Donald Schaefer wasn't necessarily joking when he called our part of the state the "shithouse."[5] The radical left turn of the Obama administration was a movie we'd seen over and over again, projected from our state capital of Annapolis as they ran roughshod over the interests of our rural communities in favor of those who lived across the Bay Bridge from us. We realized Chesapeake Bay wasn't just an estuary bisecting the state, but also the demarcation line between the more conservative lifestyle preferred by those on Delmarva and the liberalism associated with urban areas.

As we departed the bus and walked the remaining few blocks to the Mall, there was the sense that something historic was occurring. I think the closest metaphor I could relate would be that of walking into a packed major league baseball stadium just as the home team rallied in the late innings. The cheering came across to me almost as much as a wave of sound than the sound itself, and there was no question in my mind that our time had arrived. Surely we were a force to be reckoned with; a movement that I had only climbed aboard that April 15 when a rainy Salisbury joined hundreds of other cities in hosting a Tax Day TEA Party – fittingly enough, ours was held at the steps of our city-county government building.[6]

Before I get too far along here, though, I should bring you up to speed on the origins of this book you're holding and how I came to be a willing participant in the TEA Party.

My writing background has its roots as far back as creating a newsletter for the Republicans living in my precinct in Toledo, Ohio two decades ago. Eventually this talent went online after I moved to Maryland: I made a name as a political blogger focusing on state and national affairs, and some may have said back in the day I was a pretty fair writer. Yet by the time the TEA Party movement began, my life was undergoing a significant upheaval: after 22 years in the architectural field, my layoff the previous December had led me to a different avocation I was just starting out with that February. (On the other hand, the Santelli rant came just two weeks after my first date with my wife. Every cloud has a silver lining.)

So, while I was maintaining my blog, political activism wasn't foremost on my mind. However, I posted on the day he spoke out that I thought Rick Santelli would be the next guy on the unemployment line:

> I'm not sure how this guy is going to keep his job after what went on today. Mocking the all-important stimulus package on a cable network not named FOX?
>
> (At this point I embedded the Santelli video.)
>
> Rick Santelli is his name, and in many respects he's exactly correct. Why should I, a guy who's played by the rules and financed my home in a prudent manner, be the one who's left holding the bag?
>
> It's especially true now that I've gone into business for myself. If I succeed to any reasonable degree (which I have confidence that I will) all that may get me is a higher tax bracket. Is that the American Way?
>
> We have tried three different styles and types of stimulus packages now – first direct payments to the taxpayers, next bailing out the banks to create more credit, and now the Keynesian spending of government money to prime the economy. You can see on the bottom of the video in the occasional scroll that the markets REALLY love this – otherwise would they be scraping the bottom of the barrel at levels unseen in several years? And it's funny that no one is blaming Presidential

policies for the market tanking.

What do we do next if this latest stimulus doesn't work? Will there be any businesses left to create jobs? I don't want to find out but I'm afraid I will.[7]

Needless to say, my circumstances led me to declare a couple weeks later:

The best I can hope for is that the country's not in some sort of internal armed insurrection come 2013. I hold out exactly zero confidence that anything Barack Obama is doing will improve the economy in and of itself. Now we may bounce back to some extent simply based on the fact that pent-up demand can only be suppressed for so long but it's my contention that doing what Obama is doing will only lengthen the suffering. This stimulus was a bad idea under Bush and even worse under Obama because he's throwing more money at the problem!

The lack of confidence is signified by the utter collapse of the Dow Jones and NASDAQ markets, which have seen their overall value eroded by about 1/3 just since Obama was elected. That's billions or maybe even trillions in aggregate personal net worth, vanished in the proverbial blink of an eye. And while it's true that huge mistakes were made in the financial sector – mistakes which helped bring about the recession we now suffer from – I'm arguing that the steps government has taken to "solve" the problem will only make things worse down the road. Even our nation is not too big to fail.[8]

As you could guess, I was utterly frustrated and looking for any port in a storm. A few days later I received a press release in my e-mail that spelled out the first set of Tax Day Tea Parties (interestingly enough, it came from the Portsmouth Tea Company) which I reprinted as a blog post with some additional comments.[9] At the time I hadn't heard of one for my hometown of Salisbury, but sure enough a local TEA Party was brewing – I finally got word of it a week beforehand.[10]

Once we got together we had a lot of sound and fury during those heady days back in 2009, vowing that we would make the Washington insiders pay in the 2010 elections. Few students of conventional wisdom truly believed this turn of events could happen, but the TEA Party followed through and shocked the world when the Democratic Congressional majority – a majority that Bill Clinton's political adviser James Carville believed would once again be as long-lasting as the one that Democrats enjoyed for four decades before the Contract With America brought it all crashing down in 1994[11] – was instead wiped away in just four years by the midterm wave election of 2010. In turn, TEA Party regulars themselves assumed this midterm victory was just the first step in a generational political change.

Instead, the TEA Party movement has, at least outwardly, been shown to be just as fleeting and temporary as the Democratic majority in Congress was. As one who still believes in the TEA Party's mantra that we were Taxed Enough Already, I think it's almost criminal that a movement that had such promise lost its way. Since I also believe that we are doomed to repeat history unless we understand how we got into the situation in the first place, it compelled me to study the rise and fall of the TEA Party and perhaps give readers the idea of where we can go at a nadir when neither of the major-party Presidential selections in the 2016 election cycle when I began writing this seemed to have the faintest idea of how to limit government. For his part, Republican Donald Trump had a valid plan to lower taxes, but warned this modest change was just his initial negotiating point.[12] It was very likely that his rates would end up much higher, said Trump, the process more complex than the single-page form he initially promised working-class taxpayers.[13] (It turned out the future President was pretty much on the money in describing the events leading up to and the effects of the Tax Cuts and Jobs Act passed late in 2017.)

Trump's campaign, in my view, was the terminus of this stage of the TEA Party saga in spite of his surprising success, and the overriding question that needs to be answered now is how those who were part of the most conservative/libertarian political movement in over a generation (since Ronald Reagan's ascent to the presidency in the late 1970s) could turn around and back a candidate who supported Hillary Clinton's Senate campaigns,[14] had little idea of the workings of the Constitution,[15] and pledged to do nothing with some of the most fiscally troublesome aspects of government like Social Security and Medicare.[16] For many of those who made up the TEA Party the selection of Trump as a preferred candidate after his liberal predecessor was elected seemed to be counter-intuitive, although I think we had a valuable clue regarding those programs many see as entitlements. Yet the ascent of Trump is instructive on the true political leanings of the rank-and-file membership of the TEA Party, too.

While I'm arguing the story of the TEA Party as a useful and relevant conservative movement ended with the ascendance of the "alt-right" and the election of a populist in Donald Trump, I have to admit its legacy lives on in some of the most unlikely ways. At its most visible, consider one counter-balance left-wing reaction to Trump called the Indivisible movement and their insistence that their model of disruption for the Trump agenda is the TEA Party. From the *Indivisible Guide*:

> The authors of this guide are former congressional staffers who witnessed the rise of the Tea Party. We saw these activists take on a popular president with a mandate for change and a supermajority in Congress. We saw them organize locally and convince their own (members of Congress) to reject President Obama's agenda. Their ideas were wrong, cruel, and tinged with racism – and they won.
>
> If a small minority in the Tea Party could stop President Obama, then we the majority can stop a petty tyrant named Trump.
>
> To this end, the following chapters offer a step-by-step guide for individuals, groups, and organizations looking to replicate the Tea Party's success in getting Congress to listen to a small, vocal, dedicated group of constituents. The guide is

intended to be equally useful for stiffening Democratic spines and weakening pro-Trump Republican resolve.[17]

As the book unfolds, I'll delve deeply into the Indivisible narrative that the ideas of the TEA Party were "wrong, cruel, and tinged with racism." One disadvantage the TEA Party labored under was the fact that much of its media coverage came from journalists and reporters who could neither hide their agenda nor their displeasure that people in flyover country wouldn't embrace what these political experts thought was best for our nation: the policies of Barack Obama and his allies in the Democrat-controlled Congress. While the TEA Party movement was far from unblemished, neither was it simply a reaction based on "white privilege" or the fact that a President who identified as a black man (despite being of mixed parentage) was elected. In my opening chapters, you'll find that the roots of the TEA Party long predate the Obama presidency.

I don't think it's a stretch, though, to categorize the left-wing resistance to Trump as "wrong, cruel, and tinged with racism." Unlike the TEA Party, the progressive activists haven't been satisfied with the disruption of GOP Congressional members' town hall meetings or with their own gatherings in Washington, D.C. and other places around the nation. As the Trump presidency has progressed, their side has gained a number of less savory fellow travelers, most particularly radical members of the Black Lives Matter group that arose from the seeds of white-on-black police-involved shootings during the Obama administration and the "black bloc" or "Antifa" radicals who have devolved to violent and disruptive actions to put a heckler's veto on conservative or right-leaning speakers and gatherings. These counter-protestors were mostly missing during the heyday of the TEA Party, but with the inauguration of Donald Trump they were emboldened to come out of the woodwork as the resistance. So while Indivisible claims it's using the tactics of the TEA Party against the Trump administration, they've upped the ante significantly to a point where violence is becoming a new normal at political events. In certain areas and situations, it's become dangerous to be a Trump supporter at a "peaceful protest."[18]

There is a saying generally credited as an ancient Chinese curse: "May you live in interesting times." At the infancy of these most interesting political times, the 9/12 rally I attended was not just a high point of my political life, but it also seemed to be the highest swell in the tide of conservative protest activism. Some of the players who served as the "leaders" of what was a grassroots movement without a true standard-bearer have faded away, but others have become just the sort of entrenched inside-the-Beltway types they railed against during those early TEA Party days. To paraphrase The Who, the new boss has become the same as the old boss.

Michael Johns, who was one of the 22 participants in the original TEA Party conference call, noted in a retrospective he wrote in 2015 that, "All the Tea Party movement founders from (#TCOT originator Michael Patrick) Leahy's first conference call are impressive in their own ways, and have their own personal stories about what sparked their leadership in this now historical movement."[19]

I agree completely, and this leads to another aspect of my book: I wanted to get the perspective of those who were there at the beginning. In the initial, heady days of the TEA Party phenomenon there were about 100 activists who, it could be argued, got in on its ground floor. Just like those original investors in a company like Microsoft or Starbucks, a few parlayed their involvement into great fame and fortune but most who still believe in the ideals the TEA Party expressed are doing so far from the limelight. I believe those who have shunned the spotlight and weren't worried about who got the credit for positive change are the ones who will best tell the story of the rise and fall of the TEA Party because they were there at the beginning and exhibited the most passion about its ideals – more than most, these otherwise ordinary Americans lived and breathed this stuff but did so as a means to improve the land they love, not their bank accounts.

Fortunately, I was able to unearth a surprisingly large sample of their thoughts via their own writings at the time. I also reached out to many who were still active or willing to talk about that portion of their lives. To those out of that group who have chosen to share their thoughts and stories with me, I owe a significant debt of gratitude.

Most casual observers credit financial reporter Rick Santelli with the birth of the TEA Party because he coined the modern incarnation of the phrase. But its roots go back well prior to Santelli's February, 2009 rant, and even predate the election of Barack Obama. Indeed, the genesis of the TEA Party may be the handiwork of a longtime political gadfly whose son was a beneficiary of the movement a few years later. But even that beginning point came as a result of influential men and women who passed on well before the TEA Party rose in the last decade, and my aim is to sift through all those tea leaves and make sense of it all as this modern-day tea party came into being, developed into what seemed like an unstoppable political juggernaut, then just as suddenly became the subject of scorn as it slid into the irrelevance that ended with many of its most passionate leaders backing a candidate who was accused of working against the movement when it was at its peak of power.[20]

This, then, is the story of the rise and fall of the TEA Party. May it be only a short time before it rises from the ashes of history because we need it more than ever.

# ORIGINS AND INFLUENCES

*Before our rights are lost, we must work to change the policies of 70 years of government interventionism. And the longer we wait the harder it will be.* - Ron Paul, *Mises and Austrian Economics: A Personal View* (1984)

On February 19, 2009, CNBC reporter Rick Santelli passionately criticized the idea of paying for his neighbors' mortgages via a proposed government program called the Homeowners Affordability and Stability Plan live on the floor of the Chicago Mercantile Exchange. While they had little to do with taxes, Santelli's on-air remarks fired up the group of traders working that day, leading him to exclaim, "We're thinking of having a Chicago Tea Party in July! All you capitalists that want to show up to Lake Michigan, I'm going to start organizing!"[1] To most Americans, what became known as "Santelli's Rant" or "The Rant of the Year" has also come to be considered the beginning of the TEA Party movement.

Santelli's diatribe, spoken as it was in the midst of the Great Recession, struck a chord with Americans who were taken aback by the developments of the previous two years. These remarks addressed a president in Barack Obama who, like his predecessor George W. Bush, was overly fond of taxpayer-funded solutions to private-sector problems. Even as Bush was considered a politically moderate-to-conservative Republican, his admission a few months earlier that, "I've abandoned free-market principles to save the free-market system"[2] in order to bail out General Motors and Chrysler set the table for people to be angry about what they considered a meddling federal government exerting too much influence on the economy. The fact that it was the government – and not the overall economic market – that was selecting which businesses and industries were "too big to fail" rubbed a lot of people the wrong way. Through most of our nation's history, spanning wars, economic panics, and depressions, there was no such thing as "too big to fail" in America until the 2008 financial market catastrophe. Fortunes had been made and lost for decades and the federal government stayed away. But not this time.

Months before Santelli spoke out, at a point when the 2008 presidential election was looming, the economy was in a state unseen in decades. Aside from a few bumps in the road, such as the mild recession in 1991 then-candidate Bill Clinton falsely called the worst economy in the last 50 years,[3] the slight hiccup thanks to the tech bubble bursting and worries about Y2k issues in the late 1990s, and even the uncertainty in the months following the 9/11 attack, the American economy had been more or less steadily prospering since the early 1980s. The Reagan tax cuts of 1981 and 1983 set the job market on a course where new employment peaked at over 1.1 million new jobs for the month of September, 1983, and overall employment increases of 300,000 or more per month were common during the Reagan years. (Bear in mind, too, that the labor force of the day was roughly 2/3 of its present size – 300,000 then would be equivalent to well over 400,000 now.) Even the tax increase pushed through in 1993 by President Clinton didn't fully derail the American economic train – although it was one factor in the Newt Gingrich-led Republican takeover of the House of Representatives in 1994 after an unprecedented four straight decades of party control in the grasp of Democrats. No longer would Republican leadership have to apologize from the actions of their more activist backbenchers[4] because those activists were now the leadership.

While the Gingrich revolution was an earnest try at reining in the size and scope of government – and became the catalyst for a brief spell of years where the federal budget was considered in balance – by the turn of the millennium Republicans began proving they were just about as careless with taxpayer money as the Democrats were. So despite an economic boom fueled by post-9/11 wild speculation and rapid appreciation in the real estate market and aided by the Bush tax cuts in 2001 and 2003 which assisted in unemployment dropping under the 5% mark economists at the time considered full employment, the Jack Abramoff campaign finance scandal and a War on Terror gone sour allowed the Democrats to regain the majority of Congress in 2006. And yes, that passing of the gavel back to Nancy Pelosi and Harry Reid occurred just in time for the housing market to collapse.

When the housing bubble burst – as was bound to occur sooner or later – thousands of construction jobs vaporized with it. Eventually the trouble in that sector wormed its way through the economy through higher overall unemployment, while plunging values in the housing market pinched homeowners who had counted on the equity they had built up, thanks to continually rising home prices, to backstop the second and third mortgages and refinancing they had done as they wagered their home's value would continue its upward climb and give them still more equity. As the economic house of cards built up by the false increase in home values continued to implode, by December, 2007 America was officially declared to be in a recession.[5]

Unlike the smaller bumps in the road we had managed to overcome in the previous quarter-century, this sharp downturn would come to be known as the Great Recession. As venerable financial institutions over-leveraged by easy credit and risky investments in mortgage-backed securities fell by the wayside, there was the palpable fear this recession would usher in a replay of the 1930s. Panic in the financial markets led the federal government to take unprecedented steps to bail out private sector enterprises they deemed could not collapse, resulting in historic levels of deficit spending.

A large source of that spending came from earnest but misguided and basically unsuccessful attempts to avoid Great Depression 2.0. Beginning in 2008 Uncle Sam tried to goose the slowing economy with a number of Keynesian ideas as a means of "stimulus."

One solution proposed by President George W. Bush came in the form of a direct payment to millions of Americans. In the spring of 2008 over $150 billion[6] was sent out as an advance of the tax refund most Americans would eventually receive later that year. Not only did this stimulus package arouse the wrath of conservatives, the modest payments did little to assist those who were jobless and already behind on bills. And instead of spending the money to boost the economy by purchasing goods and services as the Bush administration had hoped, nearly half of those recipients surveyed used the advance simply as a means of catching up on overdue bills.[7] It may have been great for bill collectors, but the guy laid off from the steel mill wasn't getting the benefit of demand for his product.

Later that summer, as Wall Street and the American financial system in general were believed to be teetering on the precipice of collapse, the target changed. Rather than hand out a few hundred billion to the taxpayers, the Bush administration and Congress felt compelled to spend $700 billion on what became known as the Troubled Asset Relief Program, or TARP for short. This money was intended to purchase the mortgage-backed securities rendered all but worthless by the housing crash. (As it turned out, "only" $431 billion[8] was dispersed before the program was deemed closed in 2014. Resale of the assets allowed the government to get away with a small net loss of $24 billion.)

For his part, Dick Armey, then head of FreedomWorks, believed that TARP fight was the real beginning of the TEA Party. Of course, it was all their doing, too:

> In retrospect, September 29 (2008, the day of a failed House vote on the TARP bill) is clearly the day the Tea Party movement was reborn in America…
>
> There was a massive wave of spontaneous grassroots outrage that rose up against the government's proposed actions, temporarily taking back the people's house from the political elite. While FreedomWorks, our tiny coalition of like-minded organizations, and a handful of true blue legislators toiled away, surrounded on all sides by the Beltway establishment, the citizens of America – for a few days at least – took their country back.[9]

Seeing the failure of that refund advance program and the unpopular bailout of

Wall Street with the TARP scheme, incoming President Barack Obama campaigned and won the 2008 election by promising a broad agenda for "hope and change" aimed squarely at frightened Americans who were worried more about their economic security than the principles of liberty or disadvantages of increasing the size and scope of government. It was more than enough for an overwhelming electoral victory over Senator John McCain, the hapless Republican nominee who could not escape the unpopularity of President Bush and his ongoing wars in Iraq and Afghanistan, or the fatigue common with Americans grown restless after one party controls the White House for two terms. (In a tribute to his legacy, Ronald Reagan continues as the only President to escape that pattern in the postwar era, with his popularity even after two terms allowing Vice President George H.W. Bush to succeed him in the Oval Office.)

Days before he took office, President-elect Barack Obama warned Americans that, "I don't believe it's too late to change course, but it will be if we don't take dramatic action as soon as possible. If nothing is done, this recession could linger for years."[10] Obama's attempt at fixing the economy was a much larger and broader package of federal spending than Bush proposed. The American Recovery and Reinvestment Act of 2009 (ARRA), which simply came to be called the "stimulus" bill, included a grab bag of tax cuts, direct payments to states, and some investment in infrastructure that as originally proposed would total $787 billion, with subsequent tinkering pushing the package past the $800 billion mark.

In his remarks proposing the bill, which came just as the incoming Congress was setting to work in early January, the President-elect said, "There is no doubt that the cost of this plan will be considerable. It will certainly add to the budget deficit on the short term."[11]

"It is true that we cannot depend on government alone to create jobs or long-term growth," continued Obama, "but at this particular moment, only government can provide the short-term boost necessary to lift us from a recession this deep and severe."[12] The Democratic-controlled Congress worked quickly to pass the ARRA and it was signed into law on February 17[13]– just two days before Santelli's impromptu commentary.

Despite the belief from Washington that a mortgage assistance program filled the needs of thousands of Americans who were having difficulty with their mortgage payments, Santelli's criticism of the latest in what had become a growing list of big-government solutions to private-sector problems echoed the concern of millions of Americans. Those nationally televised remarks, made as a spur-of-the-moment gut reaction to yet another likely Keynesian failure, were the same being made with less fanfare by all those who understood that a government big enough to provide for your every need was also the government that could take it all away in the blink of an eye. In their view, our nation was rapidly approaching the point where too many among us were becoming too dependent on government as the provider of their sustenance. That cross-section of skeptical Americans was the nucleus of what became known as the TEA Party.

But prior to the TARP battle joined by FreedomWorks, and before the Obama campaign and its promise of "fundamental change" for our republic began to gather much steam – and draw opposition from the forgotten men and women in middle America – there was already a liberty-based movement which reflected many of the principles that eventually guided the TEA Party, and its leader was a longtime critic of federal government influence and policies.

Ron Paul was first elected to Congress in a special election in 1976 to finish the unexpired term of a Gerald Ford federal appointee: an election he lost initially in a jungle primary but won five weeks later in a runoff. Paul served just six months, only to be ousted in seeking a full term in November, 1976 by his earlier special election opponent. (He lost by just 268 votes out of nearly 200,000 cast.) Undaunted, Ron avenged his defeat two years later, returning to the House fold for three terms beginning in 1979 – stepping away for an unsuccessful run for the U.S. Senate in 1984 – and came back for a third stint in 1997. In the second interregnum Paul ran for President as the Libertarian Party nominee in 1988.

One might consider Ron Paul more of a career politician than the Founding Fathers intended – although he balanced that with a long-standing practice as an obstetrician – but his advocacy for small government, an isolationist foreign policy, and a general reputation as a contrarian[14] who was often among a small group of dissenters to otherwise popular feelgood legislation that, in his view, didn't pass muster with the idea of limited, Constitutional government (for example, being the lone vote against a House resolution commemorating the 40th anniversary of the Civil Rights Act in 2004,[15] claiming it "did not improve race relations or enhance freedom")[16] made him a hero to the pro-liberty movement.

With that in mind, Ron Paul formally announced a second run for the White House in March, 2007, but this time seeking the Republican nomination.[17] His was a campaign driven by passionate people who were quick to support him financially but didn't have the sufficient physical numbers to regularly boost his polling out of the single digits. Because Paul had such diehard supporters, his modest electoral success in the 2008 Presidential race came primarily from the states which held caucuses rather than primary elections.

However, when it came to raising money through small donations, Ron Paul was the undisputed champion in the 2008 primary season. Using an online presence with great success, he was one of the first national candidates to engage in a "moneybomb" strategy of fundraising, with an event timed for the birthday of the legendary English anti-government figure Guy Fawkes on November 5, 2007 raising $4 million.[18] (A stylized version of Fawkes' face with its pencil-thin mustache is what you see on the masks worn by the "Anonymous" hacktivists and other protestors.) Based on that success, it was clear that another fundraiser would be a good idea.

That second "money bomb" eventually was set on another commemorative date: the anniversary of the Boston Tea Party on December 16. Naturally it was dubbed the Ron Paul Tea Party of 2007.[19] It turned out to be a smashing success, eclipsing the single-day fundraising mark set by Paul with his first "moneybomb" a month earlier – as well as the more conventional fundraising effort by John Kerry the day after he won the Democratic nomination in 2004 – by taking in over $6 million.[20] Yet Paul supporters also used the occasion to do their own re-creation of the Boston Tea Party, dropping symbolic tea chests into Boston Harbor and creating an event that featured several speakers. One Boston speaker was Ron's son Rand, who would eventually be elected to the Senate from Kentucky two years later and make his own presidential bid in 2016.

Because of the Boston namesake event, many of Paul's libertarian acolytes like to take credit for beginning the TEA Party – and they certainly can stake their claim.[21] [22] But to consider the origins of the TEA Party we also have to look at two separate but complementary ideas from the more distant past: first, the principles of life and liberty that led to the very founding of this nation and, secondly, the influence on the economic side of the equation derived from the Austrian School of economics and its disciples such as Milton Friedman and Ludwig von Mises.

The nation that became the wealthiest and most powerful among nations was born as a response to the tyranny of a distant king. Using the inspirations of ancient Greek and Roman democracy, the English *Magna Carta* and parliamentary system, and the belief that mankind was endowed by its Creator with certain inalienable rights, a small group of men steered the development of a nation unlike any other in the world at the time. And while the original Boston TEA Party would be considered a revolutionary act against the British Crown which occurred because a threepence tax on tea was placed on colonies unrepresented in Parliament, it occurred 16 months before the first shots of the actual American Revolution were fired a few miles away in Lexington.

Shortly after that initial skirmish, in July, 1775, the Continental Congress adopted the *Declaration of the Causes and Necessity for Taking Up Arms*, a treatise written by John Dickinson and Thomas Jefferson:

> With hearts fortified with these animating Reflections, we most solemnly,

> before God and the World, declare, that, exerting the utmost Energy of those Powers, which our beneficent Creator hath graciously bestowed upon us, the Arms we have been compelled by our Enemies to assume, we will, in defiance of every Hazard, with unabating Firmness and Perseverence, employ for the preservation of our Liberties; being with one Mind resolved to die Freemen rather than to live Slaves.[23]

But the resentment of the overbearing governance of the Crown that led to the American Revolution had built up over a number of years beforehand. For example, John Adams famously wrote on his objections to the Stamp Act in 1765,[24] while Benjamin Franklin, after a brief moment of support early on, openly flouted the levy[25] and testified against it to Parliament in February, 1766.[26] Thomas Jefferson outlined a series of complaints as part of the outline of the rights of "British America" in 1774,[27] while Thomas Paine published his pamphlet *Common Sense* a few months after the Revolution began in February, 1776.[28] All desired to have the yoke of tyranny removed from the American colonies, but even after independence was won at the cost of nearly a decade of struggle with the British and their allies, there was still the fear that in our independence we had simply replaced one bad system of government with another based on the Articles of Confederation that served as our nation's original rules of the road. Unlike the Constitution which would come later, the Articles provided for a fairly weak federal government run at the behest of the states.[29]

Eventually this loose binding of the colonies had to be replaced, and over the course of the spring and summer of 1787 delegates from twelve of the thirteen colonies worked out our Constitution and the root of our present form of government. When some feared the new Constitution would result in an overly powerful federal government – despite the checks and balances written into the original document – it was amended with the familiar first ten amendments known as the Bill of Rights. These initial ten amendments came along a few years after the original was written, in 1791. (Two other proposed amendments did not make the cut of being ratified by a sufficient number of states, although one stipulating that Congress could not increase their salaries until an election had intervened was eventually ratified two centuries later as the 27th Amendment.)

We know that both our Declaration of Independence and Constitution have the inspiring language of all men being created equal with certain inalienable rights endowed by our Creator. But the TEA Party brought with it a long-overdue resurgence of interest in our founding documents, with one example being a pamphlet I acquired called the *TEA Party Primer*: it had the Declaration of Independence, Articles of Confederation, the Constitution, and a number of related documents including a discussion of the Constitutional convention in the summer of 1787. To read and study this particular tome would probably be the equal of a mid-level college course, yet it was a subject that suddenly piqued the interest of thousands of like-minded Americans during the first few months of the TEA Party.

Just as the original Tea Party focused on a levy the American colonists felt was unfair, the modern-day equivalent was based on TEA as an acronym for Taxed Enough Already. So we return to Ron Paul, whose idea of economic policy was based on the Austrian model that contrasted with the Keynesian school most prevalent in our government. Paul made news with his prediction of the housing bubble that created the Great Recession years before the fact,[30] but even before that, in a pamphlet he wrote in the mid-1980s called *Mises and Austrian Economics: A Personal View*, Paul stated his reason for seeking a seat in Congress in the first place was to influence policy with the ideas of Austrian School economist Ludwig von Mises:

> I decided to run for Congress because of the disaster of wage and price controls imposed by the Nixon administration in 1971. When the stock market responded euphorically to the imposition of these controls and the closing of the gold window, and the U.S. Chamber of Commerce and many other big business groups gave enthusiastic support, I decided that someone in politics had to condemn the controls, and offer the alternative that could explain the past and give hope for the future: the Austrian economists' defense of the free market. At the time I was convinced, like Ludwig von Mises, that no one could succeed in politics without serving the special interests of some politically powerful pressure group.
>
> Although I was eventually elected, in terms of a conventional political career with real Washington impact, he was absolutely right. I have not developed legislative influence with the leadership of the Congress or the administration. Monies are deliberately deleted from routine water works bills for my district because I do not condone the system, nor vote for any of the appropriations.
>
> My influence, such as it is, comes only by educating others about the rightness of the free market.[31]

While the more modern incarnation of this theory is neatly summarized in the bumper sticker slogan "Taxation is Theft," the principles behind the Austrian School treat taxation as something that both retards the potential for economic growth[32] and creates, in a never-ending contest of "can you top this?" an incentive for more creative ways for entrepreneurial individuals to avoid paying and for government to come up with new and different revenue schemes and streams. For example, despite all the heinous crimes reputed gangster Al Capone was accused of committing, the one which put him in prison was tax evasion.

To further buttress this point, a significant part of Austrian economics can be traced back to works relatively contemporary to the era of our nation's birth: Adam Smith's *The Wealth of Nations* was first published in 1776 while Jean-Baptiste Say's *A Treatise On Political Economy* came out in 1803. It's notable that our Constitution originally had a prohibition on direct taxation that was eliminated by the Sixteenth Amendment; thus, our nation spent most of its first 150 years using other means of sustenance. Implementation of income taxes were attempted at various points within that time frame, but they did not become Constitutionally valid until 1913 when the Sixteenth Amendment was ratified.

In the ensuing decades after its passage, the income tax moved from a toll on the exceedingly wealthy of the era to a headache average Americans must endure every spring.[33] As the government's appetite for revenue increased, the earnings of more and more Americans were ensnared by Uncle Sam at increasing rates. Not only that, beginning in 1943, the midst of World War II, the government re-instituted backup withholding as a permanent way to make sure it was paid first, before you could take home a dime of your check. If you were fortunate enough, you could get all you paid in and then some at the time you filed your taxes – but don't expect interest on the loan you gave the government!

Was it any wonder people were frustrated with the situation?

It wasn't until Ronald Reagan came to office that we at least began the downward trend in income tax rates that has held for the last three decades; arguably the Reagan-era supply-siders were just borrowing a facet of Austrian economics to make their case about lower tax rates increasing economic growth.[34] Yet the taxation problem wasn't necessarily confined to the federal government because state and local levies were on the rise; meanwhile, the Keynesian solutions applied to the Great Recession meant even more deficit spending, which in turn raised the prospect of the federal government either taxing us overtly through higher rates, changes in tax brackets, or elimination of so-called "loopholes" (such as consecutive presidents Reagan, Bush 41, and Clinton did) or taxing us covertly by inflating its way out of debt.

And as if the concern about the specter of perpetual deficit spending wasn't enough, those most interested in the role our government played in their everyday lives worried that President Obama's policy proposals and philosophy of government would lead us to a world not unlike the fictional characterization in Ayn Rand's dystopian 1957 novel *Atlas Shrugged*,[35] where entrepreneurs and producers were hounded by a government interested in fairness at the expense of innovation – just swap out Net Neutrality for the patent for Rearden metal and our energy industry for the railroads Dagny Taggart struggled to maintain and the novel's premise can indeed be modernized.

Ayn Rand didn't contemplate the exact alphabet soup of agencies that exerted greater and greater influence on state and local governments as well as private business, but the idea of *The Strike* (as her novel was originally called) was echoed by the reluctance of employers to expand to a staffing level that would put them in the crosshairs for Obamacare or by the disappointment of the worker who gets his annual COLA raise only to see it eaten up by a higher tax bracket and increased health insurance costs. It seemed as if we had entered a time when no good deed went unpunished and government just didn't care. Lamented writer and TEA Party organizer Michael Patrick Leahy:

> The deliberative accountability of the seventeenth-century New England town meeting was nowhere to be found in modern America. In its place stood a cynical system in which elected political officials spoke words they didn't believe to secure the votes of people they wouldn't listen to after the polls closed, in order to maintain the power that benefited themselves and the special interest groups that gave them the funds to maintain their power.[36]

With all these influences, factors, and concerns at work, the powder keg of frustration was set for the spark Rick Santelli created with his impromptu remarks on the Chicago Mercantile floor. But anxious Americans throughout the country and from many walks of life decided on their own they couldn't wait until July to continue this movement – in fact, they already had their own gatherings in the works.

# TRULY ORGANIZING FOR AMERICA

*"I gather I'm the father of the Tea Party."* - Barack Obama in his farewell address, January 10, 2017.

It's likely that fewer than 100,000 Americans were watching CNBC's *Squawk Box* when Rick Santelli called for his tea party along the shores of Lake Michigan, and many among them drinking their morning coffee probably didn't begin to pay attention until the traders in the background reacted as strongly as they did. By the time the business day ended, though, millions had heard about what went on that morning as the word about "Santelli's Rant" spread on the World Wide Web. Much of that internet audience applauded the honesty in Santelli's remarks and expressed their agreement with his sentiment, but there were a fair number around the nation who went further, taking the TEA Party idea Santelli promoted and running with it.

A common perception – one that's become common because there's a grain of truth to it – is that government works slowly because they have to go through a plethora of steps and labyrinth of bureaucracy in order to get things done. Just ask yourself how long it takes them to patch up a pothole on your street, for example, then imagine it magnified to a scale of thousands as the federal government tries to solve problems America's (and sometimes the world's) citizens claim to be victimized by.

In this grand scheme of government, preservation of one's livelihood seems to be Job One so things which deviate from that scheme don't become priority items. And that creates a paradox: every problem government solves obviates the need for the department, bureau, or administration put in place to take care of it, so you get such phenomena as "mission creep" in order for the Gordian knot of bureaucracy to remain tied. Thus, the ship of state doesn't change course readily and those steering it try to avoid these corrections as best they can.

On the other hand, look at the private sector and the power of motivation for a cause. In this particular case, February hadn't come to a close yet when the first post-Santelli TEA Parties were put into the annals of history. In just a few days organizers turned their protest plans into action and drew sizable crowds in a number of major cities. Granted, anyone can plan a protest march or gathering at any time, but having the sore subjects of a stalled economy and a government seemingly clueless about the correct methods to address the problem meant the turnout was bound to be more than just the usual activists, complainers, and cranks. Nor did it hurt to have an alternative media looking for newsworthy items; an outlet organizers employed to fantastic effect.

Among the first organizers of the protests which became the template for a local TEA Party were two people who didn't fit the standard image eventually created by the media. To the mainstream press locked in their Washington-New York axis worldview, the picture of the average TEA Party event organizer came to be one of a middle-aged pot-bellied white male; a hayseed, rural redneck blue collar working man with a gun rack in the crew cab of his pickup truck. This composite organizer's protest wasn't over government, but in the minds of the media was rooted instead in the racism of opposing our newly-elected first black president. In reality, though, these two women who organized these precursor events to the TEA Party were more like the rest of us: one squarely from the Baby Boom generation and the other born at the tail end of Generation X. Working independently of each other on opposite sides of the country, their one piece of commonality was a distrust of the direction this nation was being led in.

Our first organizer was modest in her goals. Florida transplant Mary Rakovich was a furloughed engineer who had moved south from Michigan with her husband to take care of her family. Fresh off a FreedomWorks training session she had completed mere weeks before, she found out President Obama was coming to her part of Florida to promote the stimulus on February 10, 2009. Rakovich took action by organizing a small protest – small, but vocal enough to land her on Fox News that evening. Seventeen days later, she assisted with the first group of TEA Parties and continued to grow her group as the months went on.[1]

Out on the Left Coast, Keri Carender was an Oxford-educated housewife and mother who spent her spare time as a blogger who went by the pseudonym "Liberty Belle." Carender had already contemplated ways to gather conservatives in her area together[2] and just days prior to "Santelli's Rant" had organized a rally near her Seattle home against the "Porkulus" bill. While the pet name created by Rush Limbaugh for the American Recovery and Reinvestment Act was cute, in truth ARRA turned out to be yet another misguided attempt to stem the economic bleeding. And while Keri was pessimistic about her chances of success in stopping the bill, she felt she had to start the ball rolling:

> Make no mistake, the President will be signing that bill tomorrow, I have no illusions that he will actually listen to us. BUT, maybe, just maybe we can start a movement that will snowball across the nation and get people out of their homes, meeting each other and working together to redirect this country towards its truly

radical founding principles of individual liberty and freedom. Maybe people will wake up slowly at first, and then quickly when they realize the urgency needed.[3]

Needless to say, the newfound attention to the limited-government cause spurred Carender to redouble her efforts: she was another organizer in the first TEA Party wave that occurred eight days after Santelli's broadcast.

But Rakovich and Carender was far from alone. In the days leading up to and immediately following the signing of the ARRA, there were other protests against its effects in Denver, Fort Myers, Florida, and Mesa, Arizona – the latter two coordinated to occur during an Obama visit to promote the stimulus bill. Rakovich traveled across the country to participate in the Arizona protest as a show of support.

All these individuals and groups seized on an undercurrent of political pressure which had began to form even before the 2008 election was completed. Because Ron Paul had done so well with the Boston Tea Party theme, there were already a number of like-minded groups kicking the idea around. In New York state, a January, 2009 protest against a soda tax saw a local Young Americans for Liberty chapter dump soda into the Susquehanna River as their preferred means of protest.[4] (YAL was the successor to the various student groups promoting Paul's 2008 presidential campaign.) A few weeks later, independently of each other as well as the eventual TEA Party, both part-time stock trader Graham Makohoniuk and investment website operator Karl Denninger renewed the old idea[5] of mailing tea bags to Congress.[6] Stephanie Jasky, a frustrated Michigan paralegal and reader of Denninger's website, ran with that thought[7] by sending a tea bag to all 535 members. (That symbolism may have influenced Santelli a few weeks later as several of the Chicago Mercantile traders who were members of these various groups had tea bags adorning their workspaces.)[8] [9]

Nor did it hurt the cause when nationally-known conservative blogger and journalist Michelle Malkin became a key cheerleader for the early events spotlighting opposition to the stimulus bill, writing on the first modest protest by Mary Rakovich in Ft. Myers, Florida[10] (as noted, a counter to an Obama rally)[11] as well as the subsequent gathering of opponents organized by Keri Carender in Seattle.[12] That event was held on February 16, three days before Santelli's remarks and the day before the ARRA was, as Carender predicted, signed by President Obama. Subsequent events were held in Malkin's hometown of Denver the next day[13] and in response to another Obama appearance[14] on February 18 in Mesa, Arizona.[15]

Malkin did her part in promoting the first wave of TEA Parties, but there was plenty of behind-the-scenes action that only came out later. A "Time Line"[16] of the TEA Party pointed out that the idea was already in place in Chicago before Santelli spoke out at the Chicago Mercantile Exchange: the Illinois Libertarian Party had only a week before set up a "Tea Party Chicago" Facebook page, presumably to carry out the idea they'd spent months discussing internally as their own.[17] Yet it's likely that, had Santelli never spoken out, the Illinois Libertarian event would have been all but forgotten by now, just as the earlier Tea Party-style events which drew very little attention outside their local area were. (Nor would there be the need for this book.)

But in less than 48 hours post-Santelli, there were several competing websites and groups trying to organize more stimulus protests – opposition that could now be packaged under a TEA Party banner.

Among the first was #TCOT organizer Michael Patrick Leahy, who quickly amassed several like-minded organizations that would later evolve into key segments of one of the first organized TEA Party umbrella groups. In a blog post (which likely was his press release as well) Leahy wrote on the afternoon of February 20:

> Online conservative activists have rallied to CNBC's Rick Santelli's call yesterday, backed by mortgage traders, for a "Nationwide Chicago Tea Party" to protest the Obama Administration's bailout plan.
>
> Moving quickly, Top Conservatives on Twitter, Smart Girl Politics, the #Dontgo movement, Americans for Tax Reform, the Heartland Institute, and *(The) American Spectator* Magazine joined forces to announce a "Nationwide Chicago Tea Party," to be held on Friday, February 27 at noon EST.
>
> The tea party will be held simultaneously in Chicago, Washington DC, at dozens of locations around the US, and on Twitter, using the #teaparty hashtag.
>
> Santelli's criticism of the Obama mortgage plan is that it rewards the irresponsible, while penalizing the responsible.
>
> As co-founder of Top Conservatives on Twitter, I believe it is very important that all conservatives move quickly and in collaboration to hold this event. In today's world, the life cycle of political events moves very rapidly. There's momentum out there surrounding Santelli's call to protest yet another ill-advised bailout of yet another group that has made bad decisions.[18]

In a related move, the NationwideChicagoTeaParty.com domain[19] was registered on February 21 by Eric Odom, a Chicago-based libertarian online activist who the summer before had spearheaded the Twitter hashtag campaign called #Dontgo (which Leahy referred to in his release) urging Congress to stay and deal with high gasoline prices by eliminating restrictions on oil exploration.

On a separate front, the TaxpayerTEAParty.com domain was quickly registered by Americans for Prosperity,[20] a group that was rooted in a predecessor free-market advocacy group called Citizens for a Sound Economy (CSE). In 2004 CSE and its affiliated foundation split into two groups, Americans for Prosperity (AFP) and FreedomWorks.[21] Both AFP and FreedomWorks were strong initial backers of the TEA Party movement, as this book will eventually detail.

In this post-rant landscape, almost overnight TEA Parties and other similar rallies sprang up like dandelions in an unattended grassy lot. Malkin had a list of over 30 events that were held,[22] with some sponsored by advocacy groups like AFP that would eventually attempt to amplify their own political power through the movement, but most brought on by local groups that quickly formed under the TEA Party banner. For example, take the case of Tea Party Patriots co-founder Mark Meckler, who later detailed how he put together the rally in Sacramento:

> I discussed the idea with my wife. "Let's hold a tea party in Sacramento, at the state capitol," I told her. I asked her to watch the Santelli video and showed her a few "tea party" Facebook pages, and she was hooked. I did the same with my retired parents, and they became hooked too. It would be a family affair.
>
> We started a Facebook page of our own for the Sacramento Tea Party and invited the few people I knew online. I started networking on the Web, calling local media, and doing everything I could think of, as an "activist" with no experience or training, to get the word out. We had no idea what would happen, and no idea if it would be just my family attending. But we were all in, going so far as to take the kids out of school to show them the First Amendment in action. If that had been it, we would have considered the event a success.
>
> On February 27, 2009, with about twenty handmade signs in the back of our SUV, we drove down to Sacramento from the Sierra foothills. We were excited and nervous. We'd never protested or done anything like this before. We'd certainly never "organized" politically, and we had no idea what to expect. Would anyone show? Would people abuse us verbally or even physically? We were without reference points, conservative Americans embarking on a new frontier: political activism.[23]

Down the coast, Los Angeles TEA Party leader Gary Aminoff worked with several others, including local radio host Tony Katz, to put together an event on the Santa Monica Pier. "We had a huge crowd come out," said Gary. Aminoff also took up the cause immediately after Santelli's rant, although as a leader in the ill-fated McCain campaign in California he was already "very upset" with Obama's policies.[24]

Across the country, in the hipster paradise of Asheville, North Carolina, there was a smaller gathering of about 40 who turned out in the rain. "The mood was very positive and many expressed enthusiasm over the potential for a repeat performance on a sunny weekend day in the near future," wrote Asheville organizer Erika Franzi under her *nom de plume* "Jane Q. Republican."[25] (Perhaps in a foreshadowing of events to come, the local GOP was a presence: Franzi noted that they provided those who gathered with pulled pork sandwiches and sweet tea.)

While a lot of TEA Party organizers, like Meckler, were new to the game, there were others who were old hands at this type of activity. Joan Fabiano, who put together a rally at the Michigan state capitol in Lansing, was a self-described "activist" herself who had put together a successful Glenn Beck-inspired "Rally for America" a few years earlier. Not only was she an early Twitter convert, but Joan was also active at the *Free Republic* website which dated from the mid-1990s.[26] In short, the TEA Party was custom-made for her skill set.

Not all the TEA Party events were as wildly successful as those Meckler, Aminoff, and Fabiano spearheaded thanks to weather like Asheville's, permitting issues, and the fact many were held on a weekday when people desperate to keep their jobs were working; despite those drawbacks the protests as a whole drew thousands of ordinary people who were frustrated by government overreaction and incompetence when it came to addressing the Great Recession.

One of those most frustrated was Eric Eisenhammer, who was already part of the anti-tax movement as grassroots director of the Howard Jarvis Taxpayers Association in California. As a co-organizer in Sacramento, Eric described his initial impetus to join up:

> I saw Rick Santelli's remarks on Fox News (after they originally aired on CNBC) and how huge Tea Party rallies spontaneously broke out across the country. My grandpa watched the countercultural protests of the 1960's and never got involved because he thought they were crazy and would therefore never actually gain power. By my lifetime they had gained power and control of much of the media, academia and government. I was inspired to see conservatives finally taking a stand.
>
> (...)
>
> More than anything I felt that our country was being run by a liberal elite that not only didn't listen to mainstream America but held us in contempt. Their out of control spending, in my view, is driven by their belief that they have a right to behave with impunity because they are above us.[27]

The interesting thing about what organizers dubbed the "Chicago Tea Parties" in a nod to Santelli is that these are the among the first nationwide protests done in the age of unfiltered coverage, with self-styled journalists doing on-the-spot reporting.[28] So while the quality of the audio and video may not have been professional-grade, the message portrayed by these amateur journalists was more sympathetic to the aims of the organizers of these events than most of the slickly-packaged segments than those local news stations which grudgingly bothered to come out and cover the dissent put on the air.

So all that on-the-spot coverage came without the filter of the mainstream media and its seeming blind support for Barack Obama, meaning we could see a number of common threads running through this initial group of protests, whether held in the pouring rain of Atlanta, the chilly snow flurries of Chicago, or just the dreary weather common in late February around the nation.

One was the frustration with an unresponsive government that seemed to have the one-track mind of spending the money our grandchildren haven't even made yet – however, the $10 trillion in debt several speakers cited now sounds quaint years later when our national debt is well more than double that. This concern with government spending led to a shared belief among those gathered around the country that what took 220 years to build was being destroyed in one month. Statements like theirs, though, oversimplified the issue and put a lot more blame on President Obama than they should have, given the previous President also tried the idea of handing out government dollars to goose the economy. However, in President Bush's defense, his initial version of stimulus was more of an advance to taxpayers on money the recipients were due to get a couple months later anyway.

When compared to the Bush approach, though, it was clear that in its first few weeks the Obama administration was going full-tilt Keynesian on America, and the $75 billion Homeowner Stability Initiative[29] that led Santelli to speak out, piled on top of the $800 billion-plus ARRA stimulus package that had been signed two days prior to his remarks,[30] added fuel to the firestorm of resentment. "Your mortgage is not our problem," read one protestor's sign. What proponents of the stimulus considered as a hand up was, to those opposed to "porkulus," just another big-government handout. When it came to shoveling taxpayer money at our basket full of economic problems, those who attended the TEA Parties felt enough was enough.

Second was the unified opposition to the idea of bailing out private-sector companies and industries considered "too big to fail" while small businesses were being crushed by the economic downturn. Unlike Wall Street, General Motors, and Chrysler, mom-and-pop shops with nowhere near enough clout and capital to be able to influence policy were going bankrupt. Those small businesses, which combined added up to millions of productive, dedicated workers – even more so than the big boys had – didn't enjoy any prospect of the degree of government assistance taxpayers ponied up to keep the largest entities afloat. There's no way of knowing just how many of those attending these rallies had the time to spare because they were thrown out of work thanks to the oft-repeated scene of a factory or office full of workers getting a collective pink slip as their employer closed up shop, but it's safe to bet a lot of them were looking to the TEA Party movement to bring the change needed in order for them to get hired somewhere else. So there was a certain sense of desperation present at these events.

Part of that desperation came from a third factor: the notion that neither major party really was all that interested in restoring the idea of fiscal responsibility and implementing the pullback of federal government intervention required to hasten the necessary recovery and to allow the market to correct itself. There was already a latent cynicism out there among the disaffected, including Meckler:

> As I followed political news, over the years I noted that something strange happened to politicians after they got elected. Not only did they forget about the people who sent them to Washington, they also seemed to forget about the principles that built this nation, and the oath they swore to uphold those principles. Republican or Democrat – it did not seem to matter which side was in power. Either way our government kept getting bigger, our liberties kept getting smaller, and our nation kept moving away from the ideas that made it great. The speed with which we drifted away from the founding principles ebbed and flowed, but the direction never seemed to change.[31]

Another common lament at these first TEA Parties was that Democrats, led by Obama, were in the process of fundamentally transforming the nation, and it seemed like the GOP was only acting as token opposition while this was going on. "The Republican Party is gone!" shouted one protester in Chicago, and many in the initial wave of protestors believed that a third party, perhaps one that stood for a more conservative fiscal policy and consumption-based taxation system, was the way to go.

Yet there wasn't the complete partisanship at this first wave of TEA Parties that we had seen at typical political rallies, as several speakers gave credit to the more centrist "Blue Dog" Democrats for standing up to their leadership against the fiscal onslaught of red ink, and chastised Republicans for a lack of spine. In Chicago, organizer Eric Odom rebuffed the request of RNC Chair Michael Steele to speak to the event, telling Steele, "Thanks but no thanks. You're welcome to come and listen," said Odom. "But we're not interested in hearing you speak. Frankly, you need to understand what we're telling you because so far, we don't think you do."[32]

Those attending the initial TEA Party events also held a lot of suspicion for the mainstream national media, which they accused of being lapdogs for the new Obama administration. (Only Fox News was spared from their wrath.) Their interest extended to how these individual events were covered by the media, recording and sharing the (mostly local) news coverage of their events just as the Santelli rant eventually spread like wildfire. As noted above, these non-traditional scribes also logged their reports on the World Wide Web, eventually being linked and publicized through more established outlets and bloggers like the aforementioned Michelle Malkin, as well as *Pajamas Media* and *RedState*, to name a few.

But if you looked past the generally handmade signs with their pleas for fiscal responsibility from the federal government and the yellow Gadsden flags which eventually became the symbol of the TEA Party, you found everyday people who were stirred to action as never before. "I've never protested in my life, but I am taking a stand," said Susan Brubaker, a Kansas protester interviewed on her local news.[33] And while the gatherings were fairly modest, those attending were eager to learn and listen: they signed up for e-mail lists, were alerted to the websites of various advocacy groups both existing and new (AFP and FreedomWorks were joined as key sponsors of some of the earliest events by recent online startups Smart Girl Politics and eventually the nascent Nationwide TEA Party Coalition) and encouraged to continue the fight. "We need to make this our new hobby," said Dallas TEA Party co-organizer and speaker Ken Emanuelson.[34] "Every one of us needs to decide that this trumps just about everything else." And while he went on to say that the subject of Washington fiscal responsibility was boring and dry, Emanuelson had the correct idea this would be an extended fight.

On her blog, Fabiano described part of her experience with the event in Lansing, which attracted over 300 people: "You could feel the energy in the air. The camaraderie of being gathered together with like-minded citizens caused most to linger even after our program was over, discussing politics and our new movement. And myself and my fellow co-organizers were thanked over and over again."[35]

Indeed, thousands of people were truly being organized for action. Bolstered by the success of the first initial wave of TEA Parties, a group of protests originally intended to be a one-time series of events instead spawned hundreds more. These new organizers joined the fold over the next few weeks and set their sights on a second set of nationwide rallies to be held on Tax Day, April 15.

Looking back at that interim period when the April events were being planned, TEA Party organizers Jenny Beth Martin and Mark Meckler explained their approach.

> So how did we grow from twenty-two people to 1.2 million people in less than two months?

> We did not fully realize it at the time, but we were organizing the Tea Party movement along the lines of an *open-source* community. In the world of computer software, open-source communities develop and improve ideas organically, based on concepts and practices that work.
>
> (...)
>
> (Open-source) provides the fastest possible rate of improvement for ideas, and in the case of the Tea Party movement, this notion was fundamental in the development of a true political revolution. (Italics in original.)[36]

At the same time, though, the grassroots sponsors that promoted the original set of TEA Parties and had formed the Nationwide TEA Party Coalition were joined by two others with more star power. Newt Gingrich and his American Solutions organization began their "partnering" with the Nationwide Tax Day TEA Party group to promote these events in mid-March. "I believe that April 15 is a great day to remember historically that Americans have stood up against bad government, they've stood up against high taxes, and in our generation we can get back to creating jobs by doing just the same," said Gingrich in a promotional video.[37]

That's not to say, though, that Gingrich's entry wasn't viewed as a double-edged sword by organizers like Leahy:

> A week after the success of the Nationwide Chicago Tea Party...I received a private direct message on Twitter from Newt Gingrich. Would we, he asked, be interested in having his American Solutions group join the Nationwide Tea Party Coalition... as the fourth sponsor of the Tax Day Tea Party?
>
> If Gingrich's group was added as a sponsor, it would add jet fuel to the movement. So far we were perceived as a group of activists on the margin, even though our message of the limited government ethos reflected the views of the majority of the American people. With the former Speaker of the House would come increased media visibility, and inevitably interest from Fox News, where he was a featured contributor. But Gingrich's record was viewed by many as questionable. He had been an able articulator of the limited-government ethos when he championed the Contract with America, which had propelled him to the speakership in 1994 during the Clinton administration. However, the perception was that during his four-year tenure, his accomplishments toward that goal had not matched his rhetoric.[38]

Leahy wasn't the only one viewing Gingrich with suspicion. Oklahoma's Sandie Crosroe was also a skeptic:

> We formed as a group when we saw top down techniques being used in what we thought was a collaborative effort. Then we did the research and found that globalist Newt Gingrich was being promoted as our leader and web pages directing shared lists and fundraising around his organization. We purposed to not drive traffic to the national website for that reason and will do everything in our power to keep the movement safe in local hands. But you will have to be vigilant and help. Groups are welcome to help and promote to their own lists and attend and participate. Glenn Beck is now promoting the movement as well, but he is not asking for your lists and money and is to be commended for that.[39]

Additionally, Crosroe exhorted TEA Party groups to "be sure that your… effort stays grassroots and nonpartisan." Surely she was disappointed with what was to come, but I'll get to that.[40]

Also stepping up its efforts in the second round was the group founded by Ron Paul, the Campaign for Liberty. In a show of solidarity with the cause by Campaign for Liberty supporters, more and more of their signs began popping up at various events, while Paul himself was a featured speaker at the TEA Party held in his district.[41] Campaign for Liberty president John Tate was quick to remind people about their role in the original 2007 Boston Tea Party moneybomb and protest held during Paul's presidential campaign.[42]

With the additional time to get organized, the Tax Day TEA Parties would become a spectacle that dwarfed the original February effort, with reportedly over 750 rallies nationwide.[43] In the larger cities, these protests drew crowds in the thousands, but even more impressive was the number of small communities which had more modest gatherings for the first time – places like Greensburg, Pennsylvania,[44] Monticello, Arkansas,[45] or Millersburg, Ohio.[46] Those three communities represented small town America quite well as your average county seats, and while there may have only been 100 to 200 people at their events, they remained united with the common purpose of petitioning for a redress of grievances.[47] (My local Tax Day TEA Party in Salisbury, Maryland drew 400 to 500 people on a chilly, rainy April afternoon. I covered the affair on my own website.)[48]

But within that seven-week period between the initial February protests and Tax Day, the TEA Party moved beyond a protest of "Porkulus" and mortgage relief programs into a full-blown indictment of the nation's overall financial situation. By selecting a day where Americans were expected to have their pound of flesh extracted by Uncle Sam this change could be expected, but many of the attendees were most concerned about the effect the burgeoning national debt would have on the fate of their kids. One speaker at the Richmond TEA Party contended that her children would be 17, 15, and 12 in ten years and have a projected $17 trillion dollar deficit on their heads by that point.[49] (Sadly, it turns out that she was too optimistic: we went beyond $20 trillion in debt with 18 months or so to spare before that decade was up.)

While the smaller communities generally maintained local organization for their TEA Parties, some of the larger cities began to attract celebrities drawn to the cause: Fox News (and nationally syndicated radio talk show) host Sean Hannity broadcast his evening show from the Atlanta TEA Party,[50] while his Fox network cohort Neil Cavuto appeared at the California TEA Party in Sacramento. Yet it was a local blogger to whom Cavuto pointed out the events weren't party-based, but "country-based."[51]

With all that airtime, some on the other side of the fence politically believed Fox News was doing more than covering the TEA Party – they were putting their thumb on the scale.

> In Fox and affiliated conservative outlets, the Tea Party took on meaning not only as a political grouping, but also as a vital cultural force. Fox News assigned the Tea Party a starring role in what conservatives understand as a long-running culture war between coastal elites and middle Americans… Tea Party members think of the elite not primarily as an economic category but as a cultural stratum, a coterie of liberal intellectuals and bureaucrats who wish to impose ideas and schemes about matters such as economic redistribution and environmental regulation on unwitting regular Americans. Fox News coverage of the Tea Party both draws upon and fuels this potent interpretation.[52]

The authors go on to explain the significant change in attention brought on by Fox's wall-to-wall Tea Party coverage. As an example, CNN went from openly questioning their competitor's cheerleading in the weeks leading up to the Tax Day TEA Party rallies to promising more full coverage as the event neared – including a guest appearance by Chicago TEA Party organizer Eric Odom on April 14 – to the further steps of embedding a reporter on the first Tea Party Express (TPX) tour later that summer and eventually broadcasting, among other things, the 'Tea Party response' to President Obama's 2010 State of the Union address and a Republican presidential candidate debate co-sponsored with TPX in September, 2011.

However, argued St. Louis organizer Dana Loesch, "Our progress isn't measured by whether or not CNN loves us, but (it) can be measured by how badly certain outlets want to shut us up."[53] If you watched the remaining network nightly news, you were told this vast amount of unrest, involving tens (if not hundreds) of thousands of people, could be boiled down to one sentiment: sour grapes from the conservative Right, upset at losing the election.[54] They also reiterated that President Obama had made his own tax relief plan part of the ARRA which, according to the White House, "helps 95% of working families" and has "70% of the tax benefits (going) to the middle 60% of American workers."[55] (While this may have addressed the original point of Americans being "Taxed Enough Already," it didn't change the equation when it came to spending – particularly when the Democrats were known for saying that tax cuts were a cost to the government.)

The Obama Administration was asked directly about their reaction to the protests, and White House press secretary Robert Gibbs maintained that party line under the questioning:

> Q. Does the White House have any response to the protests, the tea party protests going on across the street and in other parts of the country?
>
> MR. GIBBS: I don't know if there's a specific response to protests as much as there is – I think you saw the President today talk about as candidate Obama promising to bring a tax cut to 95 percent of working families in America, and as President delivering that tax cut.[56]

Two weeks after the Tax Day protests, President Obama more directly addressed the spending concerns, telling a Missouri town hall meeting:

> So, you know, when you see – those of you who are watching certain news channels on which I'm not very popular and you see folks waving tea bags around, let me just remind them that I am happy to have a serious conversation about how we are going to cut our health care costs down over the long term, how we're going to stabilize Social Security.[57]

While 18 members of the Nationwide Tea Party Coalition accepted that invitation,[58] it's worth noting that nothing further, let alone any "serious conversation," came of it.

If the February protests were considered a shot across the bow by the Left, though, their panic in seeing the extent of the Tax Day protests meant all hands were required on deck. On the more conventional side, they took the approach of calling the protests "Astroturf" due to the Washington-based conservative groups FreedomWorks, AFP, and American Solutions taking the lead on organizing some of the larger events.[59] [60] In a similar vein, some mainstream media coverage assigned the TEA Party a proxy role as GOP shills. Erika Franzi, blogging from Asheville, North Carolina:

> Unfortunately and predictably, the media still doesn't get it. They don't know what to do with us, so they are under-reporting our numbers and repeating the false charge that we are GOP operatives. We're going to have to give them another object lesson in non-partisan activism on July 4th.[61]

Of course, this “Astroturf” argument may have covered some of the events where these national groups indeed assisted with logistics and in-kind donations, but it didn't explain why there were so many TEA Parties that seemed to independently spring up in the smaller towns and communities around the nation. St. Louis organizer Dana Loesch was fairly blunt in that regard of local organization in the face of national interest, blogging about FreedomWorks that their “netroots, frankly, sucks”:

> Their involvement in the St. Louis protest was nonexistent and while they issued press release after press release explaining how their members were available for interviews and trying to score media access so as to promote themselves, this was more of a bother than any help. It’s difficult when you’re trying to put something together to have a group you can’t vouch for running behind you, talking to the media and giving out inaccurate information while not bothering to assist with the grunt work – and assistance was welcome![62]

Since the “Astroturf” approach could be proven false, the naysayers continued the approach of crying bias about Fox News. Here's an example from the left-wing Media Matters for America:

> Despite its repeated insistence that its coverage is "fair and balanced" and its invitation to viewers to "say 'no' to biased media," in recent weeks, Fox News has frequently aired segments encouraging viewers to get involved with "tea party" protests across the country, which the channel has often described as primarily a response to President Obama's fiscal policies. Specifically, Fox News has in dozens of instances provided attendance and organizing information for future protests, such as protest dates, locations and website URLs. Fox News websites have also posted information and publicity material for protests. Fox News hosts have repeatedly encouraged viewers to join them at several April 15 protests that they are attending and covering; during the April 6 edition of *Glenn Beck*, on-screen text characterized these events as "FNC Tax Day Tea Parties." Tea-party organizers have used the planned attendance of the Fox News hosts to promote their protests. Fox News has also aired numerous interviews with protest organizers. Moreover, Fox News contributors are listed as "Tea Party Sponsor[s]" on TaxDayTeaParty.com.[63]

Remember, these were the hosts of individual shows that drew the wrath of Media Matters, not necessarily the news programs. In watching these shows, it didn't take too long for a viewer to figure out most of the Fox hosts leaned to the right politically. Considering there already was a perception out there that the other news networks were severely left-of-center in their outlook, Fox News was simply reflecting what their audience wanted to hear about, reading it perfectly. Indeed, it's likely they had a significant effect on the attendance at these gatherings, whether from having their personalities at the largest ones or as a driver of interest in the small county seats.

Yet there was one other aspect of this left-wing rejection of the TEA Party that made it an inside joke to a certain class of people, and that was the term "teabagger." Just days before the Tax Day TEA Parties, far-left MSNBC host Rachel Maddow decided it was time to take advantage of the naivete of average Americans regarding the *Urban Dictionary* definition of the term[64] – something Sir Thomas Lipton probably never dreamed would be associated with his products. In one seven-minute segment of her show[65] she barely could contain herself, mirthful about the less savory connotation of the term that easily 95 percent of the average TEA Party attendees were unaware of.

Needless to say, the Left quickly picked up the word "teabagger" as the derogatory way to refer to those Americans who were participating in these anti-tax protests, and eventually to conservatives in general. It was funny within the far-left echo chamber, but also showed they didn't have a whole lot to battle with in terms of good policy ideas given how poorly concerns about the economy were being addressed by the Obama administration they were supporting.

While the usage of "teabagger" illustrated the cultural divide among those in the rapidly growing TEA Party and those who strongly opposed it, there was a small schism among factions within the movement as well – a break which would grow as the TEA Party did. In a message stressed mostly in the more rural regions of the nation, speakers at the various Tax Day TEA Parties brought up the fact that millions of Americans were never born because of legalized abortion. While the libertarian elements who claimed they truly began the TEA Party movement in 2007 would likely be described as fiscally conservative but socially liberal – the "keep the government out of our bedroom" crowd – as the TEA Party circle in the political Venn diagram of American politics grew, it was also bound to incorporate elements within the socially conservative pro-life religious Right that agreed with the overall "taxed enough already" umbrella of fiscal responsibility but also acted as one of the legs of the oft-quoted three-legged stool of conservatism with their emphasis on religiously-based family values. Over the next months and years, this rift became a source of tension within the TEA Party as each side of this divide blamed the other for political goals not achieved.

As spring turned into summer, the planning was there for yet another wave of TEA Parties: the Independence Day holiday became the third rallying point for the group in just over four months. By this time, the number of groups participating was well over 1,000 and organizers were expecting huge numbers of Americans to attend their local events. (I was one of them, as our local TEA Party had a July 4 event, too.)[66]

Elizabeth Klimp, then a research fellow at the Capital Research Center, wrote an excellent, succinct description of these local TEA Parties that were being formed; one to keep in mind as you read on:

> Like other grassroots movements, the overwhelming majority of Tea Party activists are volunteers who are organizing activities around issues and candidates in their local communities. A typical Tea Party organization has a small organizing nucleus, or board of trustees, that oversees a larger number of volunteers. The board handles the group's communications, fund-raising and logistics, usually without any direction from a larger state, regional or national organization. Individual groups develop their own platform, objectives, and plans of action, generally without input or assistance from larger state or national coordinating bodies. The typical group is independent, but shares with other Tea Party groups a common platform of reverence for the Founding Fathers and the U.S. Constitution and support for fiscal responsibility, limited government, and personal liberty.
>
> There are state and national Tea Party organizations, but typically they facilitate communication among Tea Party groups and serve as networking agents rather than try to stage or direct local grassroots activities. These larger organizations also try to attract national attention to the movement. They organize its larger rallies or series of rallies, train activists on practical aspects of organizing, and propose themes or platforms that can galvanize Tea Party support.[67]

Ironically, Independence Day of 2009 turned out to be the high-water mark for this localized phase of the TEA Party movement as plans were already underway to hold a set of massive, nationwide demonstrations the weekend after Labor Day.[68] Spearheaded by the group FreedomWorks, which hatched the idea during the first few weeks of the TEA Party movement, the "Taxpayer March on Washington" expected "over ten thousand liberty-loving activists" to converge on the nation's capital, with ancillary events in other cities around the nation expected to add to the total number of people involved. As I pointed out in my introduction, it turned out their expectations of the Washington event were set way too low.

For the movement to carry on, though, it had to come under a national umbrella in more than name. By nature, these individual TEA Party groups were fiercely independent, and while they may have received assistance from national organizations like FreedomWorks, AFP, and so forth, they had their own goals and agendas to consider. So as the movement worked its way forward after the spring and summer of 2009, even as various groups tried to take a leadership role at the statewide and national levels, the overall message coordination between local TEA

Party groups became harder to come by and their efforts and tactics began to become more divergent.

For example, of those TEA Party groups which carried on after the summer protests, a number of them morphed into local AFP affiliates or aligned themselves with the Campaign for Liberty, becoming more like political clubs with monthly meetings and tactics more in line with standard party politics. This commonality with party groups included a regular diet of guest speakers such as local elected officials or representatives from one of these national groups. Conversely, other organizations kept the TEA Party name and their regimen of public protests – some carrying on for several years.[69] These bouts of outspokenness occurred less and less frequently, though, as the TEA Party matured and changed its form, with local groups eventually realizing it was okay to band together to adopt broader organizational schemes on a state or regional level in order to consolidate their political power with larger numbers. These groups, in turn, were claimed under the umbrella of a small national core of TEA Party leaders who came together in just a few different entities.

With a cause that had drawn people like Florida's Mary Rakovich, Seattle "porkulus" protest organizer Keri Carender, and Susan Brubaker, the Kansas woman who had "never protested in my life" but decided this was the place to make her stand, the TEA Party was a mother lode of political activists who were barely tapped by the established party machines and inside-the-Beltway lobbying entities. In fact, North Carolina's Ralph Reagan was one local TEA Party leader who doubled as a local Republican leader and saw this as a recruiting opportunity for the GOP.

> As Chairman I had the first Tea Party rally because I wanted to transform my local with fresh energy and pull it to the right. I had rallies until I was no longer Chairman (as) my idea of recruiting was offensive to the RINOs. And I had great opposition (from some in the TEA Party) because I was a Republican.[70]

In the minds of ambitious people and groups, some already connected to the national political establishment and some who longed to be, the nascent movement was a meal ticket to be punched – or simply rubes to be exploited. Nature abhors a vacuum, and there was no shortage of folks who wanted to fill that vacuum by leading the TEA Party.

# UPRISING: A CALL FOR LEADERSHIP

*"It seemed that the government of our country was promoting the idea that everyone deserved a bailout when they got in financial trouble. We didn't think we deserved a bailout. Like most Americans, we believed in taking responsibility for our own situation in life."* - Jenny Beth Martin, Tea Party Patriots.

It was a tumultuous first five months for the nascent political movement, but once the July 4 wave of TEA Parties passed it became quite apparent that having one thousand local groups with just as many different agendas meant a whole lot of willing workers for the TEA Party cause – the problem was that it was also a lot like herding cats. Even so, there were ambitious groups and people with different causes who were very willing to try steering the herd in order to further their own goals and careers, and with any luck perhaps even make a little coin out of the deal.

This part of the TEA Party story began a few months earlier, as the vision for the February "Chicago TEA Parties" was laid out the day after Rick Santelli took the conservative internet by storm with his CNBC rant. A group of organizers inspired by the outburst of support for Santelli "hijacked"[1] the "Top Conservatives on Twitter" (TCOT) conference call between activists and groups who were already interested in promoting the conservative cause. Some time later, author and evangelist Michael Patrick Leahy – who as the creator of TCOT was among the early group putting the protests together – placed on his personal website a fairly comprehensive list that he claimed chronicled both the participants in the February 20, 2009 TCOT conference call and the organizers of the various local "Chicago TEA Parties" a week later.[2]

In that post, Leahy also documents an e-mail exchange he had in 2011 with fellow TEA Party founder Jenny Beth Martin where he revealed that he had several goals in mind for these events:

> I would add that articulating the "strike while the iron is hot" argument I made was largely a detailed articulation of what everyone on the call probably already felt. You may recall there was virtually no pushback on that.
>
> The other elements I added were:
>
> (1) The need to focus on a simultaneous nationwide event (The Nationwide

> Chicago Tea Party) (2) With a narrowly focused theme (Repeal the Pork or Retire), which we (3) Actively promoted and then documented using video cameras and social media.
>
> On the last point, you will recall Christina Botteri emphasized the importance of digitally documenting the event, with either video or still photos. The key to the success of the February 27, 2009 "Nationwide Chicago Tea Party" held in 30 cities with 50,000 attendees was that all the participants were very careful to document the event, then kick it back to Christina and me, and we in turn disseminated the pictures, videos, etc. to all our friends in the blogosphere (Michelle Malkin, Instapundit, etc.) and any national networks that provided coverage. You may recall that both MSNBC and FoxNews provided bits of coverage for that event. Local TV, actually, did a pretty good job covering the event in almost every one of the 50 markets.
>
> You will also recall that on the February 20, 2009 call, TCOT, SGP, and Dontgo combined to form http://www.nationwideteapartycoalition.com , the group that organized and sponsored both the February 27, 2009 Nationwide Chicago Tea Party and the April 15, 2009 Tax Day Tea Party.[3]

Interestingly, in his list of TEA Party "founders" Leahy considers himself as "support" rather than a local organizer.

But in considering the fate of the TEA Party nearly a decade later, I believe it's worth pointing out that the large majority of this group of initial organizers never became known on the national scene. Surely some of the 90-plus local organizers were happy to be simple citizen activists, but there were others who found out their goals no longer meshed with those of the overall movement as it evolved. As this book continues on, you will notice a number of the names Leahy cited are repeated frequently but at the outset this was a listing of the core group of TEA Party supporters who were disgusted enough with the prospect of rampant Keynesian spending and government overreach that they took the time to organize the first wave of events. As the weeks went on these "everyday American citizens" saw their ranks increase tenfold and more as new organizers in cities large and small across the nation joined in. And while the more nationally-known players that took the reins of the overall movement determined its eventual fate, I also wanted to hear the perspective from a number of the other players, too. So they will also play a key role in telling this story.

As the February 27 "Chicago TEA Party" became a reality, there were three heretofore obscure online groups that took on the role of key sponsors and leadership in coordinating the message: Leahy's TCOT, the #Dontgo movement represented by its co-founder Eric Odom, and Smart Girl Politics (SGP), represented by its co-founder Stacy Mott. None of these groups had existed even a year earlier, but in this new wave of online organizing this trio of entities grabbed the TEA Party baton and ran with it, coming together as the Nationwide TEA Party Coalition on February 20 in order to promote the first series of events. (Also included in the initial set of sponsors were the more established Americans for Tax Reform, Heartland Institute, and *The American Spectator* magazine.)[4] It was a happy accident that Leahy, Odom, and Mott were on the conference call and became involved together.

To illustrate the latent group of Americans who were ready for some sort of defense against the progressive onslaught the previous few months had brought, it should be pointed out that the TCOT conference calls had only begun a few weeks earlier, the outgrowth of a group which had rapidly expanded from a handful of bloggers to over three thousand by the time the first TEA Parties were organized.[5] Its main *#TCOT Report* page was, as they said, "obviously modeled on Drudge" right down to the graphic style.[6] Leahy's aim in creating TCOT was to counter what he saw as the dominance of the Left when it came to social media,[7] and he chose the Twitter platform because he believed the field was more open to conservatives than was Facebook. (Even so, by mid-2008 Barack Obama was the most-followed person on Twitter.)[8]

The Obama campaign team spent months building up a social media following through the campaign, allowing him to dominate the internet on his way to election in 2008.[9] But where Leahy succeeded was the promotion of using the #TCOT hashtag as a medium for Twitter searching: suddenly there was a way for conservatives to easily share and find links to items of interest to them, and thousands of people used that shorthand to learn about the budding TEA Party movement. In his later book, *Covenant of Liberty: The Ideological Origins of the Tea Party Movement*, Leahy explained how the idea of #TCOT originated:

> (M)any of those on the now-growing Top Conservatives on Twitter list suggested that we needed to adopt a "hashtag," so that it would be easier for anyone on Twitter to follow the ongoing conservative conversation. One of our members, a seventy-eight-year-old grandmother from Welasco, Texas, Beulah Garrett, suggested that we use the abbreviation of the list's name, thus the hashtag #tcot. By the end of the second full week, there were more than one thousand names on the list and #tcot was consistently on the Twitter top-trending topics.[10]

Not long afterward the TEA Party began to spread itself over Facebook as well, conservatives finally joining the battle in social media.

On the other hand, while Eric Odom's #Dontgo movement was initially social-media based, as a hashtag and Twitter presence it was very modest – and short-lived after the initial wave of TEA Parties.[11]

Odom and the #Dontgo idea seemed to be somewhat of an odd fit for the TEA Party, anyway. Describing himself as "very libertarian," he eventually ended up denouncing several of the TEA Party organizations that sprang up as the movement matured.[12] (By the end of 2017, Odom had abandoned the political world entirely, reinventing himself as a travelogue editor and filmmaker.)[13] Moreover, the idea of #Dontgo had nothing to do with the fiscal irresponsibility of the federal government: it was formed over the summer of 2008 to back Congressional Republicans who wanted to stay in Washington over the summer and overturn a federal ban on offshore oil drilling as a way of addressing surging gasoline prices. Over time, the #Dontgo moniker was scrapped and the organization formalized and evolved into the American Liberty Alliance. That organization also had a brief lifespan, with Odom eventually acquiring a reputation as a "charlatan" among some in the TEA Party thanks to the number of changes his various organizations went through, as *RedState*'s Erick Erickson documented in 2010.[14]

The third part of this original triumvirate was Mott's SGP group, which has remained as a website and social media outlet aimed at conservative women since the earliest days of the TEA Party. It was created with a different goal in mind, but turned out to be the right group at the right time for the TEA Party. "Other organizations (aimed at conservative women) have more history, more political background," explained Mott, "and I think there are many pros and cons to being outsiders and grassroots, but I think it has helped us to reach out to other women who are similar to us."[15]

By September, 2009 SGP claimed to have 20,000 members between Facebook and the Ning social media network; they still have over 20,000 Twitter followers and close to 35,000 on Facebook. Outside of social media, for several years the group also put on a Smart Girl Politics Summit, with the first edition featuring journalist Michelle Malkin, Rep. Marsha Blackburn, and Bush-era diplomat Liz Cheney. Other notables who appeared at SGP Summits included Reps. Cathy McMorris Rogers and Michele Bachmann, commentators S.E. Cupp and Erick Erickson, journalist James O'Keeffe, the late Eagle Forum founder Phyllis Schlafly, and 2012 presidential candidate Herman Cain.

Of the three primary online groups that began the Nationwide TEA Party Coalition, SGP was perhaps the most "traditional" political group in that they were the most formally organized and held events of their own which weren't TEA Party-related. At its heart, though, it was a grassroots organization like the other two, which made it a little surprising that they were the group promoting an enhanced TEA Party alliance with a more mainstream, inside-the-Beltway organization. In mid-March Newt Gingrich's American Solutions joined the Nationwide TEA Party Coalition during the run up to the Tax Day TEA Parties.[16]

This isn't to say that more mainline conservative organizations were eschewing the original Nationwide Chicago TEA Party, but their impact was mainly limited to co-sponsoring the local Washington, D.C. affair. The accusations of "Astroturf" demonstrations stemmed from that particular event's sponsor list, which included Americans for Prosperity, Americans for Tax Reform, Young Conservatives Coalition, The Heartland Institute, National Taxpayers Union, FreedomWorks, and the Institute for Liberty.[17] By association with the Washington, D.C. event, other local TEA Parties were in turn criticized by the Left as "Astroturf." Wrote *New York Times* columnist Paul Krugman as the Tax Day editions were approaching:

> (I)t turns out that the tea parties don't represent a spontaneous outpouring of public sentiment. They're AstroTurf (fake grass roots) events, manufactured by the usual suspects. In particular, a key role is being played by FreedomWorks, an organization run by Richard Armey, the former House majority leader, and supported by the usual group of right-wing billionaires. And the parties are, of course, being promoted heavily by Fox News.[18]

A couple years later, authors Theda Skocpol and Vanessa Williamson summed up contributions made by established lobbying groups in the early days like this:

> Indeed, one of the most important consequences of the widespread Tea Party agitations unleashed from the start of Obama's presidency was the populist boost given to professionally run and opulently funded right-wing advocacy organizations devoted to pushing ultra-free-market policies.[19]

In fact, by that time many of these national organizations had jumped on board, but they were only following the grassroots effort in order to further their cause because they didn't originate it. Imagine some revisionist history: what if the Nationwide Chicago TEA Parties only drew a couple dozen people apiece to maybe a dozen cities? Would any of these inside-the-Beltway organizations would have given the remaining promoters the time of day afterward? I doubt it. Success breeds success, and these national entities were just trying to elbow their way onto the ground floor with the most ambitious organizers and original members of the Nationwide TEA Party Coalition. "(T)he involvement of FreedomWorks and Americans for Prosperity during those first months was primarily because the movement could be a source of fund-raising. In that regard, it proved to be a very effective tool for them,"[20] opined Michael Patrick Leahy.

In looking at Leahy's list of local organizers ten years on, there are a lot of names people in the conservative political world would recognize: from Sacramento came

Mark Meckler, from Atlanta came Jenny Beth Martin and Amy Kremer, Eric Odom represented Chicago, Dana Loesch from St. Louis, Katrina Pearson and Ken Emanuelson from Dallas, and so forth. New media personalities Michele Malkin, Glenn Reynolds, Jim Hoft, and Ace of Spades are still well-known today. They are some of the TEA Party survivors who used the movement as a springboard to further their ambitions.

But there were some organizers who were listed as "anonymous" on the Leahy list, whether out of lack of reliable information on their identity or a true desire to remain secret. We hadn't yet seen the sheer bullying and hatred with which some on the Left address conservatives today, but it's likely there were a few who were reticent to make it known they were the local TEA Party leaders. Perhaps they sensed in advance what the media was ready to say about this potential political juggernaut – a topic I'll visit in due course.

Meanwhile, the Nationwide TEA Party Coalition was in the process of evolving. At about the time of the Tax Day TEA Party rallies – a *Wall Street Journal* story pegs the date as April 12[21] – Atlanta TEA Party organizer Jenny Beth Martin formed a new group called the Tea Party Patriots. Over the next month as the group incorporated into a formal entity, Martin, fellow Atlanta organizer Amy Kremer, and Mark Meckler from Sacramento emerged as its leaders. However, it was not just their effort: a number of members of the Nationwide TEA Party Coalition went on to serve with the Tea Party Patriots board of directors. While the Coalition carried on for some time afterward, their original, preeminent position in leadership quickly shifted to the new organization. (As evidence, the NTPC had a website through most of 2017 but it had not been updated in over seven years and had disappeared entirely by the middle of 2018.)[22]

In essence, the purpose of the Tea Party Patriots was to give some direction to what had previously been a relatively loose, ragtag collection of groups. The system in place was fine when the TEA Party was a modest coordination of a few dozen who gathered to do what was originally figured as a one-off event, but in order to create a more lasting political impact some group was going to have to become a source of leadership. And because it was a grassroots organization, as opposed to a Beltway-based group of lobbyists like FreedomWorks or Americans for Prosperity, this was a way to maintain the trust of activists who would look askance at the TEA Party if they felt it was just another tool for the Washington establishment. That "establishment" charge rubbed the TPP founders the wrong way:

> Our detractors have accused us of being tools of the political establishment. They suggest that everything that we have done has been planned from some back room in Washington, D.C. It is only natural that they would suspect this, because it is the way *their* movements operate. They cannot imagine or accept the truth:

> that we are a true grassroots movement of citizens who joined together to defend America against politicians who swore to uphold the Constitution, but instead fed it through a shredder along with trillions of our taxpayer dollars. Our detractors cannot accept that we are who we are, because it threatens their warped worldview. And so they convince themselves… that we are an "Astroturf" group; that our leaders are manipulated by the Republican Party, or by Big Business, or any one of a thousand different entities.[23]

The existing national groups' political muscle and connections were valuable as common cause, but for the grassroots movement to succeed there had to be the impression that outsider regular folk were the ones calling the tune. Libertarian blogger Stephen Gordon made this point early on, writing on April 9, "If the big boys want to jump on board, that's fine, so long as the grassroots continue to control the message. However, I'd be the first one protesting Republican spending if Newt Gingrich or John McCain showed up at my local TEA Party."[24]

Unfortunately for them, one thing the Tea Party Patriots could not do was trademark the term "TEA Party."[25] At about the same time the Patriots were being incorporated, a second group was being formed from the roots of an already-existing organization in Sacramento, California.

When they began life as the Our Country Deserves Better (OCDB) committee during the 2008 campaign, the group that eventually became the Tea Party Express (TPX) sponsored the "Stop Obama Tour." Stopping in 35 cities in battleground states over two weeks, this campaign whistle-stop bus tour featured three main spokespeople: Gold Star Mom Deborah Johns, Sacramento radio personality Mark Williams, and singer/songwriter Lloyd Marcus.[26] Once the 2008 campaign was over, OCDB hit the airwaves with a Thanksgiving-themed ad thanking vice-Presidential candidate Sarah Palin for the common-sense conservatism she brought to the GOP ticket,[27] but as 2009 dawned they were basically a spent organization aimlessly wandering the fringes of the conservative movement until one OCDB leader attended the Tax Day TEA Party in Sacramento and quickly saw the opportunity.

You'll hear a lot more about Mark Williams as this story goes on, but this is what he told me about the scene in Sacramento:

> I had been vice-chair of Our Country Deserves Better PAC for some months and had already made one national speaking sweep in advance of Obama's 2008 election. This particular day I caught wind of a band of folks gathering at the Capitol for an *ad hoc* demonstration that they were calling "Tea Party" which caught my ear. I had participated in a 1978 radio talk-driven Tea Party campaign in Massachusetts to fight a legislative pay raise and a driver of a second one in

1989 that forced repeal of a 50% Congressional pay raise and the resignation of then-House Speaker Jim Wright (D-TX) so this idea was right up my alley. I knew the entire blueprint for success because I had helped write it and then revise it.

On the day in California it was sincere but disorganized with no clear agenda or plan so I did two things. First I called my PAC office down the street and told staff to high tail it the couple of blocks over because this was the something we needed to pull together the emerging Citizen Patriot movement that was stirring. (Think the Statue of Liberty in the second Ghostbusters movie. It was almost like that moment when the image of Liberty on the NY license plate hits them. One of those.) The second thing I did was step up, stand on a barrier, start addressing the crowd with a totally off the cuff speech and proceeded to encourage and emcee others, and took over. I guess I basically just said something like follow me, I know where we're going and how to get there. There were many things broken that had to be fixed. Sadly (this) sounds corny, but millions of others heard and answered the same call to duty and obligation as did I.[28]

OCDB quickly rebranded themselves as the Tea Party Express, taking advantage of the name recognition the movement had quickly built up. In a memo made public a year later by *Politico*,[29] OCDB's Joe Wierzbicki outlined the TPX idea, but cautioned that it may step on a few toes.

"The Tea Party Express" will be led by the leadership of the Our Country Deserves Better Committee (Mark Williams and Deborah Johns), musical performers (Lloyd Marcus who has tentatively confirmed his participation and also Rivoli Revue of "A Bailout Song" who have expressed an interest in working with us but who have yet to get back to me about their availability or their willingness to participate in the tour), key staff (Joe Wierzbicki, Kelly Eustis, and if available, Sal Russo), Gary Pon of *Free Republic* (what's a national tour without him!) and potentially one other individual to serve as a speaker (an example would be Lew Uhler of the National Tax Limitation Committee) and hopefully two additional staffers. We might also choose to invite a blogger to come along with us to blog on the tour (one who is respected by leading conservative bloggers).

At each "tea party" stop we will also invite to speak the following types of individuals: local tea party leaders, fiscally conservative political candidates, local officials or dignitaries, local talk radio hosts, etc.

It is also possible that we might invite Pajamas TV, national tea party or conservative leaders such as Michael Patrick Leahy of Top Conservatives on Twitter, or other such individuals to come with us. This will be a very sensitive matter that we will need to discuss in the coming days. We have to be very very careful about discussing amongst ourselves anyone we include "outside of the family" because quite frankly, we are not only NOT part of the political establishment or conservative establishment, but we are also sadly not currently a part of the "tea party" establishment (*i.e.* Michelle Malkin, Eric Odom of Don't Go Movement, Smart Girl Politics, Top Conservatives on Twitter, FreedomWorks, Newt Gingrich of American Solutions, etc.)

We can probably pull off a phenomenally successful tour without these big-ego establishment types, provided that we do a good job in getting the word out to local tea party leaders and grass roots conservatives who operate in their local communities independently as is – the April 15th tea parties may have been promoted by Fox News, Pajamas TV, Michelle Malkin, FreedomWorks, American Solutions, etc...however almost all of the tea parties were organized and led by individual activists in local communities.[30]

Wierzbicki went on to propose a few key Senatorial targets: Harry Reid of Nevada, Chris Dodd in Connecticut, and Arlen Specter of Pennsylvania, a moderate Republican who was chosen in large part to make the protest less strictly partisan against Democrats. He also conceded that most of the financial interest would be concentrated on the individual expenditure accounts opposing these candidates, since the benefits would accrue to a political action committee.

Because of this political background, the TPX had a key philosophical difference with the Tea Party Patriots: they were willing to directly support and campaign on behalf of individual candidates, while the Tea Party Patriots studiously tried to avoid choosing sides in individual races for several years. (In 2013 they finally relented and formed a PAC called the Tea Party Patriots Citizen Fund.)[31]

Thus, the Tea Party Express was born. True to their name and their original stated goal, their first major action was a coast-to-coast bus tour which began in late August and scheduled its final stop at the 9/12 Taxpayer March on Washington. That event brings in a third key early player.

While FreedomWorks – a contributing sponsor of both the February and April TEA Party events – was fine with the concept of local protests and individual action such as they had achieved during the fight over the TARP program described earlier, they had a director of federal and state campaigns who dreamed a lot bigger. As Brendan Steinhauser described it five years later, he began working out the details of the 9/12 event six months beforehand:

(By) mid-March I had already reached out to the National Park Service in DC and inquired about reserving space for a massive Taxpayer March on Washington.

We looked at various routes and locations near the Capitol, but settled on a starting point at Freedom Plaza on Pennsylvania Avenue and 13th St. NW. I chose the date September 12th, 2009 because it gave us a long time to plan a huge event, and gave the movement time to mature and get organized.[32]

With the FreedomWorks organization on board, there was a website, a Twitter handle by the end of April[33] and Facebook page promoting the event by the middle of June.[34] Unlike the other local TEA Parties put together on short notice, this major event was going to be the culmination of months of work, with scheduled speakers running the gamut from TEA Party leaders who weren't politically involved when Barack Obama was elected to inside-the-Beltway fixtures who were providing their assistance to the very movement they had pined for. (Ironically, the predecessor group that spawned both FreedomWorks and Americans for Prosperity, Citizens for a Sound Economy, was calling for a Tea Party way back in 2002.[35] Obviously that appeal fell on deaf ears, probably because national security was more of a voter priority when the 9/11 attacks were still a recent event to them.)

Thanks to coverage on C-SPAN, to this day you can still watch the Taxpayer March on Washington.[36] (Maybe if you scan the crowd you will see me there.) And whether you believe the wild early reports of over a million strong in attendance or go with the far smaller estimates of 60 to 70 thousand people, it was still an event that proved the TEA Party movement was coming of age. (I'm not a great judge of crowds, but I would estimate the real number was in the low six figures, perhaps 300,000.)

However, in the ensuing weeks after the 9/12 event we learned that not all was rosy among the groups. Amy Kremer, who was a founding member of the Tea Party Patriots, decided later that month to formally bolt to the TPX, earning her an eviction from the Patriots' board of directors and sparking a bitter feud between the two groups that took months of legal wrangling[37] to decide. As the *Washington Independent* website put the rivalry at the time:

The self-described grassroots activists in Tea Party Patriots and the American Liberty Alliance see the Tea Party Express as a sham organization, using the political heft of the movement to push a bland, partisan Republican agenda. Privately and publicly, they accuse the Tea Party Express of being an "astroturf" outfit, a scheme for Republican strategists and candidates to take advantage of a movement that was chugging along fine without them.[38]

"They are the classic top-down organization run by G.O.P. consultants, and it is the antithesis of what the Tea Party movement is about,"[39] added Mark Meckler of the Tea Party Patriots.

Another of those grassroots activists was Orlando TEA Party organizer Phil Russo, a vocal critic who blogged about his disgust with the TPX when they first came to Orlando in November, 2009.

> The Tea Party Express is being organized and promoted by a political action committee (PAC) that is not connected to the Tea Party Movement in any way. The PAC is using the emotional attachment that people have to the Tea Party name to raise funds. If they had planned this tour and called it the PAC Fundraiser Express they know very well that no one would have showed up or donated money. So, they call their bus tour Tea Party Express knowing that large crowds will turn out and people will be more willing to give money if they think that the money is going to support the Tea Party movement or candidates approved by the Tea Party movement. We in Orlando find this to be disingenuous at best and outright fraud at worst and we are not alone in our feelings. The Houston Tea Party and other Tea Party groups are also boycotting the Tea Party Express stops in their respective cities. The PAC is paying two real Tea Party leaders to be on the bus with them to lend legitimacy to the tour. Also, the local Tea Party leaders are not "planning" these events *per se*. Local leaders are being asked to secure locations and permits but the program is predetermined by the PAC. All the music and speakers and the message... is determined by the PAC.
>
> When the Orlando Tea Party was contacted by the Tea Party Express about planning the stop here in Orlando... we told them that we could not in good faith ask our members and followers to attend an event that is raising funds for a PAC that will be going to candidates that are not in Central Florida and have not been vetted by the Orlando Tea Party. If we were going to hold such an event, which we would not, we would ensure that the money raised would go to candidates in Central Florida that were approved by our members and we would ensure that people donating knew to what candidates their money would go.[40]

Russo wasn't through with what he called the "Astroturf Express" though. A month later he was appalled at the expenses the group racked up in their visit to Orlando.

> I caught a lot of hell from the AstroTurf thieves that did not like the fact that someone was telling the truth about their little scam. Well, I should have titled this blog post "Vindication" because we now have proof that I was right. The PAC that organized the bus tour published their financial records recently. Every PAC is required by law to disclose their expenses. We now know how much of your money was spent to "get conservatives elected" and how much went into the pockets of the people on the bus.

While they were here in Orlando they went out to dinner at a restaurant called "Black Olive" and they spent more than $4,000. This is for one meal!!! Another night here in Orlando the gang ate at the Citrus Club, one of the most expensive restaurants in downtown Orlando, but don't worry they only spent $2,000 of YOUR money that night. Tens of thousands of dollars went straight into the pockets of the people on the bus, even the person who sanctimoniously told me that she wasn't getting paid to be on the bus! Tens of thousands more of your dollars went to a consulting firm owned by one of the people on the bus.

It really makes me want to puke that these people sent out emails exploiting our attachment to the Tea Party movement and our patriotism so they could raise money and live like rock stars for a month.[41]

There's a lot more discord and rancor where this came from; for gosh sakes, I'm only on the third chapter here.

Needless to say, Russo's view wasn't a lone voice crying in the wilderness:

The president of the Greater Boston Tea Party dismissed (them) as a group of 'entertainers,' and other Tea Party activists have complained that the Tea Party Express is not grassroots.

From the perspective of the Tea Party Express, the lack of much grassroots interest and close attention may be a good thing. Grassroots supporters provide a colorful popular backdrop for (TPX) to attract media attention and collect more contributions to spend on candidates and affiliated business operations – without any pesky accountability to local leaders.[42]

But perception is reality in politics; in the public eye there was just enough being revealed about the TEA Party and just enough slick marketing going on behind the scenes to make it look like the TEA Party was still primarily a bottom-up organization. (A case could be made that assertion was true through the 2010 campaign. After that, as you'll find in reading on, things changed for the movement.)

In the meantime, there were smaller groups looking for their own piece of the pie. Early on, Eric Odom had founded the American Liberty Alliance (ALA), which came out of his TaxDayTeaParty.com website. Unlike many of the other TEA Party groups, it was a for-profit enterprise that, over a relatively short period, rolled over into the Liberty First PAC and by the end of 2010 morphed into a "news and activism" site called Liberty.com.[43]

Odom's groups, though, struggled for success. A bus tour co-sponsored by the ALA (along with another former Odom employer, the Sam Adams Alliance, and the small inside-the-Beltway group Americans for Limited Government)[44] struggled to reach the finish line, losing participants and sponsors along the way.[45] And Liberty.com went through a number of iterations before finally folding in 2013. (That domain name now links to an international cable and satellite TV provider.)

Another smaller entity was Tea Party Nation (TPN). Formed by Tennessee attorney Judson Phillips at about the same time as the other groups, TPN's claim to infamy was the ill-fated attempt at the first Tea Party convention in early 2010.

It's not that the idea of a more formal TEA Party meeting wasn't sound, particularly as the focus began to shift from the outdoor protests that culminated in the late-summer 9/12 gathering to the prospects for making real political change in the 2010 midterm elections. But the fact that Phillips was charging convention-goers a hefty $549 price[46] to attend the event – much of which went to cover the appearance fee charged by keynote speaker Sarah Palin – didn't sit well with those who still considered the TEA Party a grassroots effort and didn't have that type of disposable cash laying around. "I'm not gonna throw my money around for that," said one activist.[47] Added *RedState*'s Erick Erickson, "I think this national tea party convention smells scammy."[48] While the show eventually went on despite the loss of several sponsors – as well as secondary speakers Reps. Michele Bachmann and Marsha Blackburn[49] – its fallout landed Phillips in court as financial backer Bill Hemrick, a trading card magnate, sued him over Palin's fee.[50] A second attempt at a TPN convention in Las Vegas, slated for the summer of 2010, never got off the ground, leaving Phillips liable for nearly $750,000 in unpaid bills and interest when the case settled two years later.[51]

All these groups were just beginning the fight for relevancy when the political world was shaken to its core. On August 25 the 60-seat filibuster-proof liberal majority in the Senate that the Obama administration was counting on to legislate its agenda became a thing of the past. The Lion of the Senate, Ted Kennedy, was gone.

# WHAT CAN BROWN DO FOR US?

*"It was a miracle moment...(Scott Brown) went from zero on the radar screen to what everyone was paying attention to."* - Christen Varley, Greater Boston Tea Party.

The death of Senator Edward "Ted" Kennedy on August 25, 2009 saddened the nation because it signified the end of the "Camelot" era initiated by our 35th President, a youthful John F. Kennedy. It also reminded America once again of the tragedies his family faced at the hand of assassins twice in less than five years, as well as other (often self-inflicted) misfortunes associated with the Kennedy name.

But in a political sense Kennedy's passing threw a monkey wrench into the Democrats' plans for enacting the Obama agenda by temporarily eliminating the 60-40 leftwing supermajority they could use to avoid Republican attempts to stop legislation via filibuster by invoking cloture, which required 60 Senators to agree.[1] Originally it was feared by Democrats that they would have to wait nearly six months for the results of a special election in Massachusetts to fill the remainder of Kennedy's term, but some legislative legerdemain by Bay State Democrats (requested by Kennedy himself as his health finally failed)[2] enabled them to avoid that crisis. After the succession law was changed, on September 24 loyal Democrat Paul Kirk, Jr. was installed as a four-month "caretaker" for Kennedy's seat.[3] As a condition of appointment, the 71-year-old Kirk promised he would not seek the remaining two-plus years of the term, and the election was set for the following January 19.

It was another change in Congress that would give the TEA Party its first true electoral test, though. In June President Obama had tapped moderate Republican Rep. John McHugh of New York to be his Secretary of the Army; McHugh resigned his House seat upon confirmation September 21. Although it was expected since the day McHugh was tabbed for the position, his resignation formally placed the 23rd District seat, representing the farthest reaches of upstate New York along the eastern shore of Lake Ontario and the nearby Canadian border, on the 2009 off-year ballot. Here was a chance for the TEA Party to see just how much political muscle it had.

However, there were some parameters within this campaign which made it different than a standard political effort. While Obama's intention to select McHugh became known in June, his confirmation languished as the Senate took care of other business and enjoyed its annual summer recess. Despite this uncertainty, the leading candidates were selected by local party officials as they were for an earlier special election in the adjacent 20th Congressional District.[4]

So while the 23rd District Democrats tried to convince a number of local elected officials to run, their collective refusal eventually led the party to eschew three previous failed aspirants for the seat and select lawyer and Air Force veteran Bill Owens as their candidate.[5] After all, the Democrats had little to lose since the region historically was so solidly Republican that portions of the 23rd hadn't elected a Democrat to Congress in over a century.[6]

On the other hand, the Republicans and TEA Party-influenced conservatives in the district had differing ideas.

Republican county chairs representing the eleven counties of the 23rd District came together in July and vetted a pool of interested candidates. Among this group were State Assemblywoman Dede Scozzafava and Doug Hoffman, a CPA and former Army reservist making his first bid for office. Knowing the district was a long-standing GOP stronghold that was trending toward the political middle – it narrowly supported Obama in the 2008 election, although the centrist Republican[7] McHugh was re-elected with ease – the county chairs decided to go with the experienced, more socially moderate[8] Scozzafava. (Also in her favor: she represented a portion of the 23rd in the state legislature; meanwhile, Hoffman actually resided just outside the district boundaries.)

Although Hoffman initially wished Scozzafava the best of luck in her effort,[9] a few weeks later he opted to go before the Conservative Party – which has its own ballot line in the state of New York – and got the blessing of their leadership to secure their nomination for the Congressional seat. As events unfolded, this made the race a three-way contest and a test of whether the TEA Party could make the transition to a viable political organization.

Eventually this otherwise obscure Congressional race became a cause among conservative and Republican leaders, with much of the TEA Party gathering on Hoffman's side while a handful of Republican regulars took what they considered the pragmatic approach in backing Scozzafava. Included in the latter group was erstwhile TEA Party backer Newt Gingrich:

> The special election for the 23rd Congressional District is an important test leading up to the mid-term 2010 elections. Our best chance to put responsible and principled leaders in Washington starts here, with Dede Scozzafava…

> This special election...could be the first election of the new Republican Revolution, but we need the momentum to get it started.[10]

Yet Gingrich and GOP regulars were swamped by an outpouring of support[11] for Hoffman: included in that number were Dick Armey of FreedomWorks, former Presidential candidate Steve Forbes, and potential 2012 White House hopefuls Michele Bachmann, Fred Thompson, Rick Santorum, Tim Pawlenty,[12] and – most importantly in TEA Party circles – Sarah Palin, who noted in her endorsement that Hoffman "has not been anointed by any political machine."[13] As the campaign continued into October, Hoffman's poll numbers surged thanks to the influx of TEA Party money and support – so much so that by month's end a clearly frustrated Scozzafava decided to withdraw, seeing she had lost her backing and that "victory was unlikely."[14] Yet while she said in her withdrawal announcement, "I am and have always been a proud Republican," Scozzafava endorsed the Democrat Owens a couple days later as an "independent voice...he will put our interests first."[15]

On Election night, November 3, it appeared Hoffman trailed Owens by over 5,000 votes, so he conceded the race. This allowed the Democrat to be sworn in by week's end and help push Obamacare through the House; however, the results were briefly thrown into doubt due to counting irregularities.[16] As it turned out, though, the unusual New York rules about ballot access and candidates running on multiple ballot lines allowed Owens to pick up enough votes to win as he was cross-endorsed by both the Democratic and Working Families parties – on a strictly Democratic line Owens came up short of the Conservative Party's Hoffman.[17]

While the national politicians that were angling for eventual TEA Party support took sides in the race, out of the various national TEA Party groups only the Tea Party Express endorsed Hoffman. (However, they didn't include Hoffman's district on their concurrent tour.) The others mostly maintained their "no endorsement" stances, either due to concerns about their tax exemption status or the idea of allowing their members to decide rather than a group endorsement.

Individual TEA Party volunteers, though, deluged the Hoffman campaign,[18] and to some observers that nationalization of the campaign was part of the problem. Local issues (in this case, Fort Drum and bridge repair)[19] and local municipal-level elections[20] matter, analysts said. They also contended the outsiders' tactics alienated a swath of the voters from this "very proud, self-assured area"[21] who resented the influx of out-of-state money and volunteers who supported Hoffman.

But other national leaders and TEA Party advocates from other parts of the country saw it differently. Conceding that local issues were a sore subject in the race, FreedomWorks' Dick Armey complained that time simply ran out on Hoffman: "He just got there late, that's all," said Armey.[22] Meanwhile, the Club for Growth, another inside-the-Beltway group looking to court TEA Party money and volunteers for their efforts, blamed it all on Scozzafava. "It turned out the Republican was the spoiler in the race," said the Club's Executive Director David Keating. "We can't control what others do in any event." Reportedly, the Club for Growth spent over $1 million on the Hoffman race.[23]

But across the country there was another Congressional race that most of these groups and workers ignored. Perhaps California's 11th District was considered too much of a shoo-in for Democrats, but there was a strong TEA Party presence in that part of California between Sacramento and Oakland and the Democratic opponent to GOP aspirant David Harmer was the state's lieutenant governor John Garamendi, a career politician who was jumping jobs (and lived outside the district.) So the national GOP provided little help,[24] and aside from a stop from the Tea Party Express – with the district in the back yard of its Sacramento headquarters, this wasn't much of a stretch[25] – neither did the TEA Party. Yet Harmer took a race where Democrats had over 64% of the primary vote between six candidates[26] and lost it by just 10 points.[27] (In 2010, Harmer would run in an adjacent district and lose by just over 1%.)[28] In the end, though, by the Friday after the election both Owens and Garamendi were sworn into Congress, providing two of the narrow margin of votes that got the Affordable Care Act (a.k.a. Obamacare) through the House.[29]

While the TEA Party was 0-for-2 in these off-year Congressional races, their effect was felt like an earthquake in local and state races. In both New Jersey and Virginia, Republicans won: the firebrand Chris Christie stopped 8 years of Democratic control of the Garden State by beating incumbent Democrat Jon Corzine, while Bob McDonnell regained the governorship of Virginia for the GOP for the first time since 2001, when Jim Gilmore left office. McDonnell beat Democrat Creigh Deeds handily, by 17 percentage points, in the race to win a four-year term. The GOP in Virginia also maintained its lieutenant governor, picked up the attorney general's office, and gained six seats in their House of Delegates in its statewide elections.

These local elections, which largely escaped the notice of the national GOP, proved a point made by defiant blogger and Los Angeles TEA Party organizer Stephen Kruiser during the days leading up to that offyear election:

> The argument is always that the desperately needed moderates won't be attracted to a conservative candidate, which is a truck load of manure we can no longer allow the GOP higher-ups to dump on us any more.[30]

But this series of elections also dictated a direction the TEA Party would subsequently take. You may recall that, among the early arguments between movement partisans, there was the debate of whether to create a third party. While the Conservative Party in New York was an established party with a ballot line, the fact that it was a minor party meant its ballot placement was disadvantageous.[31] "Coming off Line D, it became increasingly difficult to get out of the 40s,"[32] said Watertown mayor Jeff Graham. New York's ballot at the time was grouped by party, with the Democratic Party line on top (line A), followed by Republicans on line B, the Independence Party on line C, then the Conservative and Working Families parties on lines D and E, respectively. It was intentionally grouped to make straight party-line voting easier.

So while there were some TEA Party members and groups who gravitated to existing third parties such as the Libertarian, Constitution, or Reform parties, most decided consciously after the Hoffman fiasco they were better off trying to work through the Republican Party despite its flaws. Thus, new political activists had to learn about the Buckley Rule, named after *National Review* founder William F. Buckley: he preached the idea of supporting the most right-leaning candidate who was viable in a general election. Those who supported Dede Scozzafava in the 23rd District race obviously believed they were simply following the Buckley Rule as Hoffman was just a little too conservative for such a centrist district. While the Buckley Rule concept would make John Birch-style conservatives – especially those in the TEA Party – scoff and accuse the establishment of selling out, the idea behind Buckley was to at least move the needle in the right direction by getting a slightly less desirable winner as opposed to letting the perfect be the enemy of the good and losing entirely thanks to an extremist candidate who repelled too many voters.

> This was a bitter pill for some TEA Party regulars to swallow, though. A few days after his defiant remarks, Kruiser added, "The reality is that overhauling the GOP and getting it to focus on conservative principles and candidates ***is*** the pragmatic approach."[33] (Emphasis in original.)

Thanks to Ted Kennedy's passing and the subsequent special election, the TEA Party would soon enough have an opportunity to be pragmatic, Buckley style.

In many places, Scott Brown would not be considered TEA Party material thanks to centrist views on certain social issues, like abortion – in fact, based on his Massachusetts State Senate voting record, political analyst Dr. Boris Shor argued Brown was even farther left than the rejected NY-23 Republican candidate Dede Scozzafava.[34] But because the locale was the royal-blue state of Massachusetts, the election was a non-standard special balloting at an odd time on the political calendar, and the need was dire because a Democratic win would allow them to maintain their 60-40 filibuster-proof edge in the Senate where bad bills could steamroll their way through, Scott Brown was the TEA Party's choice in the early days of 2010. He was definitely the "right-leaning, but viable" candidate of that moment.

The election for what many pundits called the "Kennedy seat"[35] was a special election that would be held at a time on the calendar unusual for balloting outside of Presidential years – and even in those instances, it wasn't until the 2004 election cycle that Presidential primaries were first held in January. So once the off-year 2009 election was over, all eyes began to focus on this Massachusetts race, which held its primary on December 8. As expected, state Attorney General Martha Coakley beat three other Democrats to win their nod while Brown, who had the political background of being a state senator, won handily on the GOP side over a perennial candidate.

Early on, the polls suggested Coakley would be the winner, with the Intrade market-prediction service giving her a nearly 90 percent chance of winning as late as nine days before the election.[36] Just like Coakley's campaign, the Left was smugly sure they would keep the seat:

> Sorry rightards, but Intrade gives Coakley a nearly 90 percent probability of winning...Yep, read and weep. Martha Coakley, a Democrat, will replace the Honorable Ted Kennedy. The Obama-thon continues.[37]

Undaunted, the TEA Party put together a two-pronged effort to assist Brown, who was a naturally good retail campaigner in his own right. Initially criss-crossing the state in his old GMC pickup truck, Brown ran his campaign reminding people it wasn't the "Kennedy seat" but the people's seat. (He even had the break of the Libertarian candidate for the Senate seat having the Kennedy surname, which may have affected the chances of that gentleman being a spoiler.) To assist Brown, hundreds of volunteers from around the nation came to Massachusetts in the dead of winter to knock on doors and do political grunt work on his behalf. They were "freezin' for a reason," and that reason was to provide the 41st Senate seat for the Republicans and slow down the ultra-left Obama agenda.

Brown was certainly not a purist conservative, and there was an element of the local TEA Party that remained opposed him on principle,[38] but many of the volunteers, whether they came from the suburbs of Boston, drove from Missouri two days to get there, or were making a political run of their own,[39] were made pragmatic by the November failure of NY-23's Doug Hoffman and were determined not to make the perfect the enemy of the good.

On the other end of the scale, once Brown was formally endorsed[40] by the group, the money that was pouring into the TPX coffers through their Our Country Deserves Better PAC was being put to good use. OCDB spent nearly $350,000 on the Brown race, and most of it was committed to a campaign of carpetbombing the airwaves with pro-Brown commercials. Even so, their spending was dwarfed by groups supporting Coakley, who attracted nearly $1 million more than Brown in a race where independent campaign spending totaled $6.2 million.[41] This spending gap made far more important the disparity in volunteer work between the enthused backers of the Brown campaign and Coakley's forces, who were going through the motions because they figured the election was in the bag. Ten days out, the Coakley folks received the rude shock of a Public Policy Polling survey that had Brown up in the race for the first time, 48-47.[42] Yes, the candidate endorsed by the "extreme right-wing Tea Party group"[43] was winning in reliably blue Massachusetts.

One asset the Tea Party Express had that others in the TEA Party movement did not was their political savvy of running previous campaigns. For example, as the Massachusetts Senate election drew closer local television spots became harder and harder to come by, and they were getting more expensive – pricing was approaching the cost of national spots. So TPX shrewdly paid the little bit extra and bought the national spots,[44] which had the dual effect of getting out the message and further nationalizing the race as it became more of a referendum on Obamacare and less about local Massachusetts concerns. (Contrast this to what happened in NY-23: rather than a rural Congressional district, the city of Boston has a media market which covers most of the state and is accustomed to national attention for a variety of reasons.) In an election that was supposed to follow the usual Massachusetts script of a lopsided Democratic win, the fact that President Obama had to come in and do some last-minute campaigning[45] for Coakley revealed how caught off guard the Democrats were regarding the race.

Even then, Brown proved to be quick on his feet. When the President complained about Brown being in the pocket of Wall Street and poked fun at his method of transportation, saying "Forget the truck. Everyone can buy a truck," Brown retorted, "Mr. President, unfortunately in this economy, not everybody can buy a truck. My goal is to change that by cutting spending, lowering taxes and letting people keep more of their own money."[46] In essence, this soundbite was the mainstream TEA Party root message of being "Taxed Enough Already" and it propelled Scott Brown to a surprisingly easy win on January 19.

As it turned out, though, Scott Brown was sort of a "flavor of the day" for the TEA Party. It didn't take long for him to split from the movement on some key issues[47] and by the time Brown's 2012 re-election campaign rolled around (since Ted Kennedy was last elected in 2006, the 2009-10 special election was to complete his term) the TEA Party was much less enthused about helping him. Also factor in that Brown was running for re-election in the midst of a Presidential campaign with the entirety of the House and over 1/3 of the Senate also on the ballot, and you'll realize his race wasn't quite as unique the second time around. January, 2010 was a special opportunity for the TEA Party and in that case they came together with the GOP, swallowed some of their independent pride and stubbornness, and did a job that needed to be done in denying the Democrats more or less free rein in the Senate.

Yet the other effect of Brown's victory was to serve as a wakeup call to the Left which believed the TEA Party was a passing fad or just too extreme for the electorate at large. In reality the TEA Party was closer to the political center than the progressives were, but a set of narratives about the movement that started taking shape in the spring of 2009 became the Left's major talking points as the 2010 midterms approached. Of course, they had a willing set of accomplices in the mainstream media.

# THE STORY SLANTED

*"The Tea Party's right-wing populism is the perfect kind for corporate news outlets at a time when the wealthy elites who own and support them feel threatened by more authentic populist impulses."* Fairness in Accuracy and Media newsletter, May, 2010.

Once the reality of Scott Brown's upset win in Massachusetts sank in, the media and leftists (but I repeat myself) quickly realized this momentous event occurred in a place that was about as safe of a Democratic state as there was in the country, at least in terms of its Congressional delegation. With the prospect of an already rocky midterm election staring them in the face, preserving power in the face of a potential electoral bloodbath became an all hands on deck and no holds barred situation for the Left. No fact was safe nor was truth necessarily an objective – it was all about the narrative and preserving the Democrats' majority in Congress to keep the "fundamental transformation" of America going.

In one respect, however, fortune was on their side. With the various personalities and groups who were jockeying for position in the TEA Party as it developed over the last half of 2009 and into 2010, there were ample opportunities for a political press corps who originally saw the TEA Party as an isolated event to exploit some of the fissures within the movement and develop their own narrative. I've already pointed out some of this media treatment of the TEA Party's formation back in my second chapter, but it's worth revisiting as we continue on.

This attempted rewrite of history began with the charge that the various local TEA Party events weren't spontaneous, but coordinated by national conservative groups. Writer and author Jeffrey Feldman was one of those who originally attempted to equate the corporate sponsorship of one event in Washington, D.C. with the entire nationwide movement. According to Feldman and his *Frameshop* blog site, the whole thing was just a Republican plot:

> The Republican revolt is called Tea Party U.S.A. and the idea is that Republicans will stage protests against government spending, today, to send the message to Washington that the American people are tired of taxation without representation – or something like that.[1]

As it was, the Washington D.C. event was sponsored by a number of inside-the-Beltway interest groups, including AFP and FreedomWorks. But the same was not necessarily true around the country.

Feldman's piece was the initial salvo in the drive to paint the TEA Party as just a phony movement based on its corporate sponsorship. Just weeks after the first set of anti-stimulus events, writers Mark Ames and Yasha Levine went to the most unusual of investigative outfits, *Playboy* magazine, to boldly claim that Santelli's February 19 rant was, "a carefully-planned trigger for the anti-Obama campaign."[2] Their journalistic snooping led them to infer the following:

> ChicagoTeaParty.com was just one part of a larger network of Republican sleeper-cell-blogs set up over the course of the past few months, all of them tied to a shady rightwing advocacy group coincidentally named the "Sam Adams Alliance," whose backers have until now been kept hidden from public. Cached google *(sic)* records that we discovered show that the Sam Adams Alliance took pains to scrub its deep links to the Koch family money as well as the fake-grassroots "tea party" protests going on today. All of these roads ultimately lead back to a more notorious rightwing advocacy group, FreedomWorks, a powerful PR organization headed by former Republican House Majority leader Dick Armey and funded by Koch money.[3]

Ames and Levine noted that original TEA Party founder Eric Odom was the new media coordinator of the Sam Adams Alliance for a time in 2008-09, but he departed the group several weeks before Santelli spoke out. Later, Odom denied the allegations regarding any connection with the Koch family and called the story by Ames and Levine a "hit piece (that) was 100% fabricated and contained no reality whatsoever. Yet, its content was used to drive media narratives against the movement that still exist today."[4] (The original article was quickly pulled from *Playboy*, given its potentially libelous accusations about Santelli.[5] But Odom is correct in noting that it served the Left's narrative well and is still often used as a reference.)

Indeed, the brothers David and Charles Koch are favored whipping boys of the Left simply because they use a portion of the fortune they built up in the business world to promote initiatives and ideas which they believe will benefit all businesses, theirs included. If anything, history shows they lean in a pro-liberty direction: the prime example is David Koch's run for Vice-President with Ed Clark on the Libertarian ticket in 1980 – prior to Gary Johnson's two efforts in 2012 and 2016, that election served as the Libertarians' high-water mark in national balloting. Thus, a political movement that featured advocacy for lower taxes and less government spending would be something the Koch brothers would logically support based on their political beliefs, just as other businessmen such as George Soros, Peter Lewis, and Tom Steyer back left-wing interests and issues. Similarly, as noted previously in this volume, FreedomWorks was a major backer of the initial TEA Parties because they had common interests with the organizers.

Because the backlash against the stimulus programs addressed by the original February rallies was real and tangible, the Left had a perception problem. In order to provide a counterpoint to the caterwauling by John Q. Public – without conceding that the solutions offered by their allies Barack Obama, Harry Reid, Nancy Pelosi, and other Democrats in Congress were indeed unpopular – it required the usage of the "A" word.

As the April 15 TEA Parties approached, more far-left websites, such as *ThinkProgress*, began to play up the term "Astroturf."[6] Then the phrase was picked up by *New York Times* columnist Paul Krugman, who called the upcoming round of protests "AstroTurf (fake grass roots) events, manufactured by the usual suspects,"[7] which meant it became part of the spin for mass media distribution to the Left's echo chamber.[8] With that, Nancy Pelosi obviously felt free to make the comparison in her own district.[9]

There were some minor attempts to correct this false narrative – you know, from actual eyewitnesses that showed up for the events, such as this one in Seattle from observer Don Ward:

> These aren't the dime-a-dozen insta-rallies we've seen over the last eight years put on by professional protestors. Instead average people took time off from work, many of whom have never attended a political demonstration in their life, to exercise their right to petition the government for a redress of grievances.
>
> Seattle Police estimated that about five hundred protestors packed into Westlake Park to protest higher tax and the intrusive nature of the federal government into the daily lives of average Americans. The event was peaceful and festive, marked by patriotic music and handmade signs harkening to the 1773 Boston Tea Party.
>
> A few things were different. There were no drum circles. No one wore a mask over their face to hide their identity. Instead of taunting police officers, as usually happens when protestors from Evergreen or Seattle Central Community College crash a rally, the Tea Party folks thanked them. The ever present stench of reefer wasn't hovering in the air. The event started with the Pledge of Allegiance and ended with a singing of "God Bless America."[10]

*Seattle Times* writer and columnist Bruce Ramsey agreed, noting that his city's original "porkulus" protest was not put together by some large organization, but by

29-year-old math teacher and stand-up comic Kari Carender. In Washington state, the protests grew by Tax Day to involve a local radio station and a libertarian advocacy group, but they were still homegrown grassroots. “Some AstroTurf,” wrote Ramsey.[11] Multiply that by hundreds of cities around the nation and it's hard to fathom that there was a corporate hand up the puppet's back in each and every case.

As a whole regarding the Astroturf accusation, I happen to agree with writer and blogger Liz Mair:

> (I)rrespective of what you may think of the tea parties, the people who frequent them, or the underlying objections being raised by tea party attendees, the simple fact is that the people who are claiming this is all the product of some top-down organized astroturf effort are talking out of their rear ends and need to do some homework.[12]

So who are you going to believe? After all, the classic definition of Astroturfing involved the creation of front groups that encouraged willing dupes to perform some action such as submitting a form letter to their legislative representatives to create the illusion of a groundswell of support. (The political usage of the term is credited to former Senator and Democratic VP candidate Lloyd Bentsen of Texas, in response to a deluge of mail he received advocating for a particular issue on behalf of the insurance industry.) Unlike the rent-a-mobs associated with protests on the Left, though, the TEA Parties were far more spontaneous.

Moreover, once you got past the initial idea about governmental fiscal responsibility, local TEA Party organizations exhibited a lot of leeway on other subjects, particularly social issues, and also disagreed on the degree of government restraint required. While they could all agree the stimulus was a problem, hard-core libertarians and those protestors under the age of 30 had a very different perspective from the more traditional conservative Republicans who felt the government needed to keep its promises on extra-Constitutional programs such as Medicare and Social Security despite their effects on the budget.

That distinction, though, wasn't going to convince those on the Left to see the TEA Party as a legitimate petition for a redress of grievances. Even when the key organizers of the TEA Party moved away from the established political groups and formed the Tea Party Patriots, the existence of the competing Tea Party Express which was rooted in the stridently anti-Obama Our Country Deserves Better PAC – a group that regularly promoted GOP candidates – allowed naysayers to maintain the Astroturf line about the entire TEA Party, not to mention identify it as just another sector of the Republican Party. Add to this the for-profit aspects of other groups like Tea Party Nation and the American Liberty Alliance, and the seeds of doubt[13] could be planted among those in the middle who weren't quite sure what to make of these protestors and their demands.

The TEA Party, as it grew, also became the home of certain elements the Left loved to pick on. Take this example from reporter Ben McGrath at *The New Yorker*:

> As spring passed into summer, the scores at local Tea Party gatherings turned to hundreds, and then thousands, collecting along the way footloose Ron Paul supporters, goldbugs, evangelicals, Atlas Shruggers, militiamen, strict Constitutionalists, swine-flu skeptics, scattered 9/11 "truthers," neo-"Birchers," and, of course, "birthers" – those who remained convinced that the President was a Muslim double agent born in Kenya. "We'll meet back here in six months," (Glenn) Beck had said in March, and when September 12th arrived even the truest of believers were surprised by the apparent strength of the new movement, as measured by the throngs who made the pilgrimage to the Capitol for a Taxpayer March on Washington, swarming the Mall with signs reading "'1984' Is Not an Instruction Manual" and "The Zoo Has an African Lion and the White House Has a Lyin' African!"[14]

Yes, McGrath had to get those signs in, even if they represented just a small fraction of the signage (and sentiment) of the event. But his story brings up a very good point: one issue with the TEA Party was the fact their local leaders were often common folk unaccustomed to the ways of marketing and telling the news. Since the TEA Party was born without an established group of people to handle PR, the job fell onto others whose interests didn't always square with the philosophy.

> The pressing need to find media spokespersons for the Tea Party was, of course, awkward, given that the Tea Party has never been more than a disunited field of jostling organizations. A lot of Tea Party activism goes on in localities, states, and regions – and even at the national level there are no true chieftains of any global Tea Party entity.
>
> (…)
>
> (N)aturally, there are always ambitious national politicos and advocacy elites, who, in this particular case, like to see themselves as 'Tea Party leaders.' After the 2010 elections, especially, a lot of self-designated Tea Party leaders were happy to make themselves available for public statements or performances. Supply met demand.[15]

The "Astroturf" accusations about the TEA Party continue to this day – although we were treated to a shrill declaration of "final proof" back in 2013[16] – but they grew louder as the loyal opposition became more and more dominated by the nationwide groups, whether based inside the Beltway or not, that took charge of the movement in the time period leading up to the 9/12 rallies. As a prime example, FreedomWorks was criticized early[17] and often during the summer of 2009, and whether it was Dick Armey not answering a question regarding their common cause with the Tea Party Patriots to a “gotcha” journalist's liking,[18] trying to recoup its expenses for the Taxpayer March on Washington by charging speakers $10,000,[19] or just advocating for more participation at the summer's frequent townhall meetings held by Congressional representatives in their districts,[20] they (and to a lesser degree, Americans for Prosperity)[21] were made out to be the poster children for inside-the-Beltway influence by most of the left-leaning commentary sites.

But the second and much more damning charge against the TEA Party came from the Left's usage of the good old race card. It didn't take long for the first accusations of racism to come out of the leftist media, based simply on the fact predominantly white TEA Partiers were condemning the policies of a black (but in reality, mixed-race) President. The day after the Tax Day events, Keith Olbermann of MSNBC's *Countdown* welcomed as a guest the activist, comedian, and onetime Air America radio host Janeane Garofalo, and she planted the seed of the racist narrative. After watching the video of the crowd at an event in Pensacola, Florida booing a speaker who blamed the Republican Congress for overspending, Garofalo remarked:

> You know, there's nothing more interesting than seeing a bunch of racists become confused and angry at a speech they're not quite certain what he's saying. It sounds right and then it doesn't make sense. Which, let's be honest about what this is about. It's not about bashing Democrats, it's not about taxes, they have no idea what the Boston tea party was about, they don't know their history at all. This is about hating a black man in the White House. This is racism straight up. That is nothing but a bunch of teabagging rednecks. And there is no way around that. And you know, you can tell these type of right wingers anything and they'll believe it, except the truth. You tell them the truth and they become – it's like showing Frankenstein's monster fire. They become confused, and angry, and highly volatile.[22]

That message provided an undercurrent which slowly cut into the overall TEA Party message. William Jelani Cobb, a professor at Spielman College, returned to that narrative shortly after the reported sighting of racist signs at the 9/12 rally. “Now we have a black president,” Cobb told CNN, “which means, on its most basic level, that a black man has more power than any single white citizen in this country.”[23] This despite the fact the vast majority of the 9/12 speakers and signs stuck to the original call for governmental fiscal responsibility and restraint.[24]

But it's not unfair to say that there was an element of the white supremacist extremists who saw the TEA Party as a good ground for recruiting, nor can it be completely dismissed that some of the e-mail chains[25] and signage at the TEA Party events[26] was politically incorrect when it came to race issues. Regarding the recruiting aspect, the Anti-Defamation League also attempted to tie in the libertarian side of the TEA Party:

> As they have done with other political and social issues, for example, promoting the Ron Paul campaign and using the immigration debate, white supremacists and anti-Semites are planning to exploit Tea Parties to disseminate their hateful views and recruit a larger following.[27]

Remember, one thing Ron Paul was best known for was voting against a Congressional resolution commemorating the Civil Rights Act of 1964.[28] So he was an easy target.

Over the years, this particular strain of the racism accusation has moved on to cling to the Donald Trump campaign and presidency so it's nothing new – all that has changed is the verbiage and, more recently, the degree of reaction from the Left. What once tarred the TEA Party now taints Trump and the "alt-right" but the white supremacist cast of characters is basically the same.

So as a complement to the "Astroturf" contention, the racist narrative was now also being set. And every time the TEA Party or one of its leaders did something remotely questionable in the runup to the 2010 midterm elections, it was yet another chance for that not-so-subtle accusation to be driven home by the media.

Let us look first at a March 20, 2010 TEA Party rally at the Capitol. Dubbed "Operation Urgent Care" by the Tea Party Patriots,[29] it was held just hours before the final House vote on Obamacare was to be decided. After the event, Rep. John Lewis, a longtime civil rights icon, made the claim that he was called a "nigger" by one of the TEA Party protestors. "They were shouting, sort of harassing," Lewis told reporters. "But, it's okay, I've faced it before. It reminded me of the 60s. It was a lot of downright hate and anger and people being downright mean."[30] (Lewis was not a speaker at the event; he was simply walking through the gathering – not that he had to.[31] It was almost as if he was daring those gathered to create the controversy.) The same group also allegedly called gay Massachusetts Rep. Barney Frank a "fag," but reports noted the offender was admonished by others in the crowd.[32]

Yet when Andrew Breitbart challenged the leftists to put up video proof of someone using the n-word toward Rep. Lewis, no one stepped forth – even when he upped the ante by pledging a $10,000 donation to the United Negro College Fund.[33] But no one needed to supply the proof – not that there was any, since several different videos and eyewitness accounts showed the opposite[34] – because the accusation was as good as gold to the leftist media as it fit their narrative like a glove. “A weakness in (the TEA Party was) that the establishment media could find somebody presenting themselves as a Tea Party leader to say something crazy and then use those isolated instances to smear all of us,”[35] said Sacramento TEA Party leader Eric Eisenhammer.

Although he did more than “present himself” as a TEA Party leader, this was especially true in the case of Eric's fellow Sacramento TEA Party leader and radio host Mark Williams, whose remarks and writings were continually referenced by the movement's opponents as proof positive the whole lot of them were racists just barely this side of the Ku Klux Klan.

Williams' fall from grace began when CNN broadcast a phrase he used in a blog post calling Barack Obama “an Indonesian Muslim turned welfare thug and racist-in-chief.”[36] When Williams, who probably should have known better given he worked in the media, feebly replied that it was the way Obama was behaving, the trap was set. Regardless of the context, anything Williams said over the next few months was viewed through that lens.

Even after he stepped down as the leader of the Tea Party Express[37] a few months later, in June, 2010 – in large part due to his reputation and the distraction he was becoming – the media continued to seek him out, perhaps in the hopes of another PR disaster they could glom onto for their next news cycle. On July 14, 2010, they hit paydirt.

A day earlier, the NAACP, at its annual convention held that year in Kansas City, issued a resolution calling on the TEA Party to repudiate the “racist elements” within.[38] Naturally, Williams was in demand for his commentary, so he was a guest on CNN's *The Situation Room* program with host Wolf Blitzer and CNN contributor Roland Martin when he said, in response to the tag team of questions and accusations about the TEA Party from the NAACP regarding the issue, “Racists have their own organization. It's called the NAACP.”[39] Shortly thereafter Williams doubled down on the sentiment, penning a parody letter from “we coloreds” addressed to President Lincoln claiming that “we don't cotton to that whole emancipation thing.”[40]

Sensing a PR disaster in the making, the National Tea Party Federation quickly ousted Williams and the Tea Party Express from their ranks.[41] “Our members were offended by what he wrote,” said NTPF's Christina Botteri. “The Tea Party movement is much more important than this kerfuffle and we couldn't do nothing."[42]

In response, Williams called the tiff with the Federation a “personality conflict” with “some of the minor players on the fringes” hoping to advance themselves by taking him down, and told the media he was done talking about it[43] – invariably that's seen like blood in the water for the media sharks. Now they had their "proof" that the entire TEA Party was simply based on racism and the Left wasn't going to let it go.

Looking back years after the fact, Williams was contrite about his impact. Let me set this up by stating up front that I consider all of the TEA Party organizers heroes, so this is reflected in the reply:

> Thank you for considering me a hero but, please, do not let that you stop reporting what you see through your own eyes and hear through your own ears. I fucked up, a lot, to go with the good I may have done. None of the latter without the help of quite literally millions of people I never met (and) never will but was teamed with. Lotta heroes in the last decade especially.
>
> And a lot of them I let down. That I regret.[44]

But I think there's a useful thought exercise in order here. Imagine everything about the administration of our 44th President: the stimulus, the Affordable Care Act (including the gymnastics needed by Congress to get it passed), cap and trade proposals, foreign policy failures, rules created by executive order, and the rest of the whole nine yards, was exactly the same but the occupants of the presidency and vice-presidency were reversed. Would there have been a TEA Party under a President Biden and Vice-President Obama? I think there would have, and I also think the media would have attempted to play the race card even if Barack Obama had only been the veep.

Policy is policy, and bad ideas come from all races and genders. But the presence of a black President was used well as a shield by the progressive movement to shout down any opposition with the cry that those who questioned their motives were simply racists. That, in turn, was offensive to two minority TEA Party leaders: Deneen Borelli and Katrina Pierson.

> "It's easier for the Left to play the race card than address the public's legitimate concerns," says Borelli, "but what the Left and the media is doing is damaging and dangerous. **It's damaging because when everything is racist, nothing is.**"[45] (Emphasis mine.)

Adds Pierson, in her reaction to the NAACP resolution:

> The existence of the NAACP, and others like it, are threatened by the existence of the Tea Party. The reality is that we colored people no longer require the assistance from other Negros for advancement in 2010.

(…)

The NAACP has been completely ineffective in my lifetime, and the lack of leadership in the black community has contributed to the ability of these groups to speak on behalf of the rest of us. The ignored and forgotten society that lives among the projects has been abandoned by the likes of the NAACP. As well as with other groups and individuals that rode in the coat-tails of MLK, they are irrelevant but continue to feed off of the co-dependence that they have created among blacks for validation.[46]

Perhaps author and TEA Party leader Jonathan Wakefield had the right idea: power through it.

(W)atching Big Government Disciples perpetuate the myth that my friends and I (in the TEA Party) are somehow racist bothered me and made me want to get out there and defend our collective name.

Eventually, though, I realized this is actually counterproductive. The Big Government Disciples would like nothing more than to trap us into spending all our time trying to convince people that we're not racist. That way Americans, especially minorities, are focused on examining us and not the abysmal record of the Big Government Disciples whose policies have fostered the poverty that many minorities struggle under today.

(…)

Instead of getting frustrated or angry with the false accusations, I say the Tea Party should be encouraged by them. They wouldn't attack us if we weren't making an impact. And because they can't challenge us on the merits of the issues, they have to play the race card.[47]

When the shoe was on the other foot, though, the media was very slow to judge – or just ignored the story altogether. After an August, 2009 town hall meeting in St. Louis, sponsored by Democratic Rep. Russ Carnahan, a video[48] emerged of two SEIU union members beating a black man, Kenneth Gladney. The much-smaller Gladney was, depending on which account you believe, either giving out or selling Gadsden flags and other TEA Party-related merchandise when he was accosted by the much larger union members, one black and one white. A witness stated the black attacker asked Gladney, "Why is a nigger like you handing out these flags?"[49]

For Gladney, the incident turned out to be his fifteen minutes of fame as he was embraced by the TEA Party as a hero. However, despite the video evidence, his assailants were acquitted in a jury trial that didn't occur until July, 2011 – nearly two years after the incident and fifteen months after the SEIU pair pleaded not guilty. Writing at his *Gateway Pundit* blog after the trial, Jim Hoft noted that the Gladney case was the prosecutor's first jury trial and the defense put Gladney's credibility on trial to counter the video evidence.[50] Had this occurred in the other direction, it's certain the media would be screaming about a mistrial.

But race wasn't the only issue placed as an obstacle to the TEA Party: anyone who had a grudge against the government or perpetrated evil acts against it was automatically assumed to be a TEA Party-supporting far-right winger. This was the case in February, 2010 when disgruntled engineer Joseph Andrew Stack flew his single-engine plane into a building that contained the IRS office serving Austin, Texas. His suicide note blamed the IRS for many of his issues,[51] but could be interpreted more as a diatribe against the 1% which would become more common a year and a half later with the Occupy Wall Street movement.

The media's template regarding Stack was furthered when they found that Stack was a right-winger based on his Facebook page – only the page wasn't really his; it was a fake page set up as a plant within hours after the incident.[52] When people actually asked the Austin Tea Party leadership, they found out that Stack was neither a member of their groups nor was he even on their contact lists.[53] It didn't matter to the media, though, as each side blamed the other for influencing a clearly disturbed man desperate enough to wish harm on others in his final act.[54]

For several years afterward, any and all such outbursts of violence were blamed on the TEA Party – more often than not, though, it was eventually learned that the perpetrator was politically left-of-center. A good case in point was the Aurora movie theater shooting in July, 2012, where ABC's Brian Ross was forced to apologize for suggesting on air that shooter James Holmes was a TEA Party regular. The accusation turned out to be a case of mistaken identity, but Ross was led by how the other, innocent TEA Party sympathizer Jim Holmes fit well within the media narrative that the TEA Party was a violent group of Second Amendment supporters.[55]

Even though we have moved on from Obama to Donald Trump, violence is still blamed on the alt-Right (which is regarded as a successor group to the TEA Party despite having little in common) even as Antifa, Black Lives Matter, and other left-leaning groups have rioted in the streets around the nation. Recall that President Trump was absolutely blasted by the Left – and a good percentage of the establishment Right[56] – when he condemned "hatred, bigotry, and violence on many sides"[57] for the August, 2017 rioting and tragedy in Charlottesville.

The overall point is: an "Obama good, TEA Party bad" message was perpetrated by the Left once the TEA Party showed its political worth by electing Scott Brown.

Reflecting on her 2010 electoral bid, Nevada Senate candidate Sharron Angle noted her press treatment:

> I was constantly aware that we only had a short time to convince the electorate to vote for me and I was impatient over the loss of valuable time.
>
> Yet much of the press focus was not on issues but "buzz." Some came to make their name on the national scene by trying to capture the footage that would launch their careers on the national stage. I spent a day with one reporter who got a call near the end of the interview. He exclaimed, "I've made it big. I just got a call from CNN and MSNBC. They want all my footage."
>
> (…)
>
> My first encounter with the press in D.C. was outside a Republican Senate lunch. In my packed schedule for the day, no one from the press had made an appointment, yet nearly fifty media people crowded to take pictures and shout questions as I left the luncheon. I smiled, waved, declined an interview because of my schedule and got into the third floor elevator. Reporters raced one another down the stairs, and as I exited on the first floor, equipment flew across the floor in front of me. They rushed me as I entered a waiting vehicle. The story that day was "Angle Runs from the Press."[58]

And whether it was an investigative series from the *Huffington Post* detailing "The Anatomy of the Tea Party" in sinister tones,[59] an "aw-shucks" interview given to a grandmotherly TEA Party volunteer by David Letterman,[60] or the books written as an instant analysis of the movement by authors on the opposite side of the political spectrum[61] to glowing reviews,[62] the message was continually pounded in that the TEA Party wasn't truly part of the mainstream, or, in the case of a PBS/*Christian Science Monitor* story from April, 2010, alleged that it was a political movement which only had about 67,000 members and thus was receiving outsized coverage.[63] Yet, on the other hand, when it served the purposes of the media the TEA Party was portrayed as a "full-fledged independent political movement, (with speculation) whether it might even be an alternative to the two major parties."[64]

Meanwhile, the frustration was evident on the TEA Party side as well. Los Angeles TEA Party co-organizer Stephen Kruiser put it this way:

> Since last February a rather rapid shift has been taking place on the Right. Conservatives who used (to) express their displeasure with the GOP by simply staying home on election day (see: 2006 & 2008) decided to get out of the house and start putting faces and voices on our angst at Tea Parties.

> Nobody but us got it. Elected officials and GOP party insiders ignored us. With no support at all from within the ranks of establishment Republicans, the Tea Party movement has battled an unceasing barrage of lies and attacks from Democrats at all levels, the MSM and every entertainment industry lefty thought-barfer in America.[65]

Certainly the TEA Party wasn't truly part of the Republican Party. Those in GOP leadership circles were fine with the help when it served their interests, as it did for Scott Brown, but bear in mind the TEA Party had to swallow its pride and back a candidate for political expediency. Unfortunately for the GOP leadership, primary voters are a fickle lot and, once emboldened, they didn't always make the choices the leadership preferred. The next chapter shows just how the party elites dealt with those TEA Party voter selections.

# BACKLASH FROM THE BELTWAY

"*Democrats like to blame the Tea Party for everything because it satisfies their conviction that the GOP is captive to extreme interests; the Republican establishment does so because it allows elites to evade blame for the party's electoral and philosophical failures.*" - Molly Ball, writing in *The Atlantic*, March 19. 2014.

As the TEA Party's fortunes waxed, the rest of the nation found out the movement's collective angst wasn't just over the economic situation and the prospect of higher taxes, but also a frustration with how things had moved so quickly in that direction. Part of the reason for the fast pace of events was a once-in-a-generation shift in political fortunes that was benefiting Barack Obama and his fellow progressive Democrats.

After the 2008 election votes were counted, not only was Obama elected President but the Democrats expanded their Senate dominance as well. Going into the 2008 election, the body was deadlocked 49-49 between the two parties, but the two independents in the Senate – Al Gore's 2000 Democratic vice-Presidential candidate Joe Lieberman of Connecticut and future presidential aspirant Bernie Sanders of Vermont – caucused with the Democrats to give them a working majority.[1] While Barack Obama was elected without a lot of suspense, his coattails were lengthened by a candidate atop the GOP ticket who didn't motivate the base in John McCain and the unpopularity of Republicans in general. Add in the fact the GOP was defending 23 of the 35 seats contested in 2008, and it was a deadly combination for the conservatives – conditions that resulted in an eight-seat Senate gain for Democrats. The immediate results from the November election made the margin 56-41 in their favor (with one seat remaining in contention) and adding the two independents pushed the bulge to 58-41.

Then in April, 2009 Senator Arlen Specter of Pennsylvania, asserting that "I now find my political philosophy more in line with Democrats than Republicans," announced he was switching parties.[2] Specter's switch pushed the Democrats to a 59-40 edge, just one seat short of the 60-seat majority they needed to avoid cloture and ramrod any portion of the Obama agenda they desired through on a straight party-line caucus vote. They finally received this supermajority when Senator Al Franken of Minnesota was sworn in July 7 after a bitterly contested election, sullied by accusations of voter fraud, was finally confirmed eight months later by the state's

Supreme Court.[3]

Meanwhile, after taking over the House in 2006 following a dozen years of GOP control, the Democrats picked up another 21 seats in 2008. President Obama's initial popularity even allowed the Democrats, who began the 111th Congress with 256 seats, to win several special elections during the first few months of his term and reach 258 seats – a high-water mark they hadn't achieved since 1992. The aforementioned elections of Bill Owens in New York and John Garamandi in California in November, 2009 pushed the Democrats to that point (and finally filled all the vacant seats) although they lost a seat in Hawaii a few months later when Republican Charles Djou won a special election to replace Neal Abercrombie, a Democrat who resigned to concentrate on his run for governor later that year. Overall, the net results of several special elections over the span of the Congressional term left the Democrats entering the 2010 midterm election with the 57-41 Senate lead (along with the two independents, Lieberman and Sanders, that caucused with them) and a 255-178 House margin (with two vacancies.)

In 2010, there were 37 elections slated for the Senate: 34 regular elections as the class of Senators elected in 2004 were completing their terms, and three special elections to complete unexpired terms scheduled for Delaware, New York, and West Virginia. Out of those three, only New York incumbent appointee Sen. Kirsten Gillibrand was standing for election to finish her term, as Gillibrand replaced Hillary Clinton when she was appointed Secretary of State. (The other two appointees, Ted Kaufman of Delaware and Carte Goodwin of West Virginia, declined to run for the remainder of their respective terms.) As I alluded to earlier in this book, this election was held at a period of time when Democratic political strategist James Carville was predicting another long period of dominance for his party.

Traditionally in the postwar period, a new President has learned to expect his party will lose ground in Congress at the initial midterm election as the post-inauguration honeymoon wears off and the opposition learns where the President's policies have the weakest amount of support. Beginning with Dwight Eisenhower's first midterm election in 1954, where his Republican Party lost control of the House for what would end up being a 40-year run concluding with Bill Clinton's first midterm in 1994, the party in the White House lost House seats in their first midterm election all but one time: in 2002, Republicans gained eight House seats and one Senate seat under President George W. Bush in the first balloting after the 9/11 attacks. On average, the President's party suffered a 25-seat loss, although the two largest losses that skewed the average came with Democratic presidents: Lyndon Johnson lost 48 House seats in 1966 and Bill Clinton lost 54 in 1994. Conversely, the Senate was more mixed in its results because so much depended on the partisan makeup of the available seats – in 2010 Democrats would be defending 19 seats and Republicans 18.

Given that information, pundits were probably correct early on in assuming the Democrats would maintain control for another two years, although the majorities Barack Obama enjoyed would be thinner in the second half of his term. What happened instead was one of the most contentious midterm elections in some time.

As I pointed out a couple chapters ago, the election of Scott Brown in January, 2010 put the Left and Democrats on notice that this midterm would not be a cakewalk of a campaign for them. Conservatives and Republicans were just as motivated by opposition to the Obama agenda as liberals and Democrats were previously spurred into action by an unpopular war, Congressional scandal, and a failing economy in 2006 and 2008. Now that the TEA Party was a proven political force and had won and lost elections depending on the degree they could influence the electorate, the 2010 GOP primary season took on additional importance.

With their newfound political muscle and a distrust of Washington insiders and candidates deemed to be too moderate, TEA Party activists jumped into races up and down the political ladder. We all know what happened on Election Day in 2010: Republicans surged back into the House majority by smashing the pre-election expectations of perhaps adding 40 to 50 seats[4] and securing a bare majority[5] by eventually adding an astounding 63 seats to their total. But Republican leaders bemoaned missed opportunities in the Senate, where six seats were won but ten were needed to provide a Senate majority for the GOP once again. In their postmortem, pundits[6] and unnamed "Republican leaders and strategists" placed the blame for falling short of a majority on TEA Party-backed candidates in four states: Colorado, Delaware, Nevada, and West Virginia.[7] GOP Chair Michael Steele, who eventually lost his chairmanship after the election, conceded there was a risk in allowing voters to select nominees.

All four of these candidates – Ken Buck in Colorado, Christine O'Donnell in Delaware, Sharron Angle in Nevada, and John Raese in West Virginia – were winners in their respective Republican primaries, but victory there came more easily for some than others. Raese handily won his primary over a large cast of otherwise barely-known characters, but the other three took their spots over more established candidates preferred by national party leadership.

And arguably the West Virginia race was the most difficult one for Republicans to win: Raese was somewhat of a perennial candidate who had lost previous Senate races against longtime fixtures Jay Rockefeller and Robert Byrd. Going out of the frying pan and into the fire, for this third bid Raese was going up against term-limited Governor Joe Manchin, who had just won re-election overwhelmingly two years earlier. But the race was close going into the last few weeks, with the one major charge from Democrats being that Raese's wife was a registered voter in Florida –

evidence to them that Raese was trying to avoid West Virginia taxes.[8]

Yet it was two commercials that turned the tide against Raese and for Manchin, neither of which Raese had a direct hand in.

In October, it was learned that an anti-Manchin commercial sponsored by the National Republican Senatorial Committee used actors who were supposed to emote a "hicky" demeanor and appearance.[9] It allowed Manchin's campaign to continue the Florida claim as well, noting "it only proves that John Raese has spent too much time in the state of Florida, living in his Palm Beach mansion and doesn't know, understand or respect the great people of this state, and what we stand for." Raese's argument that Democrats were trying to "deceive" voters because that he had nothing to do with the commercial (since it was an independent expenditure by the NRSC) fell on deaf ears.[10]

More important, though, was a spot that drew nationwide attention:[11] [12] Manchin's "Dead Aim" commercial.[13] In his effort to distance himself from a President who was deeply unpopular in his state, Governor Manchin played up his opposition to several of Obama's policies, particularly Obamacare and the proposed cap-and-trade system. The spot worked well because not only could Manchin tout his NRA endorsement but because he literally blew a hole in the cap-and-trade bill – a powerful visual image. Even a pro-Raese rally a couple weeks later featuring noted hunter (and rock singer) Ted Nugent[14] couldn't move the needle back in Raese's favor.

Polls showed Raese and Manchin trading the lead until the last two weeks of the campaign, but in the end the governor's name recognition and presentation of his significant shift to the right of common Democratic party orthodoxy allowed him to prevail by 10 points over Raese. In the end, there wasn't a whole lot the TEA Party could be blamed for, although it could be credited for making Manchin campaign to a position well to the right of most Democrats nationally. And while West Virginia Republicans didn't elect Raese, they managed to pick up one of three House seats in the state, putting themselves at an advantage in the delegation for the first time since a brief period in the 1940s.

In Colorado, Ken Buck was a former U.S. attorney who had run for and won the office of District Attorney in Weld County, a county which spans the region between the outskirts of Denver and the state's borders with Nebraska and Wyoming. His main primary opponent was former lieutenant governor Jane Norton, whose experience also included work as a regional director of the federal Department of Health and Human Services under Presidents Reagan and George H. W. Bush and a short stint in the Colorado House. In a method relatively unique to Colorado politics, Buck was placed on the ballot by the state's Republican convention while Norton eschewed the convention and petitioned her way into the running.[15]

Despite the TEA Party embrace of Buck, though, he didn't seem comfortable with being lumped with them. Early on, he was caught on tape wishing someone would "tell those dumbasses at the TEA Party to stop asking questions about birth certificates while I'm on the camera?"[16] Shortly after the primary win, Buck made it known that he "resisted" the TEA Party label, preferring to be known as a candidate of the grass roots.[17]

As a first-time candidate on a major stage, Buck quickly had to learn that every word he spoke was important because chances were someone would be filing it away for future reference. Early on, he assumed honesty was the best policy when it came to beating the press, stating to *Politico:*

> "The only way for me to get my message out and for people to understand who Ken Buck is and that I'm not the person being portrayed by [Democratic National Committee Chairman] Tim Kaine or Michael Bennet is for me to be very open. And I will answer every question," he said.
>
> "Does it look like I'm afraid of you?" Buck added, chuckling.[18]

Indeed, Buck survived a pre-primary exchange with opponent Norton where he stated, "Why should you vote for me? Because I don't wear high heels." He then stepped in it further: "She questioned my manhood. I think it's fair to respond. I have cowboy boots. They have real bullshit on them. That's Weld County bullshit, not Washington D.C. bullshit."[19] All that was fodder for a later Norton commercial[20] and ended up helping to define Buck's campaign.

Regardless of his willingness to answer questions, the media was bound and determined to push Buck away from the economic issues he'd hoped to run on and into the realm of social conservatism. Just weeks before the election came another "gotcha" question on a *Meet The Press* debate with appointed incumbent Senator Michael Bennet regarding whether being gay is a choice. "I think that birth has an influence over it, like alcoholism and some other things," said Buck, "but I think that basically, you have a choice."[21] Naturally, the Left howled because it had another scalp.[22] And while he tried to clarify his remarks by stating "I wasn't talking about being gay as a disease,"[23] the timing was not good for his campaign, and the reaction to his misstatements became known locally in *The Denver Post* as "Buckpedaling."[24]

Coverage of these statements in the local and national media took Buck off his message, which was otherwise a fairly conservative one. As described in a postmortem by Jason Salzman at the *Colorado Pols* blog:

> In assessing his Senate bid after his loss, Buck told *The Denver Post* that

Democratic trackers recorded video of him at 600 public appearances and took his words out of context.

A review of his statements, however, shows that videotapes of Buck mostly illuminated straight-forward policy positions that voters in the general election, as opposed to conservatives in the GOP primary, found disagreeable.

Many of the videos that hurt Buck weren't shot by his opponents at all, but by his supporters, eager to spread the word about Buck's ultra-right conservative views.

The statements that damaged Buck in these videos for the most part weren't gaffes but policy statements, which may never have come to light had they not been recorded on the campaign trail.

Video clips showed Buck telling various conservative audiences that Social Security is a "horrible policy," the Veterans Administration and big chunks of the federal government should be privatized, and the Department of Education abolished. He also questioned the federal separation of church and state and the federal student loan program.

One clip aired repeatedly in TV ads showed Buck telling a Tea Party group during the primary: "I am pro-life, and I'll answer the next question. I do not believe in the exceptions of rape or incest."

The passion in his voice on the video contrasted with his statements later that he wasn't campaigning on social issues, like abortion.[25]

Because Buck barely lost his 2010 bid for the Senate, he planned on making another one for 2014[26] before changing his mind[27] and successfully winning Colorado's open Fourth Congressional District House seat, a position he still holds today. So while the GOP may not have preferred Buck in that particular Senate race, they didn't mind him trying it again for a lesser office four years later. (Buck's decision was assisted by the fact his Congressman was the one seeking the Senate seat, which left the House position as an open seat in a heavily Republican-leaning district. All Buck needed to do to prevail in the Fourth was to survive the primary.)

Not so much with Nevada's Sharron Angle. While the Republican establishment was thrilled with the prospect of beating longtime incumbent and Senate leader Harry Reid thanks to the interest placed in the race by the TEA Party, they would have preferred to see longtime State Senator Sue Lowden win the nomination. Lowden, though, was hamstrung by a few unfortunate comments herself, especially one where she suggested a return to paying for health care through the barter system.[28] With

Lowden's campaign tanking at the same pace as that of original GOP frontrunner Danny Tarkanian – son of the longtime UNLV basketball coach and a perennial candidate – Angle, who previously served in the State Assembly for eight years before making a fruitless bid for Congress in 2006, was the last one standing from a crowded primary ballot.

Angle, though, also had the tendency to put her foot into her mouth. Some of her best-known misstatements: calling the $20 billion BP put into a fund for Gulf oil spill victims a "slush fund,"[29] recounting how she advised teenagers who became pregnant "that they had made what was really a lemon situation into lemonade,"[30] and telling Latino students that some of them looked more Asian.[31] Against a seasoned politician like Harry Reid and a media very willing to amplify everything which could be construed to be outside the mainstream that TEA Party-backed candidates said, Angle's explanations after the fact were basically ignored. Her biggest issue, as told to the *Washington Times* by Nevada-based political consultant Ryan Erwin, was that, "(Angle) walked into this race with very low name ID. She's now been defined by Harry Reid and now she has to redefine herself."[32]

Angle also had the unique problem of having to run against the "Tea Party." Nevada's relatively lax laws on party formation (paperwork and 250 signatures) allowed Scott Ashjian, the owner of a paving business, to create the Tea Party of Nevada and qualify for the 2010 Senate ballot[33] even though no one connected with the real TEA Party in Nevada had ever heard of him.[34] Ashjian didn't turn out to be a serious contender, as he had negligible financial support and a number of personal and financial issues during his campaign,[35] but the usage of the name was enough to perhaps confuse a few voters. (Eventually even the Tea Party of Nevada's chairman switched his support to Angle.)[36]

What gave the Washington establishment more heartburn than anything, though, was the so-called "extreme" positions Sharron was taking. ("Extreme" being defined as more in line with Constitutional principles, as I'll reveal in due course.) Yet Angle seized the lead in pre-election polling from October on, which made Reid's eventual five-point victory a surprise to many observers. They failed to consider the "turnout machine"[37] Reid had built up over the years – a group that pollsters obviously missed.

After losing to Reid, Angle unsuccessfully vied for the Senate again in 2016, falling in the GOP primary, and lost a bid to unseat Rep. Mark Amodei in the 2018 Republican primary.

Finally, we have Christine O'Donnell, the candidate who drew the most establishment Republican ire. Her sin: beating a candidate who the pundits expected would flip a Senate seat from Delaware to GOP hands for the first time since William

V. Roth, Jr. retired after the 2000 election.

With the three aforementioned candidates having already won their primaries – and Angle and Buck running into trouble on the campaign trail – Beltway Republicans had plenty of reason to feel that they needed a sure thing, and they assumed Delaware Republican voters would see this and vote accordingly in one of the nation's final primary elections. (Delaware held its Senate primary just seven weeks before the general election, on September 14.)

Instead, O'Donnell defeated the longtime moderate House member Michael Castle for the GOP nomination. Castle, whose 18 years in the House weren't even the capstone to his political career – he was the state's governor for two terms immediately preceding his election to Delaware's lone House seat – seemed early on to be the favorite to land a cushy Senate job to finish up a political career that began back in 1966 when he was first elected to the Delaware House of Representatives. In respect to the "Delaware Way" of recycling officeholders to different positions,[38] O'Donnell was the only primary opponent Castle had and she was fresh off a loss in the 2008 election for that same seat to Joe Biden, who was allowed by Delaware law to be on the ballot for both Senate and Vice-President. (It was Biden's resignation which made the special Senate election necessary.)

But Castle's moderate stance on issues – his American Conservative Union lifetime rating was a modest 52 in 2009, the last year it was determined[39] – was anathema to TEA Party voters, and it was those Republican activists in the rural southern part of the state who turned out in just enough numbers to push O'Donnell over the top.[40]

Christine O'Donnell had two strikes against her from the get-go. First of all, she was carrying a lot of baggage from her futile 2008 effort, for which she reportedly claimed to have won two of Delaware's three counties. (She lost all three, although in the rural conservative stronghold of Sussex County Christine lost by just 272 votes out of over 86,000 cast.)[41] Fallout from that 2008 campaign also allowed other rumored anomalies regarding both her political accounting and personal money management skills to become issues in 2010 – by the end of the primary season, the Delaware state GOP was in open revolt against the O'Donnell campaign to the extent they were running commercials overtly asking state Republicans to back Michael Castle.[42]

The second big sin, according to the Delaware Republican Party, was the $250,000 donation she received from the Tea Party Express. That brought accusations of campaign coordination and a complaint to the Federal Election Commission from the state party against one of its own candidates.[43] Sarah Palin could endorse whoever she wanted, but to the Delaware GOP all that national money from an insurgent organization was a bridge too far – especially one that dropped both a pro-O'Donnell and anti-Castle commercial spot, the latter urging Delaware Republicans to "defeat liberal Mike Castle."[44]

Nor did O'Donnell make a good impression on at least one important Republican pundit. "I've met her. I wasn't frankly impressed by her abilities as a candidate," said Karl Rove to a disbelieving Sean Hannity as the Delaware results rolled in. "We were looking at eight to nine seats in the Senate. We are now looking at seven to eight in my opinion," Rove concluded.[45]

So it goes without saying that the establishment in Delaware's Republican Party woke up the morning after the primary and had a collective coronary about the results. And while O'Donnell had an uphill battle to begin with, the four words that eventually did her effort in were uttered in a commercial quickly mocked around the country: "I'm not a witch."[46] Her "dabbling" in witchcraft as a young lady – which consisted of a brief dating relationship with a boy who was into such dark arts – was the last straw for Delaware voters, who rejected her on Election Day. At least this time she indeed won two of the state's three counties.[47]

With these 2010 losses fresh in mind, some experts worried about the TEA Party's effect on the 2012 Presidential election. "They are going to try to have a tremendous impact on the Republican side," said well-regarded political expert Larry Sabato. "They are going to try to pick the nominee. The problem of course is that the Tea Party is well to the right. It is further to the right than the country, there is simply no question about that."[48]

But were they really? In a research project of this size – and after all, a book like this takes a lot of study – it's easy to discern that much of the source material on these races came from outlets with an agenda not in line with the candidate's. However, in the aftermath of their campaigns, both Angle and O'Donnell wrote books to explain What Happened (with apologies to Hillary Clinton.) In the biography she penned in the wake of the 2010 election, *Right Angle: One Woman's Journey To Reclaim The Constitution*,[49] Sharron Angle spelled out the reasons for having the platform that she had.

> Drastic measures must be taken to stop these politicians in their tracks. Does this mean a revolution is in order? No, I am simply saying the American people can replace corrupt, weak, and self-interested politicians by raising the standard to that which proclaimed liberty in 1776. The 'Silent Majority' can be silent no longer. We do not have the option or the luxury to sit on the sidelines. Transition means a grassroots movement with grassroots leadership.[50]

Angle also praised the TEA Party movement as a necessary ingredient in enacting her vision:

> The TEA Party movement is Main Street America fighting for freedom in peaceful assembly that would make Martin Luther King, Jr. proud…[51]
>
> I am conveying that there is a very real awakening of the populace who are trying to communicate with the elite, unresponsive, and arrogant centralized ruling class. It is time for this ruling class to clear their ears, listen to their constituents, take these good Americans seriously, and get a grasp on the level of frustration permeating this great country of ours…
>
> The TEA Party protests are an outpouring of the fear that our country is being lost to the corruption of political greed and lust. The best solution is not to overthrow the government but to dismantle repressive laws that have fostered corruption and then enforce the laws designed to prevent it.[52]

In other words, her being at times what she jokingly referred to as "41 to Angle" for being the lone vote against a bill in the 42-seat Nevada Assembly was the proof that she would stand on principle if elected to the United States Senate, and her agenda was that of a follower of the Constitution. Written just after her 2010 campaign, *Right Angle* is both postmortem and political platform for future races that she indeed ran in subsequent elections.

On the other hand, O'Donnell and her book *Trouble Maker: Let's Do What It Takes To Make America Great Again*[53] (shades of the later Trump campaign) was less of a political agenda and more a telling of her side of the story regarding the 2010 Senate race as well as addressing the allegations of embellishing her college records, fiscal irregularities with her 2008 campaign, and other issues brought up in the wake of her upset victory over Mike Castle. Her story wasn't so much of a backlash from the Beltway – although the national GOP was as shocked by the results as their state counterparts in Delaware were, they at least assisted the O'Donnell campaign – as it was an indictment of her state party. "I think at least for the party in Delaware, the Republican leadership in Delaware," O'Donnell said in a later interview with Bill O'Reilly of Fox News, "they would rather control the way they lose than lose control of their party."[54]

But a state party is supposed to be an extension of the national leadership, and while the TEA Party had given the GOP good results in the 2010 midterms establishment Republicans echoed the sentiments of Larry Sabato: skittish that TEA Party-influenced voters would select a presidential contender in 2012 who was perceived to be outside the mainstream like Angle, Buck, O'Donnell, or Raese were made out to be.

The 2010 election season illustrates a good point about where the TEA Party eventually failed. At a time when they had the bully pulpit and could take advantage of having an unpopular President and Congress, they ran against both bodies. Opposition is all well and good in terms of comparison and contrasting – and they got a lot of mileage out of opposing Barack Obama for seven years – but once the dog finally caught the car in 2016 the TEA Party had faded as a political force, as many of their staunchest supporters early on grew tired of the excuses.

Even before the initial spring 2009 rallies when what would become the TEA Party banner was being carried by the libertarians of the political world, true believers in the cause were making the attempt to not just oppose government but also present a vision of what they would do if the reins of power were handed over to them. When people have been inculcated with the perceived benefits of an all-encompassing, overly powerful government for an entire lifetime, they need to be educated on the benefits of liberty before they can be trusted with selecting appropriate leadership to maximize what the Constitution guaranteed to them. It was why the renewal of interest in our founding documents was just the first step in what should have been a series of lessons.

People go with what they know, and it's no secret that Americans want more of whatever makes life easiest for them as individuals. Most would agree with the primary TEA Party message that they themselves are being overtaxed, but there's a whole different political movement which depends on the notion that certain income levels should pay a larger "fair share" of their income to the tax man than others. It's telling that one party always focuses their tax-cutting efforts toward the "middle class" yet the TEA Party ignored the modest tax cut which was part of Obama's stimulus[55] because it came with a truckload of spending and debt that same party also embraced.

Yet many members of the TEA Party were also foursquare with government spending and debt when it came to certain other aspects of their lives like Medicare and Social Security. (I'm going to return to this disconnect at far more length in a later chapter, let me assure you.) Politicians, who then as now wanted most of all to be re-elected, were quick to advocate for "reform" of these entitlements rather than their eventual replacement – even if that was at odds with the principles of limited government – because TEA Partiers had always known these entitlements and expected to receive them when they reached retirement age because they "paid into the system" and were "promised" the money. (The average beneficiary receives far more than they paid into the system, though.)[56]

So soon enough the Republicans discovered that they could promise people the moon as long as they were still in the opposition. Frame that in your mind as you consider what comes next: with the dawning of 2011 and the changing of the guard in the House from outgoing Speaker of the House Nancy Pelosi to Republican choice John Boehner, those who believed in the TEA Party principles were ready for a robust fight against the Obama agenda. That optimism didn't last very long, though.

# THE FLEETING TASTE OF SUCCESS

"*They say that the US Senate is the world's most deliberative body. Well, I'm going to ask them to deliberate upon this: The American people are unhappy with what's going on in Washington. Eleven percent of the people approve of what's going on in Congress.*" - Rand Paul in his victory speech, November 2, 2010.

It was understandable that establishment Republicans inside the Beltway groused about what the TEA Party did not provide – that being a majority in the Senate – but this overlooks the overall results of one of the largest wave elections in history and how much it aided the GOP.

Looking at the six who succeeded in crashing the Senate – John Boozman of Arkansas, Dan Coats from Indiana, John Hoeven of North Dakota, Ron Johnson representing Wisconsin, Mark Kirk taking Barack Obama's old Illinois seat, and Pat Toomey succeeding turncoat Arlen Specter in Pennsylvania – all of them took former Democratic seats in the process, some of which had been so for decades. (Boozman's Arkansas seat had been a Democratic stronghold since Reconstruction.) Most of them could credit the TEA Party for their success, at least to some extent. But TEA Party hearts were most sent a-patter by two Senate candidates who kept Republican seats but promised to shake up the way the staid body was run, especially since neither were candidates preferred by party brass when their campaigns began.

When Kentucky's aging, ailing, and increasingly unpopular Jim Bunning finally decided to call it a Senate career, many assumed Kentucky Secretary of State Trey Grayson would become the state's next Senator. All that stood in the way, it seemed, was the candidacy of an ophthalmologist by the name of Rand Paul.

We first met Rand back in the opening chapter when he was a speaker at the 2007 Boston Tea Party fundraiser for his father's 2008 Presidential campaign. Given the family heritage, it was no surprise that Grayson backers and establishment Republicans in Kentucky, including Senator Mitch McConnell, attempted to paint Rand as an extremist for his libertarian-shaded view of conservatism.[1] But in an election year defined by a movement that stood for limited government and fealty to the Constitution, there was no doubt Paul's message was going to find a receptive audience in the Republican camp – so he handily defeated Grayson in the primary by double digits.

Far from what passes for the big city in Kentucky in Louisville, and away from the state capital in Lexington, Paul stood at a country club in his hometown of Bowling Green (population at the time: 58,067) and told an exuberant gathering of supporters, "I have a message from the Tea Party; a message that is loud and clear and does not mince words: We have come to take our government back."[2] His Democratic opponent would be the state's Attorney General, Jack Conway – so Rand was up against another candidate who had ran for and won statewide office on a previous occasion.

When Rand's father ran for President his candidacy was regarded as more of a curiosity among Republicans and few people took it seriously because, to be brutally honest, there was next to no chance he was going to win as a complete political outsider with little name recognition outside his Texas district and the small percentage of libertarian acolytes scattered nationwide. But once Rand won the Senate primary, in a state that had reliably elected Republicans since the Clinton era despite a Democratic advantage in voter registration – well, both the establishment and media were scared out of their wits. Democrats immediately tried to take advantage of that, with DNC Chair Tim Kaine claiming, "ordinary Americans are unlikely to be receptive to extreme candidates like Rand Paul in the general election this November."[3]

Immediately Rand was pressed hard on the libertarian end of his beliefs, with the first controversy coming out days after his primary win but stemming from the pre-primary endorsement interview he did with the *Louisville Courier-Journal*. In that interview, Rand told the editorial board he doesn't like the idea of telling private business owners how to run their businesses,[4] and the comment was uttered in the context of a discussion on the Civil Rights Act of 1964. Once he won the primary, it became a hot topic for interviews on National Public Radio and MSNBC's *Rachel Maddow Show,* along with numerous media reports.[5] Eventually Rand's campaign clammed up toward the mainstream media altogether, much to the chagrin of the press.[6] Then again, the media portrayal of Rand's supporters (and TEA Party regulars in general) as "a bunch of gun-totin', Bible-bangin', anti-Semitic racists"[7] wouldn't make for a warm and fuzzy relationship with reporters, would it?

While the media was tut-tutting Paul's beliefs, many fellow TEA Party members believed they made perfect sense from a Constitutional, limited government standpoint. "Whether a sign is on a door or placed in a window doesn't change the heart of the man who owns the restaurant," said Florida TEA Party organizer Robin Stublen to *The Daily Beast*. "And first it's one thing, but now the government is telling me how much salt I should eat or whether I can have soda – why don't they just come in and burp me after dinner?"[8] Added Memphis TEA Party organizer Mark Skoda, "There is no place for racism in the TEA Party."[9] Skoda may have insisted the truth, but the narrative had long been set, as detailed elsewhere herein.

Another problem besetting Paul's campaign soon after the GOP primary: a schism with the actual Libertarian Party in Kentucky that briefly made it appear the Libertarians would run a candidate for the seat.

Rand had “gone from being an outsider candidate to a tea party candidate to an establishment candidate in the past nine months," complained Kentucky Libertarian Party Vice-Chair Joshua Koch, who was a former Paul volunteer. “It's a complete identity crisis,” he added, calling Paul and Democratic candidate Jack Conway “faces of the same bad coin.”[10] Koch may have been frustrated with Rand Paul and wanted an opponent for him, but state Libertarian Party Chair Ken Moellman quickly insisted that, despite the fact “Rand Paul is not a libertarian,” they would not run a candidate against him.[11] That turned out to be a reasonable choice.

Later in the summer, reporter Jason Zengerle, writing at *GQ*, dug up what became known as the “Aqua Buddha” incident[12] – a college prank from Rand's days at Baylor University that the *Huffington Post* breathlessly expanded on to claim the victim (who said Paul and his companion in the incident “never hurt me”) was “ABDUCTED.”[13] Rand's experience at Baylor was itself a little controversial in that he only attended the school long enough to pass the MCAT and move on to Duke Medical School, where he eventually graduated. To say he was a non-conformist at Baylor may be an understatement, but thousands of young men and women finally grow up after their college years.

The “Aqua Buddha” incident became important again late in the campaign. Fresh off a Conway campaign commercial that portrayed Rand as being soft on crime – thanks to two-year-old statements taken out of context[14] – the Democrat was finally beginning to close a long-standing persistent polling gap with Paul. So Conway doubled down with another commercial revisiting “Aqua Buddha,” a decision which was widely panned[15] and eventually cost Conway the seat, according to a Democratic analysis of the Kentucky race.[16] Apparently the fact Jack Conway couldn't separate himself very far from Barack Obama's record had nothing to do with his defeat, despite the fact he skipped out on attending a visit by Vice-President Joe Biden to Louisville citing “scheduling conflicts”[17] but heartily welcomed the far more popular Bill Clinton to the state.[18]

In any case, it was the TEA Party favorite Rand Paul who defeated a young up-and-comer in the Democrat ranks who tried to run as a moderate and away from Barack Obama. Score one for the good guys.

Similarly, most figured in the early stages of the 2010 campaign that incumbent Florida Republican governor Charlie Crist would be an easy victor. Crist, who was forgoing a re-election bid to the governor's office for a second try for a Senate seat –

ironically to succeed his former campaign chief of staff George LeMieux, who Crist appointed when Senator Mel Martinez resigned 18 months out from the end of his term – was described in a *New York Times* piece detailing the Florida Senate race early on as a "governing pragmatist who was once seen as a winner who could reclaim the political center for Republicans...a popular governor with crossover appeal among Democrats and independents."[19] Often departing from Republican orthodoxy to embrace liberal policies such as allowing felons to vote or Barack Obama's "cap and trade" idea, Crist was reviled by those Floridians who were beginning to organize into the numerous local TEA Party chapters springing up across the state. Coincidentally or not, the timing of their rise was perfect for Marco Rubio's nascent Senate campaign.

So while pundits dismissed the chances of the Speaker of the Florida House – after all, how many people in any given state know who the speaker of their House is, let alone his or her politics – the various TEA Parties began to consider the more conservative Rubio as their Senate choice. But there were other factors at work that made Rubio more palatable to the establishment Republicans once the groundswell of support began to coalesce behind him.

The first and foremost factor aiding Rubio was his backstory: he was a first-generation American, the son of Cuban immigrants who both toiled in working-class jobs to assure their children would succeed in life. Marco did just that – attending college on a football scholarship, graduating with bachelors' and law degrees, and eventually serving his fellow citizens through politics. Having photogenic good looks and a young family didn't hurt, either.

But there was more than that: for a Republican Party that was seen as the bastion of old white people, Rubio was a person of color who they could show as a new face of the party. It didn't take long for the Left to begin calling Rubio the "Republican Obama,"[20] although his policies were generally in direct opposition to the President's. In that respect, Rubio could very well serve as a bridge between the GOP establishment which would be calmed because he had nearly a decade's worth of political experience under his belt in the state legislature, working his way up the ranks to become speaker over the last few years, and the TEA Party, which would be pleased with the more conservative political philosophy Rubio exhibited.

As Rubio's popularity grew and the Florida Senate race became more national in scope, Crist realized his path to victory was no longer going to run through a Republican Party that was taking a hard turn to the right. "It's never been about doing what's easy," said Crist on his decision to withdraw from the GOP race and run as an independent, adding, "I am aware that after this speech ends, I don't have either party helping me."[21] Once up by 30 points in the GOP polling, Crist had fallen 20 or more points behind Rubio amongst Republican voters and his last chance was making it a three-way general election race pitting him against Rubio and presumptive Democratic candidate Kendrick Meek, a four-term Congressman from the Miami area leaving the House to try and move up to the Senate.

Yet while the path to the GOP nomination was being cleared for him by Crist's exit, Rubio's relationship with the TEA Party was showing signs of strain. A Republican debate on *Fox News Sunday* in March, 2010, several months before the primary but a month before Crist withdrew, featured an unusual question for Rubio: "Ask Marco Rubio why he refuses to be vetted by the Florida Tea Parties. I want to hear from Rubio or I will not vote for him."[22]

To be sure, Rubio's campaign was a mere footnote until the time Senator Jim DeMint took notice of it. But the June, 2009 endorsement from DeMint and the Senate Conservatives Fund seemed quixotic at the time – an aide to one Crist-backing Senator noted, "When you have all the Senate GOP leaders standing behind Crist, and he has Jim DeMint, it only reinforces this idea that this isn't a serious primary. He's only appealing to the far right of the party, and that's reflected in low poll numbers."[23] It was that DeMint endorsement, though, that enabled Rubio to leverage support from people sympathetic to the TEA Party from around the country, which built upon itself into an unstoppable force that went beyond the parochial concerns of some of the state's TEA Party leaders. Not even six months after that unnamed, hapless Senate aide dismissed Rubio's chances, Marco Rubio and Charlie Crist were tied in the polls. By the time Rubio got the blessing[24] of the TPX in April, the race was all but over as Crist was on his way out.

Thus, it could be safe to say Rubio wasn't the same shining TEA Party star in his home state of Florida as he may have been on a national scale. Certainly he was the most conservative of the three remaining major candidates in the Florida Senate race, but the fact that Marco had a legislative record that could draw ire and concern from some quarters (unlike Rand Paul, who had the purity of no voting record thanks to having never held political office) left a nagging question about the amount of local TEA Party enthusiasm there was for Rubio. Fortunately, the polls during the final weeks of the campaign projected fairly smooth sailing for the Republican as Crist and Meek were splitting the liberal and moderate vote.

The only true challenge Rubio could have faced is one that turned out never to be – but not for lack of trying. Seeing how a similar tactic worked in New York's 23rd Congressional District the year before against a similar conservative insurgent, former President Bill Clinton secretly worked behind the scenes to get Meek to withdraw in the campaign's final days and endorse Crist so as to build his chance of winning, but Meek resisted.[25] (As the election turned out, it would have been possible for such a coalition to win for Crist, but he would have needed a highly unlikely 95%

of the Meek vote to do so.)

Rand Paul and Marco Rubio were the first case studies of how to use the broad support of the TEA Party nationwide to overcome hurdles in both the primary and general elections and hold Republican seats at a time when they needed to build back toward the majority while trying to push Congress in a more conservative, Constitutional direction. Add to that success a number of first-time winners in the House, and Republican party leaders should have been pleased with the results.

Success didn't just come with these candidates, though. As the TEA Party movement continued to evolve from localized, loosely organized groups that had a wide range of goals in mind for governance to more of a political machine, the Tea Party Patriots (TPP) and Tea Party Express (TPX), which began to take lead roles in the summer of 2009, consolidated their positions at the top of the TEA Party food chain. However, the TPP organization, which remained active as the umbrella group for the hundreds of local TEA Party chapters that were still making their own way, was still in its phase of not formally endorsing candidates or fundraising on their behalf at that time. Their success was more behind the scenes, and they were carefully trying to avoid being too partisan in their operations – a tension that would result in personnel issues not long down the road.

It was around this time as well that the large mega-rallies of 2009 began to fade into distant memories. Certainly there were smaller repeats of the Tax Day rallies in 2010, but the groups working within the realm of the TEA Party rally a year earlier such as FreedomWorks, Americans for Prosperity, the Campaign for Liberty, and so on had taken the e-mail listings they gathered over the period when people were most passionate and tried to keep the fires going in the far easier manner of stoking them through e-mail appeals. Obviously there was no shortage of scary subjects to feature in the subject lines.

In other instances, however, local Republicans and/or support groups like AFP just tried to "hijack and crush" local efforts. A good example: Shelli Dawdy of Nebraska complained vehemently when their local AFP and Republican Party tried to merge their Tax Day 2010 festivities with her Grassroots in Nebraska organization. "When we organize a Tea Party," wrote Dawdy, "we will abide by the no political party, no politician policy we've had since the beginning."[26] Rules like that didn't sit well with groups that coveted the TEA Party's passion and activism.

A couple of the larger groups also borrowed an idea that became the new trend in TEA Party rallies, first brought to us by the TPX.

From a humble beginning and ambitious goal of concluding their cross-country journey at the 9/12 Rally in Washington D.C. barely a year earlier, by November,

2010 the Tea Party Express had grown to the point that by the time the election had concluded, it had wrapped up four nationwide bus tours which included over 150 different stops in 40 states. About the only region of the contiguous 48 states it had missed in making its stops was the mid-Atlantic south of Washington, D.C.

In its first two tours, the TPX seemed to intentionally attempt to cover as much of the country as possible. (However, my lobbying for a local Delmarva stop didn't bear fruit.)[27] Its first effort, which started in late August and indeed finished September 12, began with a sendoff from their Sacramento home base and zigzagged across the mid-South and Midwest over the next 2½ weeks on its way to Washington.[28] Just six weeks later they were at it again, but this time with a title ("Countdown to Judgment Day") on a trek that would take them up the west coast, through the northern plains, and eventually down to the Deep South and Florida over a nineteen-day run.[29]

Reconvening for the spring of 2010, their third edition, dubbed "Just Vote Them Out," crossed the country from Harry Reid's Nevada to Washington just in time for a Tax Day anniversary TEA Party, but it spent a solid week in the Midwest – a region especially hard hit by the Great Recession. In Michigan alone the TPX made 10 stops over parts of four days, with some being proverbial "whistle stops" but others set up to be full-fledged rallies.[30]

Lansing TEA Party organizer Joan Fabiano rode along for part of the Michigan journey, which she claimed was originally targeted at Congressman Bart Stupak. Stupak, it should be noted, was the pro-life Democrat who received a promise from Obama that the Affordable Care Act would not fund abortions via a future executive order – however, just days before TPX 3 came to Michigan Stupak announced he would not seek re-election.

During her ride, Joan asserted that she "asked a lot of questions" but in the end called it "a moneymaking system for the organizers," who were in it more for themselves than the local TEA Parties. She did note, however, that those TPX stops were a great place to meet like-minded people.[31]

At the end of that third journey, the TPX revealed what it called its 2010 "target list" of candidates they were both supporting and working against, with one surprise being it was a bipartisan support list thanks to the inclusion of one Democrat. The idea, said TPX chief strategist Sal Russo, was "rewarding our friends and punishing our enemies."[32] Among that list of "friends" were Senate candidates Sharron Angle of Nevada, Chuck DeVore of California, Rand Paul of Kentucky, Marco Rubio of Florida, and Pat Toomey of Pennsylvania. House members on the "friends" list were Michele Bachmann of Minnesota, Marsha Blackburn of Tennessee, Tom McClintock of California, Walt Minnick of Idaho, Mike Pence of Indiana, Tom Price of Georgia, and Joe Wilson of South Carolina. Of those on the "friends" list, all except Minnick were Republicans.

For a final push before the 2010 election, the TPX put together its fourth nationwide tour, "Liberty at the Ballot Box." True to their word, four initial stops in Nevada were placed to support their endorsed hopeful Sharron Angle against the TPX's number one enemy, Senator Harry Reid, while another on the enemy list from their home state of California, Senator Barbara Boxer, had three California stops placed for her. But GOP Senate hopefuls got a lot of independent support: there were dates for them in Arkansas, Kentucky, Missouri, two in Illinois, Ohio, West Virginia, Pennsylvania, Delaware, Connecticut, and New Hampshire.[33] Out of those twelve, seven were successful – eight of thirteen if you count John McCain in Arizona, who had two TPX stops and probably didn't need or want them. Whether the TPX was of much assistance or not to the winners can be debated, but it probably didn't hurt to have a more or less reinforcing message.

The success of the TPX can be measured in just how many groups tried to emulate its success with bus tours of their own, with mixed results.

Just a couple days before the TPX arrived at the 9/12 rally, a coalition that included Eric Odom's American Liberty Alliance, the Sam Adams Alliance, American Majority, and Americans for Limited Government began their own cross-country bus tour, the American Liberty Tour, which included appearances from Samuel Wurzelbacher (a.k.a. "Joe the Plumber" of 2008 campaign fame), Erick Erickson of *RedState*, and frequent TPX performer Lloyd Marcus. Intended more for being "on the ground organizing the grassroots" than for rallying interest, the tour ended up being a one-off deal.[34] (It even impersonated the TPX to the point of starting from Sacramento like they did.)

On the other hand, Americans for Prosperity (AFP) took the bus tour concept to a different level. While a given AFP tour didn't have the star power or promotion that the TPX tours did, and was often limited to a particular subject – for example, an earlier rendition from 2006 was called the "Ending Earmarks Express" and focused on pork-barrel spending – the repetition (and focus-grouped, slick packaging)[35] made bus tours like the 2010 "NOvember is Coming" affair very successful for AFP.

Even the Left stood up and took notice as they defended the proposed Affordable Care Act and other socialist policies with their own bus tours. The Obama front group Organizing for America toured with the message "Health Insurance Reform Now: Let's Get It Done"[36] to create a "person-to-person, neighbor-to-neighbor, friend-to-friend conversation" even if attendees weren't quite certain about the message they were supposed to receive.[37] More clear with their message was the AFSCME union, which had their own "Highway to Health Care" jaunt to combat the "venom and misinformation" they claimed Obamacare opponents from the TEA Party were presenting.[38]

Issue advocacy groups were getting in on the act as well. The Susan B. Anthony List, the pro-life flip-side to the pro-choice EMILY's List, put together a modest bus trek through the Congressional districts of six Democrats who claimed to be pro-life but voted for Obamacare.[39] The prospect of the "Votes Have Consequences" tour may have upset Democratic Indiana Rep. Joe Donnelly so much that he had to reiterate, "Since coming to Congress, I have been a tireless advocate for the unborn, and my voting record reflects this." This after debuting an ad where he claimed he "don't work for the Washington crowd," in a race where he was up 17 points at the time.[40]

Joe Donnelly survived the 2010 massacre of "blue dog" Democrats in the House by the skin of his teeth, winning by just 2 percent over his GOP challenger. He'll have a cameo as the book goes on because of his involvement in a future race, but overall that summer and fall of 2010 was perhaps the most exciting time for a politically attuned conservative, Constitutionally-minded American since the upstart Ronald Reagan presidential campaign of 1976 against appointed incumbent President Gerald Ford.

As time has passed since the heady days of 2010, though, a sober assessment of the TEA Party after that election would lead one to conclude that the TEA Party only succeeded in re-centering the political landscape after it tilted wildly to the left in 2006 and 2008. Of course, it also could be argued the reason we were back to the center was that the TEA Party was just as extreme to the right as the Obama administration was governing to the far left. Furthermore, states this line of argument, the reason so little gets done in politics these days is that neither the so-called progressive, Indivisible movement on the left nor the TEA Party on the right will give an inch to compromise and get things done. Naturally, the true believers and organizers within the TEA Party thought their side had compromised more than enough over the last century or so, particularly with respect to following the Constitution, and that's the reason America is in its present condition.

Furthermore, the TEA Party proved themselves more than willing to put in the time and effort for change, as Michael Patrick Leahy wrote in the wake of the 2010 elections:

> This significant political victory (in 2010) was the result of two years of tireless work from hundreds of thousands of volunteers, many of whom spent during that time anywhere from $1,000 to $20,000 of their own money on travel,

organizational materials, press release fees, and the like. On average, these volunteers devoted between ten and fifty hours a week to the cause, and this includes those who had full-time or part-time jobs.

> The Tea Party movement, among its supporters, has redefined the concept of citizenship, specifically by increasing the amount of time, money, and other resources citizens should consider it to be their duty to devote to political engagement. The change, quite simply, involves an order of magnitude.[41]

So TEA Party regulars were ready for a sea change in American politics when the 2010 election results came in. Unfortunately, that's not the reception they received:

> (W)ithin a week of the 2010 midterm elections, the conservative chattering class had already broken the Eleventh Commandment (and at least one of the original ten) by openly deriding the Tea Party movement. All three legs of Reagan's coalition – along with a few extra – were broken off and aimed at us.[42]

This concept of fealty to Constitutional principles was quite the departure for the Republicans, who were at the time less than a generation removed from the days when genial old Bob Michel was the loyal but hapless Minority Leader, a real-life Washington General who could perhaps work around the edges a little bit on legislation to make it less damaging but in reality was just part of the problem. It took the bomb throwing of Newt Gingrich to make Republicans relevant again on a legislative level, and TEA Party regulars fondly remembered the way Gingrich engineered the previous Republican wave election at the 1994 midterm – just like 2010, that balloting was the reaction to a President who lurched too far to the left and enjoyed the honeymoon of a Congress which gave him pretty much everything he wanted.

But over time, the ways of Washington held sway with the "Contract With America" GOP majority, too. Gingrich was forced out due to recurring scandals both personal and professional less than five years after becoming Speaker, spending edged back up under the Republican George W. Bush, and 2006 brought the whole charade crashing down on the Beltway GOP. Four years later the TEA Party played a major role in what could be considered the "broken window" theory of Republican politics because they essentially put the Republican Party back to where it was a decade earlier – perhaps not in raw numbers, but in the sense of being able to control legislation. Problem was, the House could pass all the legislation it wanted but those bills would be filed in a desk drawer someplace in Harry Reid's office and willing accomplices in the media would give the 112$^{th}$ Congress its reputation as a "do-nothing Congress," particularly blaming the House for the troubles.

Some significant portion of that inertia, though, came from those who were supposedly on the TEA Party's side. Imagine this scene: after winning a resounding election, you come to the political table and take your seat, only to find out those already sitting there don't want the time of day from you. This is how the leadership of the Tea Party Patriots recounts their meeting with House Speaker-in-waiting John Boehner in the days leading up to the 2010 election, a point when it looked like a majority was within reach for the GOP:

> Just prior to the historic 2010 election, we met with then minority leader (John) Boehner in his large, ornate Capitol Hill office. Members of the Tea Party Patriots had asked us to meet with him to let him know what was expected if and when the Republicans took the majority. Surrounded by multiple staffers with pens and pads at the ready, we sat down with Boehner and delivered a very simple message from the Tea Party Patriots.
>
> Our members had voted and they expected "bold" and immediate leadership on the budget. They wanted an immediate return to fiscal responsibility. They wanted the soon-to-be-Speaker to propose a return to the spending levels of the last budget under President Clinton, a time when the budget was balanced and there was a surplus.
>
> Upon hearing this plan, Boehner threw his head back and laughed a deep and resounding laugh. As he regained his breath, he smiled a condescending smile, took a deep draw off of his cigarette, and with the smoke wafting out of his mouth, said, "Well, that sure is bold!" We knew at that moment exactly what to expect from the incoming Republican majority leadership.[43]

So the TEA Party had to defend not only what would become a limited and spotty record of legislative accomplishments with their people in charge, but also deal with some of the struggles and foibles of people who were considered its leaders.

I touched on the Mark Williams "We Coloreds" incident a couple chapters back, but the way it perpetuated the "racist" narrative was instrumental in how the TPX handled a key Congressional race. (Williams, you may recall, was the Sacramento radio host turned Tea Party Express spokesman.) In July, 2010 Mark's reaction to reports that the NAACP adopted a resolution which, as originally introduced, decried "the racism of the Tea Parties"[44] was widely panned as *prima facie* evidence for the Left's case. Of course, for years the NAACP has been considered a lapdog for liberal causes in general and the Democratic Party in particular, so such a resolution shouldn't have been unexpected.

Remember that the TPX had on its original list of endorsed candidates for the 2010 election a "Blue Dog" Democrat, Rep. Walt Minnick of Idaho.[45] Although it was later claimed that Minnick "was never entirely comfortable"[46] with the TPX endorsement that came out a few months earlier, the satirical letter Williams wrote as a blog post – a missive that eventually led to his resignation from the TPX a few days later[47] – gave Minnick the excuse to disassociate himself from the group, hoping it would see "the error of its ways" in its not rebuking Williams.[48]

As for the TPX, they indeed rectified their error – but not as Minnick may have preferred. In mid-October, three months after the Williams incident, the group stated Minnick "has engaged in a pattern of behavior which shows he is more responsive to the Democrat Party's establishment than he is the voters of Idaho," adding that he "declined" the TPX endorsement "after receiving significant pressure from the Democratic Party's leadership." They switched their backing to the Republican in the race, Raul Labrador,[49] [50] and it's quite possible the late switch may have cost Minnick his seat: although the Idaho-1 race was lightly polled, Minnick was leading in the last two polls taken prior to the election.[51]

While Mark Williams was a TEA Party leader who occasionally made headlines because of his outspoken nature as a broadcaster, my guess is that, if you were to go back to 2010 and ask the average Joe the question: "who's the leader of the TEA Party?" Williams would not have been the number one answer. More likely to be the chief among them, thanks to her name recognition as the most recent Republican vice-Presidential candidate and sitting Governor of Alaska, was Sarah Palin.

Of course, Palin wasn't one of those who was out there in early 2009 organizing her local Wasilla community into its own TEA Party. Whether she was consciously doing so or not, though, Palin's outspoken nature and continual criticism of the Obama administration made her the face of the movement. Felicia Cravens, the founder of the Houston Tea Party Society, conceded as much: "(Palin) certainly has sucked up a lot of the oxygen in terms of the national conversation," said Cravens in a local news interview. This didn't come without its drawbacks, though, as Cravens quickly added, "Once you've allowed someone to personify your group, you end up with a limitation on you that you can't really escape."[52]

But that limitation didn't seem to stop the people from coming out in droves to see her whenever she made a public appearance (such as for the TPX), nor did any of the many candidates running as adherents to the TEA Party fail to make a big deal of it when a Palin endorsement put his or her campaign on the map, giving it a TEA Party seal of approval. (Two examples were insurgent conservative Republican candidates from my adopted home state of Maryland: Brian Murphy for governor[53] in 2010 and Dan Bongino for Senate[54] in 2012.)

"Teavangelical" author David Brody described it this way:

> (Sarah) Palin has given herself the mission of finding the best and brightest candidates out there and then putting her neck on the line for them. And her Teavangelical pedigree really shines through when it comes to deciding which candidates to back. Typically, she chooses those who espouse Tea Party values and are pro-life. Hence, she is choosing many Teavangelical candidates.[55]

Palin, though, became a victim of her own success. Lampooned by the Left for her mannerisms and dragged through the mud by the media because of issues with her family, her selection by John McCain to balance out the 2008 GOP ticket as the more conservative of the pair spelled the end of her active political career in the sense that her outspokenness and fame made her a target. Her resignation announcement from being governor came, ironically, at a time when the TEA Party was beginning to flex its muscles, and perhaps should have been a warning of what would be to come for its leaders:

> Political operatives descended on Alaska last August, digging for dirt. The ethics law that I championed became their weapon of choice over the past nine months. I've been accused of all sorts of frivolous ethics violations, such as holding a fish in a photograph or wearing a jacket with a logo on it and answering reporters' questions. Every one of these, though, all 15 of the ethics complaints have been dismissed. We have won, but it hasn't been cheap. The state has wasted thousands of hours of your time and shelled out some two million of your dollars to respond to opposition research and that's money that's not going to fund teachers, or troopers or safer roads.
>
> And this political absurdity, the politics of personal destruction, Todd and I, we're looking at more than half a million dollars in legal bills just in order to set the record straight. And what about the people who offer up these silly accusations? It doesn't cost them a dime. So they're not going to stop draining the public resources, spending other people's money in this game. They won't stop.
>
> It's pretty insane. My staff and I spend most of our day – we're dealing with this stuff instead of progressing our state now.[56]

The fact that she quit as governor, regardless of the reasoning, would be the cudgel those on the Left beat her with. Regular people, though, still loved her in the days and months following her resignation as she wrapped up work on an autobiography and starred in her own cable TV series, not to mention frequent media appearances as a commentator. But there came a point where Palin got a little bit overexposed, the issues with her family began to resemble those of the Kardashians, and it was around that time when Palin thought better than to have a future in governing, closing the door on a 2012 Presidential run.[57] "I believe that at this time

I can be more effective in a decisive role to help elect other true public servants to office – from the nation's governors to Congressional seats and the Presidency," said Palin, which has led to turns as a PAC organizer for SarahPAC, valued endorser, and political "mama grizzly." The luxury of writing in hindsight, however, is that I know I'm getting a few months (and couple chapters) ahead of my story.

So we know the racist narrative that was present early on in the treatment of the TEA Party from the mainstream media continued apace during and beyond the 2010 campaign. But in addition, as Sarah Palin found out first hand, there was more scrutiny and investigative press against the TEA Party opposition – which couldn't even get a scrap of its cherished legislation passed – than there was coverage of the sitting President and his many questionable acts, not to mention his history and upbringing. In that respect, those in the mainstream media (defined at the time as pretty much everyone except for Fox News, the *Washington Times*, conservative talk radio, and various bloggers and websites) were more than happy to parrot the party line of Barack Obama's words and White House spin.

Governing was always going to be the hard part, and it was even more difficult with the headwinds buffeting the TEA Party's ship of state.

# MANAGING THE DECLINE

"*(T)oday you can't find a candidate running anywhere in America – Republican or Democrat – that doesn't sound like they belong to the Tea Party movement.*" - Sal Russo of the Tea Party Express, *New York Times*, September 19, 2010.

As the TEA Party entered its first full political cycle, there was a perceptible change in the movement. With the money from Barack Obama's stimulus program being divvied out to his friends, cronies, and supporters, Obamacare now law, and the GOP in control of the House of Representatives passing resolutions to repeal it, the large-scale protests were becoming a thing of the past – but now ambitious TEA Party operatives at least had a seat at the table. So why did people still feel like they were on the outside looking in?

Certainly the TEA Party had placed itself on the political map in the two years since Santelli's rant, but as 2011 dawned their attention was drawn in a number of different directions. As I noted in an earlier chapter, some of the local TEA Party organizations had, over time, morphed into or splintered off to become chapters of various larger, more formal advocacy groups such as the Campaign for Liberty or Americans for Prosperity.

This nationalization didn't sit well with some. The TEA Party "should be leaderless, a group of citizens expressing their political views," said Los Angeles leader Gary Aminoff, who added that "we felt the TEA Party should be independent and local," and focus strictly on fiscal issues. (More on that schism in a later chapter.) By the end of 2010, his group had disbanded.[1]

And while he wouldn't have agreed with Aminoff on the aims of the movement, Fayetteville, North Carolina's Ralph Reagan was also flummoxed by the national TEA Party:

> Sadly those who were financial only were warm weather warriors...The tea party went wrong by going financial only. (They also) had no clue about forming coalitions. In the end they failed locally because they didn't take into account soldiers (from nearby Fort Bragg) leave and the organization faltered.
>
> (...)

> The real problem here was they absolutely ignored the culture and had no couth or understanding of anyone's perspective. I had to look them in the face (and) browbeat them to admit I wasn't part of the problem (as a local GOP leader.) The biggest failing was their lack of thinking and inability to make coalitions.[2]

And while most of the other surviving community chapters maintained their TEA Party identity, they were largely abandoning the outdoor rallies for regular monthly meetings, a setting not unlike other local party-based political entities. Even the rancor of its first summer in 2009 – a summer where Democratic representatives learned the hard way to avoid town hall meetings like the plague – had pretty much subsided[3] in 2010 because Obamacare had already passed and those questioners were working for opponents who oftentimes ended up defeating those who voted for the bill.

There were also a number of individual members who had moved over to the political inside by running for and winning local office. As former TEA Party denizens they were now better known as members of their town councils or school boards, township trustees, or other local officeholders. By doing so, they gave the TEA Party a voice in government but also found out just how difficult steering budgets and policy in the right direction was going to be, especially when they had to work with mandates from the state or federal governments. "You can't turn the Titanic around quickly," Joan Fabiano told me, even as it was hard for the "type A personalities" of the TEA Party to adjust.[4] To repeat: governing was always going to be the hard part.

Most importantly to this narrative, though, the period of time immediately after the 2010 election was the time when the TEA Party transformed from being a more spontaneous and localized organic group and arrived at the point where some true believers feared it would be early on:[5] just another part of the clique of inside-the-Beltway lobbyists whose main goals were to build e-mail lists for sale, raise unsolvable issues to perpetuate their reason for existence, and otherwise find ways to line their pockets. Reporter Ambreen Ali, in a May, 2011 article in *Roll Call*, claimed:

> Several tea party leaders have found paid jobs for themselves in the movement as it evolves from an amateur grass-roots wave into a professional lobby.
>
> Tennessee lawyer Judson Phillips became the latest to make the jump when he announced last week that he was devoting himself full time to Tea Party Nation, a change that means drawing a salary he would only describe as "under six figures."
>
> (...)

> Former flight attendant Amy Kremer said she has been earning $4,000 per month as chairwoman of Tea Party Express, a political action committee known for its nationwide bus tours promoting conservative candidates such as failed Senate contenders Sharron Angle in Nevada and Joe Miller in Alaska.
>
> Jenny Beth Martin, who worked as a housekeeper and Home Depot manager before joining the movement, reportedly receives $6,000 per month as national coordinator for Tea Party Patriots, a nonprofit coalition group. Martin is one of six such coordinators, four of whom are paid.
>
> Both organizations have hired numerous staffers and consultants to promote the tea party principles of small government, free markets and individual liberties.[6]

Nice work if you can get it. Ali's story also asserted that TPX raised $7.6 million during the 2009-10 election cycle but only spent about $2.4 million opposing or helping candidates directly, with Senators Harry Reid and Lisa Murkowski receiving most of their wrath. In those same Nevada and Alaska races, though, the TPX, through its parent Our Country Deserves Better PAC, also spent money on behalf of unsuccessful candidates Sharron Angle and Joe Miller, respectively.[7]

Even as the groups were getting more mainstream, they were still trying to be active political players in their own ways. (Since the rival Tea Party Patriots continually stressed their political neutrality in particular races and didn't change that philosophy until they began their own PAC in 2013, TPP spending was far less and could reasonably be considered a more strict get-out-the-vote and issue advocacy effort.)

We already know that the TPX had its fair share of detractors within the movement who considered them simply a PAC that was trading on the TEA Party name, but with electoral success under its belt and a contact list that numbered in the millions from all the demonstrations, social media, and other ways people now gather information, the TPX – as well as its rival TPP – had become the two entrenched leaders in the movement. In the case of the TPX, though, 2011 was the year it arguably became the more dominant force among Tea Partiers for a number of reasons.

For one thing, the TPX began the year with a lot of momentum. Knowing that a significant news audience considered themselves TEA Party members and always interested in cutting into the Fox News ratings lead among that demographic, in the wake of the 2010 midterms CNN approached and negotiated with the Tea Party Express about co-sponsoring a Republican presidential candidate debate.[8] The result:

the first TEA Party Republican presidential candidate debate, broadcast by CNN on September 12, 2011.[9] "We're not going to sit back and just let the Republican Party hand us the nominee," explained co-chairman Amy Kremer of TPX. "We're going to choose the nominee."

Further along in the CNN story, though, after Kremer declares, "We're sick and tired of the Republican Party handing us candidates who are not true conservatives," CNN Political Producer Rachel Streitfeld repeats that same establishment bromide: "The question now is whether the tea party will push candidates far enough to the right during the primaries that it could hurt their chances at winning a general election. The failed Senate candidacies of tea-party-backed Sharron Angle in Nevada and Christine O'Donnell in Delaware may stand as a warning."[10] Somehow the successes of Senators Scott Brown, Rand Paul, and Marco Rubio (among others) didn't count?

In that TPX/CNN debate, fortunate TEA Party members got to ask the eight Republicans who participated several questions about the issues they cared about. At that point the GOP field invited to attend was a quite diverse and varied one: Rep. Michele Bachmann of Minnesota, Georgia businessman and part-time radio host Herman Cain, fellow Georgian and former Speaker of the House Newt Gingrich, former Utah Governor and Ambassador Jon Huntsman, Congressman and two-time Presidential aspirant Ron Paul from Texas, then-current Texas Governor Rick Perry, 2008 candidate and former Massachusetts Governor Mitt Romney, and former Senator Rick Santorum of Pennsylvania. (Other major candidates who were seeking the nomination but not invited to the debate were former New Mexico Governor Gary Johnson, political consultant Fred Karger of California, Michigan Rep. Thaddeus McCotter, and onetime Louisiana Governor Buddy Roemer.) While the debate mainly focused on red-meat financial and taxation issues, CNN moderator Wolf Blitzer tended to steer the questioning toward the front-runners at the time, Rick Perry and Mitt Romney.[11]

Between the announcement and the actual debate, though, the TPX was a busy group. It began the year by being audacious enough to have its own response to President Obama's State of the Union address. After Obama's speech and the Republican response from Wisconsin Rep. Paul Ryan, it was time for the Tea Party response, presented by Minnesota Rep. Michele Bachmann, the founder of the House Tea Party Caucus – a group that boasted 60 members by the middle of 2011.[12] "I believe we're in the very early days of a history-making turn in America," Bachmann assured us, even if she wasn't looking into the camera as she was speaking.[13] Overall, her presentation, which ran about 6½ minutes, stuck to the theme of opposing Obama's massive spending using two charts she presented during the telecast to demonstrate its lack of results in assisting the economy.

Just a few days later, the TPX again left the buses in the garage and embarked upon something they called the TEA Party Town Hall. Again featuring Bachmann being joined by fellow Congressman Steve King as well as Senate TEA Party favorites Mike Lee and Rand Paul, this Washington-based event was held in front of an audience, with thousands more around the country watching on the TPX website. "By ensuring concerned citizens are on the same page with our elected officials, we can find new ways to work together in advancing an agenda that will help put America on the right track," said TPX Chairman Amy Kremer in the group's release. "The issues we'll be discussing are primarily the tea party ideals of Constitutionally limited government, support for private enterprise, lower taxes, and fiscal responsibility."[14]

However, there was no way the TPX was going to abandon its bread and butter. A new wrinkle for them, though, was shining up their buses for an August mini-tour that focused strictly on the state of Wisconsin, where a TEA Party-backed reformer had learned the hard way about just how entrenched special interests would be when it came to having their ox gored.

The events in Wisconsin were a great example of the breadth of the TEA Party revolution. While there was much to be said about the success the TEA Party had in flipping the House of Representatives to GOP control, less is mentioned about their accomplishments at the state and local level. Among its beneficiaries was newly-elected Wisconsin Governor Scott Walker, a conservative who would no longer kowtow to the state's public-sector unions. Quickly bringing budgetary reforms before his state legislature, Walker had to put up with minority party Democrats who refused to go along, briefly abandoning the state to prevent Republicans from having a quorum to pass his legislative package.[15] Despite the noisy, weeks-long protests of Democrats and union leaders – who even besieged the state capitol building with a prolonged sit-in[16] – Walker got his wish. True to the adage that no good deed goes unpunished, several Republican state senators who sided with him became subject to August recall elections that threatened to cut into or eliminate the GOP's 19-14 advantage in the Wisconsin Senate. (Walker would have to endure his own recall effort for the 2012 election.)

Sensing that prospect, the TPX swung into action the weekend before the August balloting, putting together a four-day "Restoring Common Sense" tour to shore up voters in these districts. It turned out that winning four of the six races (keeping the Senators in office) was good enough to keep the Republican majority in the Wisconsin State Senate, albeit by a bare 17-16 majority. (Similar recall efforts to oust two Democratic state senators who bailed on the legislature and fled to Illinois were unsuccessful a week later, as both survived their recalls.)

The news of the Wisconsin mini-tour came just a few days after TPX revealed it was time to gather up the troops for their fifth national bus tour. This one, which was eventually given the title "Reclaiming America,"[17] would focus on early primary states, according to the TPX release. It was "expected to feature Presidential candidates, highlight core issues such as fiscal responsibility and constitutionally limited government, and generate interest and awareness for the upcoming Tea Party debate,"[18] said the group. The journey was intended to culminate at the Tampa debate on September 12, another seminal date in the history of the TEA Party.

In addition, there was a less-noticed aspect to the Wisconsin tour, but it was central to the consolidation theme of this particular chapter. Joining the TPX on this and the subsequent "Reclaiming America" tour were two key early TEA Party figures: Eric Odom, who by this time was described as the "new media director" of related groups Grassfire Nation and the Patriot Action Network, and Judson Phillips of Tea Party Nation.[19] Phillips, as you probably recall, attempted to organize TEA Party conventions in Nashville and Las Vegas which turned out to be controversial financial disasters, so in this case he was taken in by the larger, established group. If you can't beat 'em, join 'em.

Also on board for various stops of the TPX were representatives of FreedomWorks and Americans for Prosperity, which by then had stepped back from the active organizational and political advocacy aspects of the TEA Party movement; instead, the two groups viewed the TEA Party newcomers as common cause in their particular fights. By far the best example of this was Americans for Prosperity, which was taking advantage of its expanded membership to operate akin to a conventional party-based political club with over 30 state-based chapters overseeing their own local groups – a more rigid organizational structure than the TEA Party in general had.

As for those in the Presidential sweepstakes who joined the TPX along the way, the first participant was Michele Bachmann, who headed up the event in Des Moines, Iowa.[20] Bachmann may have founded the TEA Party Caucus, but she was not alone in seeking their support: later on in the tour the TPX would be joined by Thaddeus McCotter at a rally outside Detroit,[21] Gary Johnson, Sarah Palin, Buddy Roemer, and Mitt Romney at one or more of the three New Hampshire stops,[22] [23] and Herman Cain, Roemer, and Rick Santorum at stops in South Carolina.[24] Cain held court in Greenville while Roemer and Santorum shared billing in Columbia.

Even as all of these entities seemed to be on the same team, the Reclaiming America tour had its own piece of controversy. After Mitt Romney was announced as a TPX speaker at a huge Labor Day weekend event in Concord, New Hampshire, FreedomWorks turned from participant to protestor. This outburst was dismissed as a "misguided press stunt"[25] by the TPX, but FreedomWorks president Matt Kibbe noted inviting Romney was a second strike against the TPX as they had at a previous stop entertained a speech from Utah Senator Orrin Hatch, who FreedomWorks accused of being a "big-government" Senator in his own right. "If every political opportunist claiming to be a tea partier is accepted unconditionally, then the tea party brand loses all meaning," Kibbe explained. "Our grassroots activists will be in New Hampshire on Sunday to defend the tea party ideas of small government and fiscal responsibility, and to remind Mitt Romney that when it comes to policy, actions speak louder than words."[26] Despite the small counter-protest turnout,[27] FreedomWorks broke with the TPX tour at that point.

But the momentum was on the side of the Tea Party Express as they continued to hold the large-scale rallies. By year's end the TPX was even sponsoring a local over-the-air radio program,[28] although it lagged some six hundred or so radio stations short of Rush Limbaugh's reach.

Conversely, their mates at the Tea Party Patriots were at their task with a more quiet determination – at least when they weren't slugging it out in court with former TPP head Amy Kremer, who broke off with them in the fall of 2009 to join the TPX and had moved up to become its Chairman.[29] By this point, original Tea Party leaders Jenny Beth Martin and Mark Meckler were co-chairing the TPP and becoming the frequently-seen faces of that group (and, by extension, the TEA Party itself) on the cable news networks.

For the TPP, their first major success was pulling off what they dubbed the American Policy Summit.[30] Held in Phoenix in late February, 2011 to coincide with the second anniversary of the original Nationwide Chicago Tea Party protests, it was intended to become an annual gathering that would attract thousands of activists both onsite at the venue and virtually via the internet. To the extent that they drew prospective Presidential candidates Herman Cain, Ron Paul, and former Minnesota Governor Tim Pawlenty – whose abortive campaign flamed out after a dismal performance at the Ames Straw Poll in Iowa later that summer – it was indeed successful, but it wasn't enough to create demand for a repeat performance. (At least they avoided the lawsuits and bad press which plagued Judson Phillips and his Tea Party Nation when he attempted a Tea Party convention the year before.) At the event, billed as one that "organized around the group's core values and its 'Five Pathways to Liberty': education, politics, judicial, economics and culture," Cain did the best job of convincing those who physically attended the American Policy Summit of his Presidential bonafides, while Ron Paul unsurprisingly lapped the field among online activists from the Virtual Summit who voted in a straw poll taken at the event. Also among the top finishers: fellow attendee Pawlenty, who was impressive enough to come in third in the in-house poll (but way down the list online) and Sarah Palin.[31]

Later in the spring, the TPP briefly returned to its roots by teaming up with Let

Freedom Ring, Smart Girl Politics, and the Institute for Liberty and holding the Washington-based "Continuing Revolution Rally."[32] TPP co-founder Mark Meckler told the *Washington Times*, "We expect to see a bunch of frustrated, angry patriots who want to see serious cuts to government spending. I think it's a huge gut check. This is a way for us to judge them and see how serious they are and to prepare for the 2012 election."[33] Unfortunately, the turnout was abysmal thanks to a cold, rainy day, so critics from the Left speculated that the turnout "suggests the organizing group, Tea Party Patriots, isn't as powerful as it's made out to be in the media."[34] But they also conceded the spending cuts in question didn't amount to much and the TEA Party movement was doing more of its work back home, not in Washington.

Working back home was the aim of the TPP's next big idea, dubbed "Deal in the District." Since Congress was on recess, the goal was to get TEA Party members to meet with their representatives and beseech them to work on ways to cut spending. The TPP:

> ...announced that local groups across the country will be planning office visits to House and Senate Members to demand they oppose an increase in the debt limit, support the Full Faith and Credit Act and oppose any tax increases, as part of their 'Deal in the District' grassroots effort. The activists plan to visit the district offices... to share with their elected leaders the desires of their constituents and let them know they are keeping a record of their votes.[35]

In this case, the April round was enough of a success that they did a second batch in November.[36]

For another sign that the TPP was returning to its roots, the summer of 2011 also brought a new alliance with Morton Blackwell's Leadership Institute. Billed as a "50-state grassroots activism training initiative designed to equip and mobilize activists, campaign staff and candidates to turn their passion for tea party principles into effective action,"[37] the idea was to create a new generation of non-traditional conservative activists out of the Kansas housewife or the factory worker in Michigan who was passionate about fiscal values but knew next to nothing about the political process.

The TPP also remained the more "purist" organization, objecting to the creation of TEA Party license plates in Arizona because the money would be distributed by the state to TEA Party organizations the government deemed worthy. (It didn't stop them from putting words in the mouths of local TEA Party leaders, though – not exactly "bottoms up" there.)[38] [39] They also picked an indirect fight with the TPX, criticizing Amy Kremer as the "unnamed spokesperson" who said on Fox News the TEA Party would back any Republican candidate against Barack Obama, even Mitt Romney. (This was before the TPX/FreedomWorks incident involving Romney in

New Hampshire.) "A pledge of allegiance to the Republican party, or any other party, violates what the tea party movement is all about and is completely out of touch with grassroots Americans," noted TPP's Jenny Beth Martin. "The tea party movement grew out of disillusionment with both political parties who have rejected the principles of fiscal responsibility, limited constitutional government and the free market. We are independent and will remain so."[40]

In Kremer's defense, though, her remarks were taken a bit out of context. "Whoever the Republican nominee is will have to have the support of the Tea Party movement, the entire Tea Party movement...If Romney is the nominee I believe we want to defeat Barack Obama." Kremer told Fox News, adding, "There is no way that we are going to support a third party candidate. It would split the vote and it would guarantee reelection for Obama."[41] Given the history of the TEA Party and its first foray into electoral politics as backers of third-party candidate Doug Hoffman in the NY-23 race – a race where a conservative split vote allowed a Democrat to take a long-held GOP seat – Kremer was being politically astute. Moreover, for years there's been the perception that Ross Perot's presence in the 1992 Presidential race siphoned enough votes from George H.W. Bush to hand Bill Clinton the presidency; eight years later one could argue that Ralph Nader running in his own long-shot bid gave the job to Bush's son over Al Gore thanks to a few hundred Florida votes.

There's no doubt that the bitter feelings between Martin and Meckler at TPP and Kremer at TPX were drawbacks to the cause, and perhaps consciously the media tried to reinforce that rivalry in the hopes that something would be said to allow for the elimination of what they regarded as a threat to their preferred political philosophy of far-left, socialist-to-Marxist tendencies. As the Occupy movement gathered strength in the fall of 2011, there wasn't nearly the playing off of personalities within that group as there was for the TEA Party. Remember, the mainstream media already had one TEA Party leadership scalp in disgraced former TPX head Mark Williams, and that coverage angle may have clouded the public's perception as I'll shortly remind you again.

Considering all the success they were having on the political world, many would be surprised to find a larger and larger segment of the public was becoming disenchanted with the TEA Party brand. Since the spring of 2010, the Gallup polling firm had regularly asked Americans whether they supported, opposed, or were neutral to the TEA Party. Unbeknownst to the world at the time, the peak of support for the TEA Party as measured by Gallup had occurred right around the time of the 2010 election, with the TEA Party gathering the support of 32% of respondents. (At that same time, it was reported that 30% opposed the TEA Party and 31% were neutral toward it.)[42] Ironically enough, like many other trends, the point where the TEA Party became mainstream was the moment it seemed the cool kids dropped it like a bad habit.

Another casualty of this change from spontaneous local group to inside-the-Beltway political powerhouse, though, was the initial idea of being non-partisan – as the spat between Amy Kremer and the Tea Party Patriots made clear. But there was a good reason.

One, perhaps unintentional, result of the 2010 election was the all but absolute wipeout of what was known as the "blue dog" segment of the Democratic Party – most of the midterm electoral carnage came from the ranks of their centrists who had either won long-held Republican districts in the wave elections of 2006 and 2008 or came from regions which were conservative by nature but voted for Democrats because their ancestors always did, such as wide swaths of the old South. For the "blue dogs," the unpopularity of Barack Obama's policies made their party's votes in favor of the stimulus bill or the Affordable Care Act a suicide pact for their Congressional careers. Liberals who were in safe, urban districts had nothing to fear in voting for such far-left policies, but their Democratic cohorts in "flyover country" were cannon fodder for the TEA Party wave of voters. (It turned out in many cases their Congressional districts would be cannon fodder as well, since the victorious Republicans often got to enjoy the spoils of redistricting: one of the first items on the new legislative order of business was to update district lines to reflect the completed 2010 Census.)

With few centrist Democrats who might be persuaded to adopt the fiscal values of the TEA Party, if not necessarily the other limited-government attributes those citizens desired, and no appetite for a third-party movement after the experience with the Hoffman race in 2009, the uneasy marriage of the TEA Party and Republican Party was consummated with the 2010 elections. And as that relationship deepened and became more obvious, the TEA Party slowly began to lose its libertarian element – a significant portion of the very philosophy the TEA Party was originally rooted in. Remember, they came together over the Keynesian-on-steroids American Recovery and Reinvestment Act, often called the stimulus package, but as I pointed out early on the TEA Party's beginnings could be traced farther back to the latter stages of the George W. Bush administration and its increasing appetite for spending that the Pelosi-Reid Democrats in Congress were only too happy to continue accommodating.

While libertarians also craved the limited government that Republicans courting the TEA Party were promising to adopt if given the reins of power, they were just as distrustful of the interventionist foreign policy and short shrift given to civil liberties and Fourth Amendment rights by the GOP as well as the growing influence of the Republicans' socially conservative voters. So as the TEA Party drifted toward the mainstream of political thought, libertarians began to slowly filter out[43] [44] of the TEA Party movement. Many joined the chorus from the Left claiming that the TEA Party was already a sellout to the Republican Party: Orlando TEA Party organizer and blogger Phil Russo, the TPX critic previously introduced, was one of those libertarian-minded TEA Party members who eventually left. "(M)ost of the people in the tea party movement (now) are not true believers in liberty," Russo wrote in 2010.[45]

Unfortunately, the GOP wasn't all that comfortable with the TEA Party, either. Recall the words of Larry Sabato in the aftermath of the near-misses the GOP suffered in trying to take the Senate in 2010: "They are going to try to pick the nominee. The problem of course is that the Tea Party is well to the right. It is further to the right than the country, there is simply no question about that."[46] But was anyone else besides the TEA Party asking if Barack Obama was "well to the left" of the country?

At its largest point, the field of major candidates for the Republican nomination in 2012 was perhaps the heretofore most diverse in history. Members of that group were certainly mindful of the need for TEA Party acceptance, but some were more interested in appealing as a pragmatic, "electable" choice – it was the approach they had to take considering one had worked for President Obama as his Ambassador to China, another had done a commercial with Nancy Pelosi on the subject of global warming,[47] and still a third approved the template that Obamacare was based on while serving as the governor of Massachusetts. Male, female, centrist, conservative, libertarian, businessman, political insider, straight, gay: all of these adjectives and more could be applied to at least one aspirant for the 2012 Republican nomination, and the TEA Party was just one group that had to sort all of these attributes out.

# FRAGMENTATION AND FRUSTRATION

*"This would be five Senate seats basically we've blown by just nominating the least-electable candidates."* - former GOP Rep. Tom Davis.

Back in my "Backlash" chapter I outlined a number of losing 2010 Senate races and some of the pitfalls these candidates went through, oftentimes bringing it upon themselves.

But an even better case can be made, now that we have the benefit of 20/20 hindsight, that having such a loosely organized and fragmented group as the TEA Party was led to its squandering the biggest opportunity they were presented for change by not unseating Barack Obama when they had the chance. On the other hand, the TEA Party often shined in local and state elections where it could nationalize their impact and support local groups with common cause.

Early in the 2012 campaign – basically in the time prior to the 2010 midterms – the natural tendency was to anoint John McCain's 2008 running mate Sarah Palin as the 2012 GOP nominee. Yet while she was extremely popular personally among the rank-and-file of the TEA Party, as I noted earlier her electoral chances were doomed: everything from Tina Fey's "I can see Russia from my house" impersonation of Palin to the dumpster diving for dirt on her that teams of alleged journalists put forth reduced her chances of winning. Add to that Palin's resignation midway through her gubernatorial term which allowed her to be forevermore dubbed a "quitter" by the media that despised her, regardless of the validity of the reason,[1] and she was simply too much damaged goods for a Presidential run. Besides, she was having plenty of fun being a mom and getting herself all over cable TV – shrewd producers knew she had a built-in, loyal audience of TEA Party supporters in much the same demographic that later made *Duck Dynasty* such a raging success for a couple years.

But the signs of weariness of Palin could be seen rather early in the 2012 cycle. In October, 2010, a statewide convention of TEA Party members in Virginia – considered at the time the largest such gathering to date – selected tough-talking New Jersey Governor Chris Christie as their favorite in a major straw poll.[2] (Despite that victory, Christie chose instead to skip the 2012 Presidential sweepstakes to focus on his own 2013 re-election campaign. Christie would eventually fall from the TEA Party's favor when, days before the 2012 election, he incurred their wrath by embracing and commending Barack Obama[3] for his assistance to New Jersey in the wake of Superstorm Sandy.) In the last chapter I noted a similar straw poll taken a few months later in February, 2011 among those who attended a national Tea Party Patriots summit. Granted, Palin was the top non-speaker in the American Policy Summit straw poll, but her vote share still was less than 10 percent.[4]

Palin was coy about her intentions for a few months, but as time ticked away and the odds of her putting together a campaign dwindled, so did her poll numbers. A *Washington Post*/ABC poll surveyed in October, 2011, just days before she formally announced she was taking a pass on 2012, found Palin only had 9% support among Republicans.[5] Even worse, just 31% of those responding believed she should run, as opposed to the 66% who said no.[6] During the summer, as Michele Bachmann's stock rose, there were a number of TEA Party regulars who believed Bachmann was the new queen of the TEA Party, deposing Palin.[7] While Sarah was good for moving merchandise,[8] the new conventional wisdom on Palin was that she'd become yesterday's news by not sticking with her efforts in Alaska.

So once Sarah officially took her pass on a 2012 bid on October 5th, 2011, other would-be hopefuls maintained their quest for TEA Party support. Certainly Bachmann was among them, as by that point her campaign was beginning to flail and it needed the shot in the arm gaining Palin's supporters would bring.

The battle for the 2012 nomination, however, really began in late April, 2011 when former New Mexico governor Gary Johnson became the first candidate with potential TEA Party appeal to formally enter the race. (In truth, onetime political consultant Fred Karger declared a month before, but those in the TEA Party were unlikely to back a self-described "pro-choice, antiwar, freedom-for-all, spendthrift compromiser inspired by Nelson Rockefeller and Teddy Roosevelt."[9] So I'm taking the editorial license to fast-forward.) Johnson didn't have the field to himself for long, though: by Memorial Day the GOP aspirants who had made it official included (in order of announcement) Newt Gingrich, Ron Paul, Herman Cain, and Tim Pawlenty. June brought in more luminaries: Mitt Romney, Rick Santorum, Jon Huntsman, Buddy Roemer, and finally Michele Bachmann. Thaddeus McCotter made his bid known July 2 (only to withdraw 2½ months afterward, later kidding that the campaign was the worst 15 minutes of his life)[10] and Rick Perry rounded out the field by his formal announcement August 13, the day of the final Ames Straw Poll in Iowa. One day later, the humiliating loss to his Minnesota cohort Bachmann (as well as several others) at that event in his neighboring state made it clear to Tim Pawlenty that 2012 wouldn't be his year.

If you broke down the 2012 field from a TEA Party perspective, you had conservatives in Bachmann, Cain, Gingrich, and Perry, the populism of Roemer and

Santorum, and the libertarian side with Johnson and Paul. With so many choices, there was a growing concern from the GOP establishment – a shadowy group that preferred eventual candidate Romney, a man who enacted a state-level version of Obamacare, but could also have lived with the moderate Huntsman in a pinch – that none of the TEA Party hopefuls were "electable" against Obama. "From the point of view of a non-tea party Republican, the... possibility (of a TEA Party-backed Presidential candidate) is the most tragic waste. A winnable election will be thrown away on an ideological adventure," wrote columnist David Frum.[11]

Each of these "TEA Party" candidates took a turn on the polling roller coaster, leading the polls for a short period where it looked like they would be the one to take on Barack Obama. (The most suspicious polling demise among them probably belonged to Herman Cain, who fell victim to allegations of sexual harassment[12] and marital infidelity[13] that ever-so-conveniently broke just about the time he reached the top of GOP polls. His nomination would have destroyed the "TEA Party is racist" narrative in record time.)

Unfortunately for the TEA Party, there was no perfect candidate they could unite behind and force into the Republican nomination. "I have my issues with Romney, as do most people," said Christen Varley of the Greater Boston Tea Party. "However, nobody really seems to like anybody else."[14] Herman Cain may have been the closest because he was the Beltway outsider with business experience that many members of the TEA Party craved as presidential leadership material, but that dream crashed when the harassment charges came out. Earlier, Michele Bachmann was their darling – based largely on her part in forming the TEA Party Caucus and promotion from groups like the Tea Party Express – but she couldn't keep her momentum gained at the Ames Straw Poll going, fading as the autumn went on and eventually dropping out after a terrible showing in the Iowa caucuses.[15] Starting later than her peers may have cost her, just as it may have done in Rick Perry after his strong start (in part at Bachmann's expense.) Jon Huntsman also departed the race by mid-January, but few in the TEA Party were going to miss him anyway.

On the libertarian side of the ledger, Gary Johnson had departed the race for what he thought were the greener pastures of the Libertarian Party before the Iowa caucuses, which left Ron Paul as the standard-bearer for that dwindling subset of the TEA Party. Also seeking a different party nomination was Buddy Roemer, whose curious (and low-budget, as he refused donations greater than $100)[16] campaign ended up trying to start up a party called Americans Elect, then change direction in an effort to revive the Reform Party.

Thus, by the time Super Tuesday rolled around in March, the field insofar as the TEA Party (and practically everyone else) was concerned came down to four: Newt Gingrich, Ron Paul, Mitt Romney, and Rick Santorum. At that point, the TEA Party had to be convinced that they weren't being forced to eat a crap sandwich – there was a "great deal of distrust"[17] regarding Romney. "The main issue is Romneycare," TEA Party Tampa co-founder Sharon Calvert told the *New York Daily News*. "Obamacare was modeled after Romneycare and that was one of the thing the grassroots really took on as an issue. We believe it must be repealed. There's general concern whether he'd actually fight to do that. We see him as the moderate. He's the establishment candidate."[18]

But as the fight went on, it began to look more and more like either the establishment Mitt Romney or establishment Newt Gingrich would prevail, a choice that some, like columnist Jay Bookman at the *Atlanta Journal-Constitution*, believed was a failure of the TEA Party.[19] On the other hand, there was the camp that essentially chided the movement by saying that the perfect was the enemy of the good, and job one had to be defeating Barack Obama.

Representative of that latter school of thought was writer Mark Petrina, who upbraided Bookman for his assertion:

> Bookman is not only wrong, he is 180 degrees off: the Tea Party is displaying political maturity and discernment, as most of us would prefer someone else, but we are making do with the best available – and viable. Bookman's position is pure spin, wishful thinking: we did stunning things in 2010, but suddenly we're a failure because we haven't succeeded in overcoming the decades-entrenched GOP Establishment? Whatever.[20]

Also weighing in was *Washington Times* columnist, future Senatorial candidate, and second cousin once removed to Barack Obama, Dr. Milton Wolf. He succinctly defined the conundrum TEA Party followers faced in many races, including the Presidential one:

> As the race teeters between Mr. Gingrich and Mr. Romney, conservatives must make it politically profitable for either or both to do the right things. Embrace the Tea Party principles, which are – not coincidentally – America's founding principles. If either man hopes to have the enthusiastic support of the Tea Party – and he'll need it to beat President Obama in the general election – he should enthusiastically join the movement.
>
> (...)
>
> Unfortunately, both Mr. Gingrich and Mr. Romney have, at times, forsaken conservative principles. It's true. The offending list is long: Romneycare, bailouts, ethanol subsidies, government-sponsored enterprises and more. It's *mea culpa*

time, not for the mere sake of groveling, but instead to swallow their pride and convince voters that they won't repeat those mistakes. Downgraded America simply can't afford it.

Both Mr. Gingrich and Mr. Romney are exceptionally capable leaders. Conservatives have reason for optimism that either man could be an enormously successful president and usher in a new era of American prosperity and freedom. But based on their own histories, skepticism certainly is justified. Should one of these men become our next president, will he steadfastly embrace our founding principles? Or will he be too clever by half and succumb to big-government temptations? Will he fall for Washington's siren song of bipartisanship, which has bloated our government and bankrupted our nation? Or will he instead put his trust in free Americans to guide their own lives?

Our best hope is for the Tea Party to make it politically profitable for Mr. Gingrich and Mr. Romney to choose wisely between their own alternate futures and to make it politically disastrous to do otherwise. The Tea Party is a powerful band of happy warriors but not blind followers.

It's time for conservatives to quit playing checkers and start playing chess. Stop sabotaging our own candidates and instead create a path that rewards conservatism no matter who our nominee is. Newt Gingrich and Mitt Romney are both smart enough to know that while the Tea Party lights a path to the White House, the harsh reality follows that should one of them receive its support and betray it, his presidency would be over before it began.[21]

It's worth pointing out for the record that both men actually wrote their pieces before a single vote had been cast. But with Cain out, Bachmann and Perry fading fast, and no one else very palatable to the TEA Party who stood a chance, there wasn't a reason to sugarcoat things. (Rick Santorum became the flavor of the day at the Iowa caucuses, but couldn't do much to slow the Romney advance after that.) For all the bluster that the TEA Party would select the Republican nominee, the reality was that the last four men standing had done well enough without the overt backing of the TEA Party – which had divided itself up as well as chased the tails of various flashes in the pan like Cain and Bachmann – that the movement wasn't relevant for their purpose. And as the TEA Party became just another subset of the Republican Party, the question was asked from the GOP regulars: who are you going to vote for if you don't vote for our guy?

Out of those four survivors (Gingrich, Paul, Romney, and Santorum) there was no way that many of the TEA Party members who came along later as the movement built momentum were going to back Ron Paul, as author David Brody points out:

Ron Paul will go down in American history as a man whose ideas challenged the status quo and changed the conversation in this country. He's considered the godfather of the Tea Party, and his trendsetting economic message of fiscal responsibility ushered in Teavangelical support.

But don't miss these crucial points: His foreign policy positions were a major problem for the Teavangelical audience despite a certain anti-war mindset among some Libertarians and evangelicals. A major part of the Tea Party had a problem with his noninterventionist views.[22]

Nor were many interested as much in Paul's overall vision of limited government as they were in limiting just a few selected parts such as the amount of immigration, repealing Obamacare, cutting the funding spigot of favorite federal whipping boys like NPR, PBS, or the National Endowment for the Arts, and perhaps eliminating a cabinet department or two like the departments of Education or Energy. But touch my Social Security benefits? No way, Jose!

Evidence of that disconnect between the more libertarian elements present at the TEA Party's founding and those who were claiming to be supporters three years later was clear: Paul rarely saw more than 10% of the vote in a primary, regardless of field size. Even in Virginia, where arcane ballot rules set it up so that only Ron Paul and Mitt Romney were the candidates listed, Romney still won by 19 points on Super Tuesday[23] in a state that had a strong TEA Party influence. (One caveat: Virginia is a commonwealth that does not have partisan voter registration, so it's possible Romney had help from crossover Democrats who had no primary of their own.) In that most direct of contests against the so-called Establishment, Ron Paul still came up short.

Conversely, Gingrich and Santorum held more appeal to TEA Party regulars – but for different reasons. You may recall from way back when in my first chapter that Newt's American Solutions group was an early TEA Party backer. This was a double-edged sword: while the fledgling movement gained a lot of credibility thanks to Newt's lending his support, it also ushered in the beginning of the TEA Party's takeover by larger national groups, up to and including the Republican Party. Yet those who supported Gingrich and could look past his many personal foibles did so because of his constant barrage of new ideas and proposals on how America could work better. Rather than see America as a product of its past, as many Republicans who fondly looked back on the Reagan era would do, Newt kept his eye on the future: a future measured not in electoral cycles, but in generational cycles.

But after Newt won his victory in South Carolina – heretofore a predictor of the Republican nominee – negative advertising and continued momentum from Santorum in other Bible Belt states undercut his support. A subsequent loss in Florida to Mitt Romney, despite a TPP straw poll of activists that showed they favored Gingrich by a nearly 2-to-1 margin over Romney,[24] began the slow decline of the Gingrich effort. The Palmetto State and his home state of Georgia would be Newt's only two primary wins.

Santorum, on the other hand, was more of a populist. However, his campaign was also the last stand for the religious Right, which rejected Paul for his libertarianism, Gingrich for his checkered marital past, and (in some quarters) Romney for his Mormon faith. The former Senator was known for a few religious initiatives, such as supporting a religious freedom act and the teaching of intelligent design, as well as being solidly pro-life when in office, but he wouldn't have had the traction among that group that Mike Huckabee had in 2008 if both had ran. With Huckabee skipping the race this time, though, the onetime Moral Majority crowd placed that cloak of Bible Belt appeal on Santorum's shoulders. Reflecting this, Rick did his best in rural regions, winning outright in a swath of Midwestern and Southern states, but his campaign never had the funds to compete with Mitt Romney and was over by mid-April. Meanwhile, Gingrich tried to make his last stand in Delaware (of all places)[25] but was also out by mid-May. (Ron Paul never actually withdrew, with his supporters intending to place his name into nomination at the Republican National Convention – until they couldn't.)

So for all the insistence the TEA Party would pick the Republican nominee, that nominee turned out to be one of the least TEA Party-friendly candidates in the field – the guy whose state initiative was turned into the national nightmare of Obamacare. With some exceptions, such as *Salon*'s Sally Kohn who believed Romney would "be sitting in the Tea Party's lap,"[26] observers from the Left had a field day with this. Molly Ball, then writing for *The Atlantic*, intoned:

> For the movement that made its mark in 2010 chiefly by giving moderate, establishment Republicans a drubbing in primaries across the country – staking claim to the soul of the GOP on behalf of a newly energized, populist group of activists, no matter the cost – (a Romney nomination) is nothing short of a catastrophe. For the movement to achieve its ultimate goal of toppling President Obama, it now must join forces with just the kind of compromised, compromising Republican whose elimination was its raison d'etre.[27]

More tellingly, Sam Rohrer, a Republican U.S. Senate candidate from Pennsylvania interviewed by Ball, noted:

> Ultimately, they're not going to pull the lever for Obama, but… Mitt is going to have to woo them. Getting their vote is one thing; getting their impassioned commitment is another thing, and the impassioned commitment is what it takes to win.[28]

Yet others on the Left considered the TEA Party too clever by half. Writing in the *Washington Post*, author Theda Skocpol (who also co-wrote a tome called *The Tea Party and the Remaking of American Conservatism* that I often refer to) asserted Romney was a perfect candidate for them:

> In Romney, the tea party has found the ultimate prize: a candidate loyal to the movement's agenda, but able to fool enough pundits and moderate voters to win the White House at a time when the tea party has lost broad appeal.[29]

Ancilliary groups like FreedomWorks, which previously had split with the TPX over their decision to allow Romney to speak at a New Hampshire rally, also grudgingly moved into the Romney camp but hedged their bets by working more on downballot races.[30]

And instead of the ascension for their cause to its rightful place in the political pecking order that many in the TEA Party believed would occur at the Republican National Convention in Tampa, TEA Party groups were left to console themselves that the GOP platform was at least friendly to their interests.[31] "I would consider this an extremely successful convention for the Tea Party," noted TPX's Sal Russo. "We thought we shouldn't try and intrude on a convention that we're happy with."

For their part, the TPP was looking more long-term. The convention is, "more style than substance," said leader Jenny Beth Martin. "The purpose is to legally nominate their candidate. Tea Party Patriots are far more concerned about what laws are going to be passed than what they're doing at a party in Florida and Charlotte."

"As long as our values are represented," Martin continued, "we are making an effect."[32]

But those who thought the TEA Party would get credit for what they had done would be sadly disappointed in the lack of mentions during prime-time speeches,[33] if not outraged at how the party establishment manipulated the rules[34] [35] to shut out supporters of Ron Paul from even putting his name into the quixotic nomination he earned by virtue of winning enough states.[36] If ever there was an excuse for the libertarian segment of the TEA Party to split away from the mainstream as it continued to cast its lot with the establishment GOP, this was it. To that group, the shenanigans at the Republican Party convention were further "proof" the nomination was stolen from Ron Paul.[37]

Amidst the goings-on of the Presidential campaign, issues were developing with the national organizations themselves. After a three-year run at the top of the Tea Party Patriots, co-founder Mark Meckler resigned in February, 2012, citing "discomfort with the way the financial affairs of TPP have been handled... I believe that TPP is fiscally irresponsible in the way that it spends and manages donor monies."[38] Meckler also complained that, as treasurer, "I have been excluded from the distribution of critical financial information, and critical discussions about the finances of the organization." In a tersely-written statement, TPP chalked up the Meckler resignation to "months of discussions and good-faith differences on how best TPP can serve the Tea Party movement."[39]

Questions about TPP's finances were nothing new, however. Proving once again that investigative journalism is frequently employed by the Left only against its enemies, a three-part series by *Mother Jones* reporter Stephanie Mencimer written in 2011 alleged, among other things:

> Tea Party Patriots (TPP) has started to resemble the Beltway lobbying operations its members have denounced. The group's leaders have cozied up to political insiders implicated in the Jack Abramoff lobbying scandal and have paid themselves significant salaries. TPP accepted the use of a private jet and a large donation of anonymous cash right before a key election, and its top officials have refused to discuss how the money was spent. And recently, the group has hired several big-time fundraising and public relations firms that work for the who's who of the Republican political class, including some of the GOP's most secretive campaign operations.
>
> As TPP's leaders entrench themselves in Washington, local activists the group represents have accused them of exploiting the grassroots for their own fame and fortune while failing to deliver any meaningful political results.[40]

The investigation went on to note that TPP had not yet applied for tax-exempt status from the IRS[41] and accused the group of nepotism, claiming the real treasurer of TPP was Lee Martin, husband of TPP co-founder Jenny Beth Martin.[42] The latter allegation would tend to corroborate Meckler's claims. (Knowing what we now know about the IRS and TEA Party groups, though, the fact TPP was not approved for tax-exempt status at that time probably wasn't their fault. They were pleased with the settlement of a class-action lawsuit not completed until October, 2017, after the Trump administration had taken over.)[43]

Meckler left the TPP to form a new group called Citizens for Self-Governance, which left Jenny Beth Martin as the sole survivor among the trio who started TPP in 2009. She took over an organization that was trying to regain its footing, as a March "Road to Repeal Rally" in Washington, D.C. featuring Herman Cain[44] didn't draw as well as expected. It appeared the physical rally aspect of the TEA Party was pretty much tapped out.

The other member of that onetime power trio, Amy Kremer, was busy riding the buses again in 2012 as the Tea Party Express fueled up for three national tours – one dubbed the "Restoring the American Dream" tour through the nation's heartland,[45] the less-formally scheduled "Reclaiming Our Future" tour[46] that staved off the recall effort against Wisconsin Governor Scott Walker, and the final "Winning for America" cross-country effort,[47] as well as mini-tours through Florida[48] and (again) Wisconsin.[49] One new wrinkle introduced as part of these tours: a mobile phone bank where local activists could make calls on behalf of TPX-backed candidates.[50]

And perhaps there was a sense that the traditional TPX format was losing steam, but the name itself still had some cachet. Toward the end of the campaign, this mobile phone bank bus had its own tour through many of the battleground states; a tour not as heavily promoted but in their eyes vital to success. "Unlike in 2010 when the election was only driven by frustrated voters getting out to the polls, in 2012 we are seeing that those frustrated are now experienced and motivated activists working to also get their neighbors and friends to the polls," said Kremer in a release. "This bus tour campaign will accomplish a grassroots-led phone-from-home program that will allow motivated tea party activists the opportunity to engage in the political process."[51]

Kremer also added her optimism about the election results: "There is a lot of wishful thinking on Democrats' part that the tea party has disappeared, but they don't see the army of tea party activists that are manning the precincts, phone banks and victory centers," she said, adding, "They also fail to note that we are on the verge of defeating an incumbent President, gaining seats in the Senate, and retaining the historic majority in the House. It doesn't sound like we have gone away, as much as the establishment of both parties would like."[52]

More than any of the other so-called grassroots groups, though, the TPX was the group furiously shining the turd of the Mitt Romney candidacy. "For the past 12 months, we have been polling our members on presidential preferences, and Mitt Romney has consistently been leading or in the top 3 choices of our poll,"[53] they claimed.

At the grassroots level, though, there was a sense of disappointment and ruing of a missed opportunity among those who followed the TEA Party once the *fait accompli* of Romney going over the top in delegate count occurred in May.

Yet TEA Party history was about to repeat itself. You'll recall that the initial bitter disappointment of the Doug Hoffman NY-23 campaign in 2009 was followed quickly by the Massachusetts special election that propelled Scott Brown to the Senate and provided that critical 41$^{st}$ vote against Obamacare, altering the Democrats' plans to ram it through Congress. In this case, the bruising primary battles that eventually sidelined both Newt Gingrich and Rick Santorum yielded to another state-level election that had national impact because it occurred at an unusual juncture on the political calendar.

In 2011, Wisconsin Democrats and their union allies put a total of six GOP state senators up for recall, threatening what was then a 19-14 Republican majority in their State Senate which backed the budgetary reforms demanded by newly elected Governor Scott Walker – measures that included provisions to curtail dues collection for the state's public-sector unions. With help from local and national TEA Party groups, Democrats were thwarted in four of the six races, allowing Republicans to maintain a slim single-vote majority in the Senate.

But the bigger contest was still to come. Wisconsin's version of Big Labor got to work after the passage of the budgetary reform bill, racking up nearly twice the number of signatures required to put the recall of Governor Walker and Lieutenant Governor Rebecca Kleefisch on the ballot. The election dates were then set: a primary – which was needed on both sides because Walker drew a token GOP opponent while several Democrats vied for the chance to go against him – on May 8 and the general election on June 5.

Having a June election worked well for the TEA Party because it was a race with national interest conducted at a time when little else of political impact was occurring. Five states also held their primary elections on June 5, but with the Presidential race decided and no key Senate battles on the ballot in those states, all their attention could be focused on Wisconsin – just like the circumstances the TEA Party took advantage of in 2010 to propel Scott Brown to an upset win.

So Wisconsin became Ground Zero in a battle for preserving TEA Party principles on a state level, which, even before Romney wrapped up the nomination, was where many local groups were already focused.

> (M)any Tea Party supporters said that while they would work to help any Republican defeat Mr. Obama, their real passion was for electing small-government conservatives further down the ballot and building a stable of leaders who grow up in the movement rather than trying to adapt themselves to it. If that means it takes four or eight more years for them to feel any passion for a presidential nominee, they said, it will be worth the wait.[54]

The Walker recall race fit this description like a glove given his track record. So, in an effort to motivate and attract local supporters, the TPX focused one of their bus tours in Wisconsin solely to combat the recall; meanwhile the Tea Party Patriots had their own “all hands on deck” approach with hundreds of volunteers coming to

Wisconsin to knock on doors. "By (mid-May), buses will begin bringing Tea Party Patriots volunteers from all across America to start canvassing Wisconsin and motivating the voters to support fiscal responsibility, constitutionally limited government, and free markets," said TPP co-leader Jenny Beth Martin, who was by now comfortable in her role as its lead spokesperson. She also took a swipe at the establishment: "It remains to be seen if the Ruling Class...will be able to see past their own bigoted prejudices enough to pay attention."[55]

In addition, home-based activists from around the country were encouraged to make phone calls to undecided voters. As the campaign reached its end, the enthusiasm gap was clear and in Walker's favor.[56] Of course, this left the Left fuming and looking for scapegoats, two of which were the Koch brothers and their group Americans for Prosperity, which was leading a sophisticated GOTV effort independently of the Republican Party – one which happened to be already focused on Wisconsin.[57] As the Tea Party Patriots would say, it was a "partnership for liberty."[58]

So when victory came on June 5, the TEA Party took the occasion to tell America they were back. "Tonight's victory shows that the passion that moved Americans to the streets in 2009 and 2010 is as fervent as ever," exclaimed TPP's Jenny Beth Martin. "Our supporters and volunteers dedicated days and weeks of their lives to make a difference in Wisconsin, and their work has paid off. Thousands more across the country are making a difference right now in their own towns, cities and states."[59]

There were also gains to be made inside the Beltway, too – or at least so the TEA Party hoped. Because 2012 was the year the Democratic wave that took over the Senate in 2006 was up for re-election, Democrats had to defend a staggering 23 of 33 seats – meaning Republicans had a 37-30 advantage in the remaining 67 seats. Thus, to regain control of the Senate the GOP only had to win 14 of 33 races.

The odds of that, however, were a little bit longer than the simple numbers would lead an observer to believe. Nine of those 23 seats were in states that Democrats had controlled for decades, making it unlikely the TEA Party would make a dent despite good candidates. Splitting the others would still leave the GOP a couple votes short of the majority. Out of those, the TEA Party had favorites in several other states, with the prime examples being Richard Mourdock of Indiana (running in the GOP primary against incumbent Sen. Richard Lugar), Josh Mandel in Ohio, Ted Cruz in Texas,[60] and John Raese in West Virginia. Notably absent from that list: 2010 darling Scott Brown, who had angered the TEA Party with his moderate Senate voting record.

Unlike 2010, and perhaps because of what happened at the top of the ticket, there was much less angst among the party bigwigs for not gaining in the Senate – as it happened, the GOP lost two net seats to fall back to a 53-45 minority, with two independents again caucusing with the Democrats. (Connecticut independent Joe Lieberman, who caucused with the Democrats, chose not to run for another term – however, Maine's Angus King took the seat formerly held by retiring centrist Republican Olympia Snowe to maintain the Senate's pair of "independents" as Vermont's Bernie Sanders also won. Meanwhile, the Connecticut seat remained in Democratic hands.)

But there were still those who took the TEA Party to task for three particular races. They blamed the movement for abandoning a Senator they helped to elect in Scott Brown in Massachusetts, setting him up for defeat by Democrat Elizabeth "Fauxcahontas" Warren. Complaints were also bitter about losing the Indiana seat, which the establishment believed would have been held if the gaffe-prone Richard Mourdock hadn't primaried six-term incumbent Richard Lugar out of a job. By that same token, Todd Akin's oft-repeated statement about rape did his candidacy in, and the TEA Party was chastised for selecting him at the ballot box, too.

Yet it's possible the TEA Party took less blame this time around because, frankly, most of the races were blowouts. The closest two GOP defeats came from states which Mitt Romney carried but without the coattails to propel the Senate candidates, both of whom were sitting Congressmen, forward: Denny Rehberg lost to Jon Tester in Montana and Rick Berg fell to Heidi Heitkamp in North Dakota. To be honest, those races in "flyover country" didn't attract a lot of attention from national groups so the TEA Party was basically held harmless.

But the points regarding the losses of Brown, Akin, and Mourdock are still worth studying.

It didn't take long – only about a month after being elected in January, 2010 – for Scott Brown to get the TEA Party mad at him for a moderate vote,[61] but as I briefly noted back in the chapter on Brown's race you couldn't say they weren't warned.[62] His defenders argued that Brown's voting pattern was a requirement to survive in a left-of-center state like Massachusetts, but fewer and fewer TEA Party regulars took that assertion to heart as Brown sided with Democrats on more and more key issues:

> Brown had tried to demonstrate his independence from the national GOP in order to cultivate unaffiliated voters and soft Democrats. During the lame-duck congressional session, he broke with conservatives by supporting the New Start Treaty and an end to the "don't ask, don't tell" policy concerning gays in the military. Brown was a member of the Army National Guard, had advocated for veterans in the Massachusetts legislature, and had mostly sided with hawks during his special election campaign, so both votes were considered a surprise – and a betrayal by his more conservative supporters.[63]

Also mentioned in the piece from *The American Spectator* was Brown's support for Dodd-Frank and the Consumer Financial Protection Bureau (CFPB) and its initial chairman Richard Cordray – who, ironically, was selected for the job despite the fact Elizabeth Warren got the CFPB off the ground.

Despite the bluster about finding a serious primary opponent for Brown[64] in his first few months, though, no serious candidate stepped forward. Left-leaning pundits warned that losing Brown in a primary would be akin to what happened in Delaware a few months earlier, when the moderate Mike Castle – who they thought could secure a Senate seat for the GOP in a place they hadn't been successful for decades – lost to primary foe Christine O'Donnell, who in turn lost to Democrat Chris Coons in a landslide.[65]

But the biggest tell in Brown's campaign was that he didn't see TEA Party support as that important anymore – or at least one could interpret it that way. "Scott Brown is an independent voice," said campaign spokeswoman Alleigh Marre, "and while he welcomes support from all people, he is not beholden to any group."[66] As it turned out, the "support from all people" left him almost 250,000 votes short of Elizabeth Warren's total – and two years later, Brown would cross over to New Hampshire only to lose again for their Senate seat despite the GOP's wave election.

The short answer on what killed Akin's and Mourdock's chances was this: ill-considered replies to questions about rape, which themselves were backhanded ways of trying to draw candidates (TEA Party in particular, but Republicans in general) away from the message of fiscal conservatism that had fairly broad appeal and into the divisive nature of social issues, which didn't have lockstep agreement within the TEA Party itself, let alone society at large.

The Missouri U.S. Senate race was almost an embarrassment of riches for TEA Party followers, as all three of the top GOP primary candidates – Akin, a sitting member of Congress from a suburban St. Louis district, former state treasurer Sarah Steelman, and businessman John Brunner, a political neophyte running in the role of outsider – were worthy of TEA Party support and received backing from various activists around the state. In terms of national support, the candidate who received the choicest backing was Sarah Steelman, the former state treasurer who claimed Sarah Palin[67] and the Tea Party Express[68] in her corner; however, the evangelical crowd was more likely to prefer Akin based on his worldview and endorsements from former Presidential candidates Mike Huckabee[69] and Michele Bachmann.[70] Akin won the primary on a plurality vote, besting Brunner and Steelman by six and seven percentage points, respectively. It turned out that Akin was the candidate incumbent Senator Claire McCaskill preferred to face, and later it was found she had put her own thumb on the scale in the GOP primary by spending on anti-Akin commercials in order to solidify his base, believing his "extremist" views would repel moderate voters.[71]

Less than two weeks after the primary, in an interview with a St. Louis television station, Akin outraged the political world by revealing his ignorance of OB-GYN principles:

> During that (local television) interview the congressman and U.S. Senate candidate was asked whether abortion should be allowed in the case of rape.
>
> "From what I understand from doctors, that's really rare. If it's a legitimate rape, the female body has ways to try to shut that whole thing down. But let's assume maybe that didn't work or something. I think there should be some punishment, but the punishment ought to be on the rapist."[72]

Within hours the firestorm of criticism and calls for Akin to step aside were at a fever pitch, from the Romney campaign on down.[73] [74] Although Romney himself stopped short of asking Akin to withdraw, Amy Kremer from the Tea Party Express urged Akin to drop out[75] because defeating Claire McCaskill was too important and the deadline to do so without penalty was fast approaching.[76]

But as time passed, many Missouri TEA Party members became defiant about the national catcall for Akin to quit.

> I support him probably even more than I did before," said Molly Nesham, a home-schooling mother who also teaches at a Christian school and likes Akin's stand on abortion. "He made a mistake and the Republican Party abandoned him."[77]

Indeed, Akin was left hanging out to dry by the big-money Republicans. But the damage was done: Akin's polling lead he'd held through August was suddenly reversed, and while he recovered to some extent the November results were a 15-point blowout win for McCaskill most of the polls underestimated.[78]

In Mourdock's case, the postmortem on the Indiana primary focused to a larger extent on Lugar being out of touch with his home state[79] than on Mourdock's more conservative mindset. "Lugar betrayed the principles of fiscal responsibility, constitutionally limited government and free markets that must be addressed this year or the American people will choose new leaders as happened today and in 2010." said TPP's Jenny Beth Martin. "This upset is no surprise to tax paying Americans in Indiana."[80] She further explained, "It's time for the establishment to link arms with the Tea Party's core values and get in line with the rest of America."[81]

Conversely there was also the sense among opposition partisans and the media that it was an opportunity for Democrats to steal back a GOP seat. "The 2012 Democratic nominee is Rep. Joe Donnelly, and party members think his reputation as a centrist will stack up well against Mourdock," stated the *Washington Post*.[82]

"(Mourdock) says there's a problem... of too much bipartisanship, and he can be counted on to obstruct. Well, there are a lot of things wrong in Washington, but too much compromise is certainly not one of them," added Democrat Senator Chuck Schumer. "The more the Republicans embrace the Tea Party agenda and its candidates, the more they damage their chances in November."[83]

Yet the limited amount of polling in Indiana suggested the race was Mourdock's to win[84] until a debate question tipped the scales. The penultimate question of the final debate between Mourdock, Donnelly, and Libertarian hopeful Andrew Horning was on an issue most weighing on Hoosier minds like the economy – oh wait, it was about abortion. Here is the actual question and answers from each candidate transcribed from that debate.

**Dennis Ryerson, moderator:** *The issues of abortion and contraception continue to divide the country, and questions we received from voters reflected that divide. For example, one voter wanted to know your position on a woman's 'right to abortion' but not only that, but to contraception and other reproductive health services, whether government should provide those services. Another asked if you believe that life begins at conception, and in that person's view, what would you do to protect the babies who would be aborted during your term in the Senate.*

*So where do you stand on these issues? Mr. Horning?*

**Andrew Horning, Libertarian Party candidate:** Oh boy, you can imagine this is going to be a tough one...all of us up here have said we're pro-life. But what does that really mean? In terms of the federal legislature, you know, there's not really any authority granted to the federal government in matters of even murder; no, that is a state-level crime and unless it crosses state boundaries it's really not supposed to be a federal matter. In fact, I have said, you know, just on Constitutional grounds I would have to oppose *Roe v. Wade* being treated as law – it's not, it was an unconstitutional ruling and the laws which have been written subsequent to it and under the color of it have been wrong.

But, we have been doing so badly and so long that we have kind of forgotten how many other rights have been trampled with it. Men don't have any concomitant rights with it over their baby: you know you can't expect – you can't just say no to child support, for instance. We've gotten so lopsided with looking at this as only a woman's issue we forget that there are all kinds of ways around this where we can make it easier for people to adopt children – there are lots of things we can do better than what we are doing right now, but as a federal legislator I've got to tell you there is not much that I can do.

**Ryerson:** *Thank you. Mr. Donnelly?*

**Joe Donnelly, Democratic candidate:** I believe in pro-life. I believe that life begins at conception. The only exceptions I believe in are for rape, and incest, and the life of a mother. In regard to contraception, I believe that religious institutions have a right to not go against their own religious beliefs. We can't ask them to do something they simply cannot do. And so, how do we make sure that a woman has a right to that quality health care while at the same time protecting the rights of religious institutions to not violate their own beliefs. And that's what we're working on right now.

Many groups, many of them in the Catholic Church which I'm a member of, have filed suit. They have every right to file that suit. I am working on a legislative solution to it. There's also work being done on the judicial side, and we're trying to get an executive solution as well.

**Ryerson:** *Thank you. Mr. Mourdock?*

**Richard Mourdock, Republican candidate:** You know, this is that issue that every candidate for federal or even state office faces, and I, too, certainly stand for life. I know there are some who disagree and I respect their point of view, but I believe life begins at conception. The only exception I have for – to have an abortion is in that case of the life of the mother. I just – I struggled with myself for a long time but I came to realize that life is that gift from God. And I think that even when life begins in that horrible situation of rape that it is something that God intended to happen.

You know, Mr. Donnelly's comments about Obamacare and what's happening there, trying to reform it – that's good to reform it, but it should not be here in the first place. You know, the fact that we have the Catholic Church and so many institutions having to file a lawsuit to get their basic freedom – that I thought was guaranteed under the Constitution, the practice of your religion – that now there has to be an amendment put forward to somehow bring that about. If the law had never been passed that lawsuit wouldn't be in place and religious freedom today would not be today in question.[85]

What the reporting generally missed but I noticed right away in reviewing the video was the catch in Mourdock's voice and pinched facial expression when he related the part about rape. Since most people only read about the transgression, or maybe saw the five-second sound bite, they may not have noticed the change in demeanor and tenor. But it didn't matter – the Left and media had their "gotcha" sound bite they were looking for and Mourdock's campaign never recovered.

The ascension and downfall of Akin and Mourdock relates well to an issue that helped to drive a wedge through the TEA Party movement as it grew and peaked, and that's eventually going to be a significant part of this postmortem. Yet the loss of the Romney/Ryan ticket sparked a lot of finger-pointing and further upheaval in the ranks of TEA Party support groups, as well as a sea change in philosophy for one of its two most prominent organizations.

# THE TEA PARTY IS DEAD

*"The TEA Party is Dead. Good Riddance."* – Headline from a post by Erick Erickson, *The Resurgent*, September 1, 2016.

Arguably Erickson's declaration may have come a few years too late, but after the staggering blow of losing the 2012 election there was a definite retrenchment and a new tone of cynicism bordering at times on paranoia within the TEA Party.

Even before the media networks called the race for Barack Obama, the finger pointing began. One day before the balloting, TPP's Jenny Beth Martin contended that the TEA Party's appeal was to independent voters:

> It is election time again. Which means it is time again for the beltway establishment media, and politicians from both sides, to begin laying the groundwork to blame whatever happens on November 6th on the tea party.
>
> These are the same folks who convinced themselves, and perhaps convinced you, that when the tea party delivered the biggest political shift in America in 62 years – a "shellacking" by the President's own admission – that it was somehow a loss. And that so-called "loss" was the Tea Party's fault.
>
> (…)
>
> Tea Party independents left the left (-14%) and flooded the right (+13%) in the 2010 "Tea Party Elections."
>
> That's right. We appeal to the independents. Tea Party independents.[1]

Unfortunately, those independents didn't show up in large enough numbers to swing the election, so the next agenda item for Martin on election night was to blame the establishment and their selected candidate:

> We wanted a fighter like Ronald Reagan who boldly championed America's founding principles, who inspired millions of independents and 'Reagan Democrats' to join us, and who fought his leftist opponents on the idea that America, as founded, was a 'Shining city upon a hill.'

> What we got was a weak moderate candidate, hand-picked by the Beltway elites and country-club establishment wing of the Republican Party. The Presidential loss is unequivocally on them.[2]

And if that wasn't enough, Martin added the next day that the loss was also on the mainstream media:

> The dereliction of duty by the media is both dishonest and harmful to our great country. We have to keep the pressure up so the media remembers it is supposed to hold politicians accountable, not cover for them.
>
> We all know last night's results were disappointing, and the media is to blame for that. Had another politician been President, he or she would have rightly been hammered by the media for what happened in Benghazi.[3]

It was a vineyard's worth of sour grapes coming from the leader of the primary grassroots TEA Party organization. (By contrast, the one public statement coming from a member of the TPX was more philosophical: in the stable full of excrement, there had to be a pony someplace.)[4]

It was no surprise, though, that the establishment pushed back. After laying out how conservative Mitt Romney's platform was, columnist Ann Coulter placed some of her blame for Mitt's loss on circumstances, but heaped more on the TEA Party:

> Having vanquished liberal Republicans, the party's problem now runs more along the lines of moron showoffs, trying to impress tea partiers like Jenny Beth Martin by taking insane positions on rape exceptions for abortion – as 2 million babies are killed every year from pregnancies having nothing to do with rape.
>
> Romney lost because he was running against an incumbent, was beaten up during a long and vicious primary fight, and ran in a year with a very different electorate from 1980. At least one of those won't be true next time. But we're not going to win any elections by telling ourselves fairy tales about a candidate who lost because he wasn't conservative enough, articulate enough or mean enough.[5]

That all may be true, but 2½ years later Ann was one of the first behind a candidate who wasn't necessarily conservative or articulate in Donald Trump, believing he could win from the start.[6] To her, Mitt Romney was "the best (candidate) that we ever had until Trump."[7] (Perhaps his "you're fired!" reputation made him mean enough?) My apologies for getting ahead of myself, but that had to be said about the prolific and controversial Coulter.

Billed as a "former research director for the RNC," David Welch went several steps beyond Coulter in a scathing *New York Times* editorial:

> (Jeb) Bush and (Chris) Christie (as governors) best represent realistic, levelheaded conservatism. Both have crossed the aisle numerous times to the betterment of their states. Yet they enjoy sterling reputations in the party. This occurs when common sense trumps partisanship.
>
> This is not to say that the only way forward is by tying the party to bipartisanship. But it does mean a willingness to fight those who claim the name of the party but not its ethos.
>
> In a recent interview, the bête noir of both the left and the Tea Party right, (Karl) Rove, suggested that his organization, American Crossroads, might become active in Republican primaries during the next election cycle. If Crossroads and the old-guard Republican committees sided with sensible candidates early on in the primaries and, if need be, ran ads against extreme members of the party, they could do much to bring some sense back to the Republican landscape.
>
> Our modern-day Buckley's denouncement of once fringe Tea Party candidates should be forthright. Whether it's Bush, Christie or a party institution, there must be one clear message: no unserious candidate need apply.[8]

So who was correct? Was it the group that said Mitt Romney was a squishy moderate, or those who agreed the TEA Party "forced Romney too far to the right and didn't give him the room (or the trust) to move back toward the center"[9] for the election? And what about an argument presented by Republican strategist Sara Fagen, who postulated during the campaign[10] that Romney was a "bridge candidate" between the Baby Boomer generation and younger Republican leaders like Paul Ryan, Chris Christie, and Bobby Jindal?

That "bridge candidate" contention may have made more sense in the immediate aftermath of the 2012 campaign, but instead the largest plurality of Republican voters in 2016 chose the oldest man ever to become President in Donald Trump, who was the first President to be elected while in his seventies. (Had she won, though, Hillary Clinton would have been the second-oldest, about eight months younger than 69-year-old Ronald Reagan.) I'll get to some of the reasoning in a later chapter, but in the 2016 campaign Trump defeated a slew of younger conservatives – four of them still in their forties, a group that included the aforementioned Governor Bobby Jindal and his cohort Scott Walker, along with Senators Ted Cruz and Marco Rubio.

In politics perception is reality, and the biggest problem in Mitt Romney's campaign was that he was the wrong candidate at the wrong time. To be quite honest, Romney's year may have been 2008, although he would have been hard-pressed to win that election given the brutal economy and media-fueled perceptions about how George W. Bush was to blame for it (as opposed to the Pelosi-Reid Democratic Congress that came into power just before things began heading south in a hurry.) But compared to the low-energy, devoid of excitement campaign of John McCain – one where conservatives felt the bottom of the ticket (Sarah Palin) should have been the top – a 2008 Romney general election campaign would have featured a technocrat Beltway outsider with a business background and the *bona fides* of being the 2002 Salt Lake City Olympics savior[11] that may have been sold as just what the doctor ordered to address the serious economic issues at the time. With Romney as President, the TEA Party likely would have been a little-remembered libertarian-sponsored series of events because Mitt would have chosen a different path to address the Great Recession.

But in 2012 with the TEA Party in place on one side and a President that escaped significant media scrutiny[12] in Barack Obama on the other, Mitt Romney did the best he could under the circumstances – there were just too many people who believed that Obamacare would eventually work (remember, it was still a couple years away from full implementation; while its most popular reforms were already in place at that time, we had yet to completely live out what was in the bill once it passed) and were convinced the economy was thisclose to turning around. The little prosperity we had was thanks in large part to an energy boom Obama tried to thwart through regulation and lack of progress on the Keystone XL pipeline, yet take credit for on the job creation side.

With respect to the TEA Party, their lack of enthusiasm over Romney was apparent. Unlike the situation in Wisconsin a few months earlier where volunteers were readily willing to help out Governor Scott Walker, at campaign's end the TPP was forced into gimmicks and giveaways just to get volunteers to make phone calls for Romney and others on the GOP list.[13] Generally the concept of Romneycare was pointed out as a reason TEA Party regulars were suspicious of Mitt, but in truth the program was more constitutional than Obamacare, which passed muster with the Supreme Court only because the mandate involved was twisted into a tax for the sake of the decision. (That verdict made TPP leadership physically ill.)[14] Romney noted "there are a number of things I like"[15] about Obamacare, but his plan called for more state-level involvement: converting Medicaid to a block grant program was the primary example.[16] "I believe in the Tenth Amendment," said Romney, and his program would have better utilized it.[17] Obviously the few libertarian purists remaining in the TEA Party would still object to the revision of a government entitlement, but those who would complain about such a program would find it easier to do so in Albany, Sacramento, or Springfield than in faraway Washington, D.C.

The fact that Romney conceded the argument about Obamacare by vowing to "repeal and replace" it, though, put him squarely in a space where he was the squishy moderate, simply tinkering around the edges of a bill where we had not yet fully found out what was in it despite the fact it had long since passed. Those who believed that health care was a right weren't going to vote for an imitation when they had the real thing in Obama and those who believed the previous system only needed tweaking and not replacement with Obamacare were left wanting by Romney's embrace of the new system. Perhaps it worked on a state level, but New Mexico is not New Hampshire and Michigan is not Massachusetts. And Mitt Romney won none of those states, even though some believed he somehow could.

Having failed to influence the Presidential election, there may now have been the sense inside the Beltway that the TEA Party was toothless. At least Speaker of the House John Boehner thought so:

> This has been the most misreported story of my two years' tenure. We don't have a Tea Party caucus to speak of in the House. All of us who were elected in 2010 were supported by the Tea Party.
>
> These are ordinary Americans who've taken a more active role in their government. They want solutions, but we've all come a long way over the last two years. I think we all understand each other a lot better.[18]

To no one's surprise, Boehner's remarks didn't sit well with the TEA Party or their media allies. *Breitbart* writer Matthew Vadum charged that "Boehner almost immediately began waving the white flag in their view in front of the newly re-energized Democrats."[19] Thundered TPP's Martin, in a piece titled "John Boehner Just Denied You Exist": "There is no way I will let the establishment blame you for their losses."[20] But they did anyway, because shifting blame is what they do.

Later on Jenny Beth continued with the us vs. them rhetoric, adding in response to a conciliatory "Fox News Sunday" appearance by *Weekly Standard* editor William Kristol where he called for tax increases for the wealthy,[21] "(The establishment) views the GOP as a good in and of itself. Getting the Republican Party back in power is the goal of the establishment. Never mind what the party stands for, or what principles it has to abandon to gain said power. *Power* is what drives most of these people, whether they be politicians or pundits."[22] (Italics in original.) By this point, the TPP was calling for an all-out war[23] against the establishment.

(Meanwhile, the Left was striking back: Michigan entrepreneur Clint Tarver was the victim of a union-led war against his business, a battle he unknowingly entered by catering to an Americans for Prosperity group counter-protesting in a tent at a Lansing rally against a right-to-work proposal.[24] Tarver wasn't seriously injured, but his catering equipment failed to survive the onslaught.)

And while the blame game between establishment and TEA Party was in full swing, a key TEA Party support group was undergoing an upheaval. A month after the election, it was learned that FreedomWorks leader Dick Armey was resigning as chairman, citing "serious differences of opinion about the process of how you do business"[25] with Matt Kibbe, the CEO and president of the organization. Armey wasn't the only one who left, either: another key defection was Brendan Steinhauser, the man who put together the Taxpayer March on Washington (a.k.a. the 9/12 Rally) and from that success became FreedomWorks' Director of Campaigns.[26]

Steinhauser's loss was key because, under his tutelage, FreedomWorks had evolved from putting together large protest rallies to setting up the grassroots training that created political activists out of ordinary citizens. Unlike the Tea Party Patriots, which was set up as an umbrella organization to band together local TEA Parties, the candidate- and election-driven Tea Party Express, or FreedomWorks' sibling organization Americans for Prosperity with its own sponsorship of bus tours and organizational structure of its own local and state chapters – some of which were former or split off from local TEA Parties – FreedomWorks had more or less remained behind the scenes and tasked itself with activist training.[27]

While it was always argued by the Left that FreedomWorks and Americans for Prosperity were the two key reasons the TEA Party was political Astroturf – simply a mob which was bought and paid for by the Koch brothers – the fact that the TEA Party survived through three election cycles (and influenced 2016 in a different way) argues that it was larger than just these Beltway-based organizations. Certainly they worked hand-in-glove with one another, but not all local TEA Parties used the national assistance nor did every issue the movement attempt to address fall onto the radar screen of the economic platform promoted by the groups (and, by extension, the Koch brothers.)

A good case in point for this line of contention came after the tragedy at Sandy Hook Elementary School in Newtown, Connecticut. Just days before a school full of children, teachers, and staff would have been released to enjoy their Christmas break, 26 of them were instead mowed down on December 14 by gunman Adam Lanza, who began the spree by murdering his mother at their home and ended it by taking his own life at the school.[28]

Before the bodies had even been buried, there were calls from Congress for stricter gun control standards, especially since Lanza's primary weapon was a semi-automatic AR-15 "assault rifle."[29] While President Obama stopped short of explicitly calling for gun control, it was easily read between the lines in his remarks later that fateful Friday:

> As a country, we have been through this too many times. Whether it's an elementary school in Newtown, or a shopping mall in Oregon, or a temple in Wisconsin, or a movie theater in Aurora, or a street corner in Chicago – these neighborhoods are our neighborhoods, and these children are our children. And we're going to have to come together and take meaningful action to prevent more tragedies like this, regardless of the politics.[30]

Because of the reputation that preceded Barack Obama and Democrats in Congress, there were a subset of TEA Party irregulars who believed the Sandy Hook shooting was a hoax[31] [32] or blamed other factors,[33] but others saw it more as a general threat to our Second Amendment rights. Defending the Second Amendment meant that for a brief period the outdoor TEA Party rallies returned, some complete with loaded weapons. "This is the fundamental issue on the founding of our nation," said Tampa TEA Party leader Tom Gaitens to the Associated Press.[34]

Under the white-hot post-tragedy spotlight, gun control was a troubling issue for a moment. But as the uproar over Sandy Hook faded from the political conscience after the holiday season passed, Congress found other things to preoccupy it – in part because no ban on so-called "assault weapons" was going to pass in a Republican-controlled House.

These issues, not necessarily economic but important to our freedom nonetheless, became more of a rallying point as interest in fiscal issues waned. Activists were now used to the ebb and flow of government spending, and realized the impasse was now probably going to last until Barack Obama left office in early 2017.

And if more proof wasn't required that the finger pointing between the TEA Party and Republican establishment was leading to a messy divorce that would have lingering consequences, the March 2013 release of the RNC's "Growth and Opportunity Project" served as the separation papers.[35] Two key platform planks which were dear to much of the rank-and-file of the TEA Party – enhanced immigration reform and a return to a more traditional view on social issues – were tossed aside.

> We… believe that comprehensive immigration reform is consistent with Republican economic policies that promote job growth and opportunity for all.
>
> (…)
>
> On messaging, we must change our tone – especially on certain social issues that are turning off young voters. In every session with young voters, social issues

were at the forefront of the discussion; many see them as the civil rights issues of our time. We must be a party that is welcoming and inclusive for all voters.[36]

This was treated as a revelation by establishment Republicans like Jennifer Rubin of the *Washington Post*, who crowed:

Given that many of its most popular leaders endorse immigration reform this may not cause as much of a stir as it would have 6 months or a year ago. Don't be surprised, however, to see a backlash from those appealing to anti-immigration exclusionists. It would be a mistake for established conservative media outlets to pander to those voices.

(…)

These passages may very well raise the hackles of many social conservative activists and some elected officials. But by not asking for endorsement, merely toleration of a variety of positions on gay rights and marriage, the report aims to take the issue off the national political table.[37]

As we later learned with their dogged opposition to the Gang of Eight, TEA Partiers were not hungering for comprehensive immigration reform, which was indeed properly addressed at the federal level. (Their lack of motion, however, led states like Arizona to make their own attempts[38] to enforce federal laws.) Three years later, the gay rights issue was nationalized by the Supreme Court's *Obergefell* decision, which took the same-sex marriage issue off the table but ignored the idea of the Tenth Amendment and letting states decide. In that decision, the SCOTUS instead ran roughshod over the will of the people in the group of states that turned down same-sex marriage at the ballot box in recent years and created a new "right" from thin air.

Yet even as it was claimed any "very informal" ties regarding these topics weren't collusion but were on a "case-by-case basis,"[39] the TEA Party's growing orthodoxy on social issues was shooing its libertarian element out the door, too. Orlando-based TEA Party leader Phil Russo, who earlier in this book was critical of the Tea Party Express and its impact, called it quits on the movement itself in a very public way by claiming the TEA Party had fallen due to "hypocrisy and racism":

Sadly, what began as a genuine opportunity to make this country more free has deteriorated to racist name calling, fear of anyone with brown skin, and an irrational focus on Sharia law.

(...)

It's so sad to me that a movement that began as an organic reaction to big government has been hijacked by the right. The Tea Party's slogan was, "fiscal responsibility, limited government, and free markets" – but it has now become the religious right in tri-corner hats.

(…)

Hypocrisy and racism are what drove independents who voted Republican in 2010 away from the Tea Party. The same thing has happened with the Libertarians, like me, who were part of the original Tea Party. We have been driven away from the rallies and the meetings because what was supposed to be a movement about fiscal issues has become the activist-wing of the GOP. If you don't think every Muslim is a terrorist you are not a real Tea Party member. If you think that the U.S. Constitution does not say anything about drugs, and that therefore, under the 9th and 10th Amendments the issue should be left to the states, you are not a real Tea Party member. And when you use the Constitution to prove to them that they are wrong it sends them into fits.[40]

But there was also a reality libertarians had to face, too: "Tea Party libertarians may be vocal and active, but they simply don't have the numbers if evangelicals stay home," wrote author David Brody. "That's the plain hard truth."[41]

Looking at hard truth from a different perspective, North Carolina TEA Party leader Ralph Reagan, who you'll recall was also a Republican Party chair in the Fayetteville area, complained that "every time the D.C. GOP caved on something we were blamed."[42] This dichotomy between TEA Party and Republican Party eventually cost him his county chairmanship.

So as the TEA Party was losing ground with establishment Republicans, dropping libertarians like a bad habit, and shedding popular support thanks to continuing negative press, the perception of it stopped being positive and began being tossed around as an epithet by the Left – *i.e.* a conservative Republican was now a "TEA Party politician." Some politicians, such as Virginia's upset 2014 primary winner Dave Brat – who knocked out the "establishment" favorite in House Majority Leader Eric Cantor – ran away from the "TEA Party" label even if they agreed on most issues.[43] The only time the TEA Party got any love was when it went against those entities perceived to be its corporate masters, such as the birth of the "Green Tea Coalition" in Georgia[44] (and later Florida),[45] which combined local TEA Party chapters and left-wing environmental groups that supported enhanced measures promoting solar energy in opposition to each state's AFP chapter.[46]

At the same time, those who doggedly remained passionate TEA Partiers were having a harder and harder time motivating others to participate in protests. Take for example this abortive Florida protest against Senator Marco Rubio, who drew the TEA Party's ire by participating in the Gang of Eight.

> One sweltering July day, a half-dozen tea party protesters gathered under a tree in front of Rubio's Miami office, seeking shade as they denounced his support for an immigration overhaul. But the protest soon turned into more of a support group, with the four men and two women grousing to each other about how Rubio had turned into a "back-stabber," a "liar" and a "flip-flopper."
>
> Juan Fiol, a real estate broker who organized the protest, kept looking at his phone, waiting for calls from fellow tea party supporters that never came.
>
> "It was supposed to be a big event," he said as he waved a large "Don't Tread on Me" flag.[47]

The argument could easily be made – particularly with the hindsight of half a decade – that the TEA Party was successful in staving off amnesty via Congressional means, forcing Barack Obama to do it piecemeal through, among other actions, the executive-ordered Deferred Action for Childhood Arrivals, better known as DACA. These activists' behind-the-scenes action were effective enough to work in some cases – just ask Joan Fabiano, who I previously introduced to you in this book[48] – but it didn't change the perception the TEA Party was yesterday's news.

This was particularly true when the Congressional GOP caved on the prospect of shutting down the government in October, 2013. Gleeful *Washington Post* columnist Eugene Robinson gloated that "President Obama's victory this week (on the budget deal) was as complete and devastating as Sherman's march through the South."[49] (An interesting analogy to be sure, given subsequent events.) A few months later, on the movement's fifth anniversary of its Tax Day protests, Nicole Hemmer of the fading weekly *U.S. News and World Report* summarized the TEA Party as "withering" because of its "waning popularity and disastrous electoral record."[50]

This came shortly after the Tea Party Patriots hosted a fifth anniversary rally remembering the original Chicago Tea Parties in Washington, D.C. But instead of fiscal issues, a number of speakers addressed the age-old charge of racism within the movement's ranks and TEA Party favorite Rand Paul warned the group, "If we want a bigger crowd and we want to win politically, our message has to be a happy message, one of optimism, one of inclusiveness, one of growth."[51] This was a departure from the hardline message the pre-2012 TEA Party had, and this mellowing of tone, combined with primary victories for incumbents like Rand's fellow Senator Mitch McConnell, who "crushed the Tea Party"[52] later that spring, led pollster Nate Silver to declare the "Tea party has outlived its usefulness" as a political term.[53]

Perhaps the new version TEA Party may have been portrayed as looking for "smart, educated candidates" like successful Senate hopefuls Tom Cotton in Arkansas and Ben Sasse in Nebraska,[54] but simply put they were still taken as just another subset of the mainstream Republican Party.

This perceived need to compromise, at least a little bit here and there, wasn't lost on other observers of the TEA Party.

> There's no doubt that Tea Party members have not learned the art of compromise, and as the movement moves forward Tea Party congressmen are either going to have to grow their legislative majority so they can call the shots or figure out a way to compromise without sacrificing their principles.[55]

Yet our old friend Theda Skocpol warned the Left that, "The Tea Party was supposed to be dead and the GOP on the way to moderate repositioning after Obama's victory and Democratic congressional gains in November 2012...(but) Tea Party influence does *not* depend on general popularity at all. Even as most Americans have figured out that they do not like the Tea Party or its methods, Tea Party clout has grown in Washington and state capitals."[56] (Italics in original.) That much was true, but it came with a caveat.

The methods of the TEA Party, as a matter of fact, were becoming less and less distinguishable from those of the mainline Republican Party. Infighting on allocation of resources led longtime TPX leader Amy Kremer to split with the group[57] in April, 2014 when the TPX decided to back Florida Congressional candidate Curt Clawson with several days of activities to begin its ninth bus tour "Fighting For Liberty" and ignored the state of Kentucky, where Kremer wanted to back Senate challenger Matt Bevin – the one who was eventually "crushed" by Mitch McConnell. That relatively modest bus tour, and a small-scale one in Mississippi to back Senate challenger Chris McDaniel, would be the extent of the 2014 bus tours for the Tea Party Express as it backed away from the rallies and instead offered simple, far less expensive press release endorsements.

Meanwhile, the 2014 campaign cemented Jenny Beth Martin's status as one who made her living in the shadowy world of political consulting. Once the Tea Party Patriots Citizens Fund was created in early 2013, the onetime philosophy of neutrality among TEA Party leadership was no more. The fund would spread millions of dollars around for the 2014 cycle, with all of it aiding Republican candidates. Certainly Martin would try and put her spin on GOP success in the 2014 midterms, to wit:

> The tea party provided more than winning ideas to this Republican wave; our intensity was palpable in the lead-up to November 4. We knocked on tens of

> thousands of doors. We made 2.4 million get-out-the-vote phone calls in key battlegrounds like Iowa, Georgia and Kansas, often for candidates we didn't originally support or endorse in primaries.[58]

While all of this may be factually correct, it also showed the focus on the volunteers was not there like it was in 2010 and 2012. Knocking on "tens of thousands of doors" may sound impressive, but Senate races affected millions of doors in 2014; moreover, robocalls can be made a thousand or more at a time. It was more troublesome to get volunteers for GOTV efforts for these Senate races, as opposed to local and state contests where TEA Party contenders did better.

The distinction of the 2014 Senate election, though, was the number of TEA Party favorites who lost primary challenges against incumbent or more establishment-favored GOP candidates. Matt Bevin in Kentucky, Chris McDaniel in Mississippi, and Milton Wolf in Kansas were among that group of challengers who lost, with all three incumbents who defeated them eventually returned to the Senate. While the triumphs of Tom Cotton in Arkansas and Ben Sasse in Nebraska were looked at as TEA Party wins, Cotton was unopposed in his primary and several groups jumped on the Sasse bandwagon late, originally favoring Shane Osborn, the former state treasurer who bowed to Sasse in the primary.

With the preferred "establishment" candidates mostly in place, in the 2014 midterm the GOP eliminated three Senators who were seeking their first re-election (having come in on the 2008 Obama wave), defeated one Democratic appointee, and picked up the seats of three other retiring members on their way to regaining control of the Senate after eight years out of power. Just like Nancy Pelosi lost her gavel after the 2010 midterms, Harry Reid would no longer be the Senate Majority Leader and would have to endure his final two years there in the minority. It was four years and one candidate in Sharron Angle too late for those who were passionate about the TEA Party, but better late than never. (By comparison, the initial TEA Party wave of 2010 only lost two of the 12 Republicans newly elected in 2010 in the 2016 election – Mark Kirk, who represented the deep-blue state of Illinois, and Kelly Ayotte, who lost by barely 1,000 votes out of over 738,000 cast in New Hampshire. Arguably a revitalized TEA Party there would have held Ayotte's seat, although Hillary Clinton's victory margin in the Granite State was similar.)

Even with that measure of electoral success, however, there were signs of serious trouble associated with the TEA Party. A rampant factor in their demise was the rise and success of so-called "scam PACs," described in *Politico* by campaign finance lawyer Paul Jossey this way:

> A small group of supposedly conservative lawyers and consultants saw

something different: dollar signs. The PACs found anger at the Republican Party sells very well. The campaigns they ran would be headlined "Boot John Boehner," or "Drop a Truth Bomb on Kevin McCarthy." And after Boehner was in fact booted and McCarthy bombed in his bid to succeed him, it was naturally time to "Fire Paul Ryan." The selling is always urgent: "Stop what you're doing." "This can't wait." One active solicitor is the Tea Party Leadership Fund, which received $6.7 million from 2013 to mid-2015, overwhelmingly from small donors. A typical solicitation from the TPLF read: "Your immediate contribution could be the most important financial investment you will make to help return America to greatness." But, according to an investigation by *POLITICO*, 87 percent of that "investment" went to overhead; only $910,000 of the $6.7 million raised was used to support political candidates. If the prospect signs a "petition," typically a solicitation of his or her personal information is recorded and a new screen immediately appears asking for money. Vendors pass the information around in "list swaps" and "revenue shares" ad infinitum.

Starting a new PAC is easy: Fill out some paperwork, throw up a splash-page website, rent an email list, and you're off. It's an entrepreneurial endeavor. Through trial-and-error, operatives test messages to see which resonate best and are most likely to get them and their vendors paid.[59]

And so on and so forth, in a never-ending cycle of fundraising.

Erick Erickson, then of *RedState*, was one of the first to sound the alarm on this,[60] and he was joined by a larger *Politico* investigation[61] into these "scam PACs" that mainly traded on TEA Party-favored candidates and causes. The incessant fundraising off TEA Party regulars, who skewed heavily toward those 60 and over who had the disposable income to use for political causes, made consultants – a group of characters who often countered that doing mass e-mail appeals wasn't as cheap as those on the outside of the business thought – fabulously wealthy for next to no effort, while achieving little to assist actual candidates who could have used the funds if they were given directly. Oftentimes less than 10% of the money raised by a PAC would go toward candidates, with much larger amounts used to pay for more fundraising. To remind you again, look back in Managing the Decline at the disparity between the money raised and assistance provided by the Tea Party Express in one election cycle and imagine it multiplied by a factor of 10 or more.

Even a group like the Tea Party Patriots, which had separated its PAC side from its organizing side, revealed in their annual report – a glossy, full color pictorial that bragged about their key achievement, firing Speaker John Boehner – that in 2015 they had spent just under $10 million, with nearly half of that ($4,621,263 to be exact) allocated to "Recruiting & Development Communications" ($2,903,821) and "Operations and Administration" ($1,717,442).[62] By this point, argued Michigan

TEA Party leader Joan Fabiano, the TPP was "another bureaucracy (and) not necessarily organic."[63]

Yet where did the money go? Chances are it went into the pockets of those running the PAC, and not the candidate. In the meantime, the grassroots were being starved of their fiscal fertilizer:

> By sapping the Tea Party's resources and energy, the PACs thwarted any hope of building the movement. Every dollar swallowed up in PAC overhead or vendor fees was a dollar that did not go to federal Tea Party candidates in crucial primaries or general elections. This allowed the GOP to easily defeat or ignore them (with some rare exceptions). Second, the PACs drained money especially from local Tea Party groups, some of which were actively trying to grow the movement electorally from the ground up, at the school board and city council level. Lacking results five years on, interest in the movement waned – all that was left were the PACs and their lists.[64]

This pointed out another issue. A real problem the TEA Party had was having the same old people represent it in the media. When it first began, the spokespeople for the TEA Party were average, everyday people – maybe even your neighbor, the guy in your bowling league, or the lady who sits a few pews behind you at church. But now all America heard from the TEA Party came from the same old recycled guests one came to expect from inside the Beltway, and suddenly it seemed a lot less of a grassroots thing.

There were people who understood this, but they were too few and far between. Michael Johns, an original TEA Party leader from Philadelphia, explained:

> In 2015, the Tea Party and patriot movement's top priority must be communicating and impacting public opinion and explaining why and how Tea Party principles can make America great again: creating jobs and economic prosperity, restoring rigid adherence to the U.S. Constitution, and restoring a strong America that can defeat serious national security threats. We must demonstrate to the American people, as they already seem to be recognizing, that liberalism is a false religion ultimately about the manipulation of society for political ends.[65]

Joan Fabiano added that the press didn't want to interview local TEA Party organizers. They were "lazy" and once national spokespeople from the TEA Party came out, they became the go-to source – thus, the media created the spokesperson problem. "That did not sit well with TEA Party people," she added. It was "a false dynamic created by the press."[66]

But boxed into a corner by a resurgent "establishment" GOP, scammers preying on its faithful to enrich themselves, and increasingly negative coverage of the same Beltway insiders creating a poor perception for this onetime champion of the grassroots, the TEA Party was on the verge of being wasted and exhausted. To me, the tale of the TEA Party's fate was best told by Gallup, whose final poll asking about the popularity of the TEA Party was conducted in October, 2015. At that time they registered just 17% support – an all-time low in popularity[67] – so Gallup stopped asking the question.

The perfect way to complete the circle on the demise of the TEA Party is to note the resignation of Keri Carender from the Tea Party Patriots in order to raise her daughter. Back in my first chapter I introduced Carender as one of the first to hold a "Porkulus" event in February, 2009, a prototype for what would become the Tax Day TEA Parties. With her newfound passion, Carender joined the TPP later that year and, according to the release announcing her departure, "has served as a local and state coordinator, barnstormed the country, served as a spokesperson for our organization in the media, headed up our field team by providing support to the local coordinators around the country, and she injected much needed levity and humor when times were grim to remind us that we can be happy warriors."[68]

What Keri wrote in response was, perhaps, a fitting eulogy for the movement.

> I believe that the power of good people will triumph over the corruption of the evil people. I believe in the power of this movement because it comes from the millions of grassroots people across the nation, taking action and standing up for principle. And, though we've seen over and over how the corruption can ensnare so many once well-intentioned warriors that move to D.C., I am confident that the heart of the movement will not be corrupted because the heart will never live inside the beltway. We will persevere against everything the swamp wants to throw at us, and we will not be taken in. I truly believe this with all my heart.[69]

Perhaps the heart would never live inside the Beltway, but many of those who took advantage of and profited off the name were now denizens of the nation's capital. And once they got there, they seemingly forget why they were sent, succumbing to that age-old siren song of political power.

Greed wasn't the only factor in the fall of the TEA Party as a political entity, though. The next three chapters are going to look more in-depth at other causes: the effects of the infusion of social conservatives into the growing movement, those organizations that sprang up to counter the TEA Party like the Coffee Party (among several others), and finally the view of the TEA Party from across the bridge, as skeptics on the Left were quick to point out its hypocrisy and trouble with staying fiscally conservative in deeds as well as in words.

# OF GOD AND MAN IN THE TEA PARTY

"*Making people dependent on government as Provider instead of God is one of Satan's most brilliant and devastating tactics. It reduces people to slaves at the mercy of the Father of Lies.*" - Jonathan Wakefield, *Saving America: A Christian Perspective Of The Tea Party Movement* (2012).

In any postmortem of the TEA Party worth its salt, a point has to be made about the impact of the religious Right on the TEA Party. Author David Brody described this group by coining a phrase: Teavangelicals. He contended they were simply occupying their natural political home in the TEA Party but were fine with the libertarian company:

> Now it's vitally important to understand that Teavangelicals are *not* trying to take over the Tea Party movement or co-opt their agenda. Just because evangelical Christians are heavily involved in the Tea Party movement doesn't mean that they are ready to storm the gates and change their stated goals. If you think that, you're missing the point entirely. These are evangelicals who are breaking bread with the Tea Party. They are part of the Tea Party. Think of Teavangelicals as a large subset of the Tea Party movement. The truth of the matter is that Tea Party libertarians *cannot* win consistently and consequentially without evangelicals by their side. Conversely, evangelicals can't do it alone either. (Italics in original.)[1]

While survivors of the former Moral Majority and other pro-traditional values groups shared some values with the liberty-oriented economic freedom advocates who initially comprised the core of the TEA Party, sometimes they got along like oil and water. To some observers it was the one example of "diversity" in the TEA Party:

> There is… one major dimension along which Tea Party activists show diversity. Some Tea Partiers are social conservatives focused on moral and cultural issues ranging from pro-life concerns to worries about the impact of recent immigrants on the cultural coherence of American life, while others are much more secular minded libertarians, who stress individual choice on cultural matters and want the Tea Party as a whole to give absolute priority to fiscal issues.
>
> (…)

> We heard one remarkable story about a local leader who faced so many tensions in her flock that she split the group in two. She now meets separately with "the Christian Tea Party" and the "regular Tea Party."[2]

Some of this tension led to the finger-pointing I alluded to for the last several chapters; after all, it could be conclusively shown that questions about abortion – a social issue dear to religious members of the TEA Party but at best a states-rights issue to the libertarians, who more often than not believed the decision should be left to the mother – significantly damaged, if not destroyed completely, the prospects of TEA Party-backed candidates winning at least two Senate seats in 2012.

But more of it was from an honest difference in opinion that started from the very beginning. As I recounted early on, soon after the initial February 27 protests came an offer from Newt Gingrich and his American Solutions group to join the Nationwide Tea Party Coalition – an offer that its leadership warily accepted based on a perceived lack of progress when Gingrich was Speaker of the House in the 1990s.

Even with this potential boost to the movement, it didn't take long for some organizers to become furious with Newt for playing to social conservatives. Wrote Michael Patrick Leahy:

> The digital ink wasn't dry on the press release (announcing American Solutions was on board) when Gingrich caused a problem that irritated us all so greatly that there were calls to kick him out of the Coalition. We had labored mightily since the inception of the Nationwide Tea Party Coalition to make sure everyone in the movement understood that we united around the fiscal issues. We would leave the social issues off the table until the fiscal and constitutional issues had been solved…
>
> But Gingrich endorsed the American Family Association's "Tea Party" – which placed an emphasis on social values – the next day. This group had no real supporters within the Tea Party movement, but had instead merely taken the list of local tea parties we had posted at the Tax Day Tea Party website, claimed them as its own, and sent out press releases and e-mails to its e-mail list of conservative Christians touting the national tea party it was organizing.[3]

Over the last several chapters I've gone through a number of factors that fractured the TEA Party, but one key area that separated the original group of libertarian-minded activists away from the mainstream that adopted the TEA Party as it grew in stature and popularity was the argument over whether there should be a concerted effort or even a call for action on restricting abortion and same-sex marriage. After the TEA Party became the catchall for the conservative movement in the nation, there were obviously going to be those who felt the TEA Party's mandate needed to expand from that of being a strictly fiscal and role of government issues group to one also dedicated to restoring or preserving what they believed were the values befitting the moral nation our Founders envisioned.

This was a time in the game when the TEA Party leadership, such that it was, punted by maintaining their original stance. “Issues like abortion and gay marriage have little to do with our three core principles (fiscal responsibility, constitutionally limited government, and free markets), and therefore we leave those issues for other groups to advocate,”[4] said TEA Party Patriots leaders Mark Meckler and Jenny Beth Martin.

Yet this separation of church and anti-state wasn't enough for the naysayers. From its earliest stage, the religious Left chastened the TEA Party for its libertarian roots. One example is Christian author and founder of Sojourners Jim Wallis, who wrote this for the *Huffington Post* in early 2010:

> An anti-government ideology just isn’t biblical. In Romans 13, the apostle Paul (not the Kentucky Senate candidate) describes the role and vocation of government; in addition to the church, government also plays a role in God’s plan and purposes. Preserving the social order, punishing evil and rewarding good, and protecting the common good are all prescribed; we are even instructed to pay taxes for those purposes! Sorry, Tea Party. Of course, debating the size and role of government is always a fair and good discussion, and most of us would prefer smart and effective to “big” or “small” government.
>
> Revelation 13 depicts the state as a totalitarian beast – a metaphor for Rome, which was persecuting the Christians. This passage serves as a clear warning about the abuse of governmental power. But a power-hungry government is clearly an aberration and violation of the proper role of government in protecting its citizens and upholding the demands of fairness and justice. To disparage government *per se* – to see government as the central problem in society – is simply not a biblical position.[5]

In the eyes of the TEA Party, though, this “power-hungry government” was not acting like it was an “aberration.” Nor does it take cradle-to-grave socialism for a government to function as one “upholding the demands of fairness and justice.” In fact, it's likely a more limited government would do a better job in being a fair arbiter than the one we were laboring under because less was at stake for them.

That was the contention of author and TEA Party leader Jonathan Wakefield, who wrote:

> The Tea Party is a small-government movement that supports freedom of religion, not the establishment of one.
>
> Christians like me… believe in the maximum freedom possible under the minimum government required to protect us and our property. This type of system bears no resemblance to a theocracy, which is based on strict and specific religious code. It is God's – not government's – role to teach us right and wrong and our role to live by His standards. This is best done in a free society without government intervention wherever possible.[6]

So as the TEA Party gathered followers from its original cadre of pro-liberty, mainly secular activists, more and more who otherwise agreed with their principles of limited government were also advocating for more governmental restrictions on abortion and maintaining the sanctity of marriage as between one man and one woman through government edict. This wasn't a strictly-held position by any means because there was a difference in scope: one set of TEA Party regulars advocated for a blanket federal ban, such as a Constitutional amendment banning abortion and/or declaring only marriages between one man and one woman to be valid nationwide, while another faction of federalists argued that, once *Roe v. Wade* was overturned, it should be up to states to determine their own policies toward abortion. (By extension, the same would be true if a future court re-examined the later *Obergefell* decision regarding same-sex marriage.)

David Brody explains that the moral transformation of the TEA Party was a process, like water seeking its level:

> The reason many evangelicals morph into Teavangelicals is because the fiscally conservative message of the Tea Party resonates with them. We often hear about how the Republican Party is made up of social conservatives, fiscal conservatives, and national security conservatives, as if somehow they are three distinct groups. Hogwash! Just like the symbol of the Olympic rings, they are intertwined.
>
> (…)
>
> Just because social conservatives might put more emphasis on social issues doesn't mean they don't care deeply about fiscal issues.[7]

But by the middle of 2010 it was becoming clear that the libertarian roots of the TEA Party movement were being torn out[8] by the thousands of evangelicals who were finding the TEA Party to be a comfortable political home – so much so that Judson Phillips, who was making his second attempt at a TEA Party convention, was warned about avoiding a certain venue. "I told Judson [Phillips, of Tea Party Nation], don't hold it in Vegas!" said (media expert Mark) Skoda. "This is a movement with a lot of religious people – they don't want to go to Sin City! Hold it in a place that people can drive to."[9] After the Vegas convention failed to get off the ground, Skoda ended up promoting a similar event in Virginia sponsored by a large contingent of TEA Party groups in the commonwealth.

In 2010 and 2011 surveys of TEA Party members, the Pew Research Center found:

> In addition to adopting a conservative approach to the economy, Tea Party supporters also tend to take socially conservative positions on abortion and same-sex marriage. While registered voters as a whole are closely divided on same-sex marriage (42% in favor, 49% opposed), Tea Party supporters oppose it by more than 2-to-1 (64% opposed, 26% in favor). Similarly, almost six-in-ten (59%) of those who agree with the Tea Party say abortion should be illegal in all or most cases, 17 percentage points higher than among all registered voters. Tea Party supporters closely resemble Republican voters as a whole on these issues.
>
> (…)
>
> According to an August 2010 survey by the Pew Research Center for the People & the Press and the Pew Forum on Religion & Public Life, Tea Party supporters are much more likely than the public overall to cite "religious beliefs" as the biggest influence on their views of same-sex marriage and abortion. Roughly half of Tea Party backers said their religious beliefs are the most important influence on their views of gay marriage (53%) and abortion (46%). Furthermore, Tea Party supporters who cited religion as a top factor were overwhelmingly opposed to same-sex marriage and legal abortion. By contrast, 37% of registered voters overall cited their religious beliefs as the most important influence on their views of same-sex marriage and 28% cited religion as the primary influence on their views of abortion.[10]

Since those traditional views on social issues were closer to the mainstream of the Republican Party – which by then had pretty much annexed the TEA Party as a significant subgroup – than to those of the libertarians, many of the former Ron Paul acolytes departed, grumbling as they left about how the theocrats took the TEA Party away from them. In that respect, the TEA Party leadership began to lose touch with its roots and indeed became more of a GOP mouthpiece. As I've stated before and will again, the TEA Party wasn't going to go form a third (or fourth, or fifth) political party so they accepted the more common GOP platform on social issues and thus expected dozens of questions about abortion, same-sex "marriage," etc. For a Republican candidate, this was part of the on-the-job training needed to be a politician because social issues were the new third rail.

With the massive influx of socially-aware voters bumping into the public perception that people were pro-choice and for same-sex "marriage," some just pegged the TEA Party as a continuation and extension of Focus on the Family and other religiously-based groups:

> The Tea Party was just a new name coined by clever activists and the media – a rebranding that has made it much easier for Christian-right candidates to run for office without having to air their views on social issues, which are increasingly viewed in a negative light by the general public.[11]

It was no surprise that the Left called the TEA Party "theocrats" for their Biblically-correct stances:

> To a remarkable extent, today's theocrats have stopped thinking of "social issues" like abortion or gay marriage as isolated from or in competition with fiscal or economic issues, and started thinking of them as part and parcel of a broader challenge that requires the radical transformation of government itself.[12]

On the other hand, Jonathan Wakefield more properly defined the left's "theocrat" term:

> So while the Tea Party advances small-government principles, wanting to leave citizens free to make their own decisions and reap the benefits or suffer the consequences accordingly, the left pursues a system of big-government command and control. They then turn around and accuse the small-government Christian Tea Partiers of attempting to impose a theocracy in America, when it is the left's plan that is often indistinguishable from theocratic rule.[13]

Granted, some of those who were elected with TEA Party support delved deeply into religious issues, particularly at the state level,[14] but it's obvious the liberal writers of these pieces weren't very aware of the libertarian origins of the TEA Party, assuming it was a monolithic group that was already extant and forgetting the original protests had little to do with social issues. Also, as mentioned earlier, and unlike those who joined up based on the simple premises that government taxed and spent too much taxpayer money, those TEA Partiers who were most heavily into the social issue aspect may have also agreed on the basics of stopping abortion and the rush toward same-sex marriage but couldn't agree on a single solution.

TEA Party scrutiny also extended to character. It didn't matter which party they were in, but back in its infancy the TEA Party didn't have a lot of tolerance for misfeasance or malfeasance in office. While the original idea was to keep those who were of unsound moral character out of politics, as time went on and the TEA Party became more closely identified with the GOP, the foibles of one side aroused much more interest than the transgressions of their political allies. We heard a lot about the character issues of Barack Obama from TEA Party regulars, which could be expected when Obama went to extraordinary lengths to hide parts of his past and a lapdog media didn't call him out on it. Yet we haven't since seen that same level of condemnation regarding Republicans – perhaps they assume the mainstream media will cover these issues for them.

This Republican alliance proved troubling to religious arbiters like Wakefield:

> I joined the Tea Party in part because I hate politics. They disgust me, as they do the vast majority of Americans. The power structure that the two major parties have erected is largely responsible for our current crises. Because politicians are more interested in preserving and expanding their power than in serving the American people, we are where we are today.
>
> The Tea Party wants nothing to do with this.
>
> The Big Government Disciples try and convince you that the Tea Party is merely an arm of the Republican Party, but that's a lie. If it were true, then why is the Republican Party trying to amputate that arm?[15]

Yet if you consider another statement by Wakefield in this context, the idea of their original TEA Party involvement comes more into focus:

> If you ever questioned whether or not the Tea Party addressed the moral issues, question no more. Selling our children's future to China – where they limit the number of and even kill their own children – is *the* moral issue of our generation.[16] (Italics in original.)

This is a political style and charge which befuddles people who are anywhere left of center and are either agnostic or go to a church befitting their feelgood religious beliefs:

> While a traditional political party may have a line that it won't cross, the Tea Party has a stone-engraved set of principles, all of which are sacrosanct. This is not a political platform to be negotiated but a catechism with only a single answer. It is now a commonplace for Tea Party candidates to vow they won't sacrifice an iota of their principles. In this light, shutting down the Government rather than bending on legislation becomes a moral imperative. While critics may decry such a tactic as "rule or ruin," Tea Party brethren celebrate it, rather, as the act of a defiant Samson pulling down the pillars of the temple. For them, this is not demolition but reclamation, cleansing the sanctuary that has been profaned by

> liberals. They see themselves engaged in nothing less than a project of national salvation. The refusal to compromise is a watchword of their candidates who wear it as a badge of pride. This would seem disastrous in the give-and-take of politics but it is in keeping with sectarian religious doctrine. One doesn't compromise on an article of faith.[17]

Writer Jack Schwartz concludes the TEA Party is "a challenge to both religion and democracy."[18]

Maybe it's a good time to remind readers that our Founding Fathers, while often categorized as Deists or otherwise less than pious, are considered so only in the context of their time, not that of the present day when church attendance hovers near all-time lows and religion is considered a subject that should be confined strictly to church on Sundays. No secular group of today would even consider the concept of being endowed by their Creator with certain inalienable rights; instead, they would figure that rights were defined by what the government decided to give out on a particular day, and fewer of them would be given to those who are white, male, cisgender, or voted for a Republican in any election since 1956.

So a TEA Party with such reverence for our founding documents, and knowing the context of the time, was probably going to have to make room for those who believed in the God of the Bible. Perhaps the precursors to the TEA Party that existed before February, 2009 would not have cared when the "Rainbow Mafia" targeted a particular restaurant chain because its CEO espoused opinions on same-sex marriage – statements he later regretted making from a business standpoint[19] – but the TEA Party of 2012 was more than willing to back up Dan Cathy's statements and pack Chick-Fil-A for a day to show their support of his traditional values.[20] (I was one of them.)[21] And furthermore I would contend that it was an evolution which had to occur for the movement to remain true to the principles of liberty – particularly on the issue of abortion – because in order to have liberty you must have life.

And sometimes fighting for life makes sense from a fiscal standpoint. Such was (and remains) the case with defunding Planned Parenthood, the nation's largest abortion provider.

> Now, it is true that most national Tea Party leaders stayed away from the defunding Planned Parenthood debate because, in a nod to staying on message, they simply don't want moral issues to creep into any fiscal issue whatsoever. But that really doesn't matter because this isn't about what national Tea Party leaders think. You can't stop an organic, bottom-up movement. This issue gives you insight into why conservative evangelicals are joining ranks with the Tea Party. They see both the moral and fiscal dimensions of an issue.[22]

I am convinced the concepts of "life, liberty, and the pursuit of happiness" were placed in that order intentionally to place life paramount among them.

Allow me two final quotes before I close this chapter: one from Jonathan Wakefield and one from David Brody. As you may be able to tell, their books were instrumental in putting this chapter together – although it was always the plan to include a look at this topic, these volumes helped me greatly in defining the similarities and differences. I'll start with Wakefield.

> (T)he Tea Party movement isn't Christian in nature – it includes people of all faiths and of no faith – and is politically focused. I contend, though, that our movement transcends politics. The principles we espouse are not, in fact, *political* but are *moral*, as they align with the Bible and are intended to liberate our fellow citizens from the oppressions of an Almighty State by placing power with a people instead of its government. If I did consider the Tea Party a political movement, I never would have gotten involved, because I have no use for either the Republican or the Democratic Party.[23] (Italics in original.)

Brody:

> While they're praying on the (Iowa Tea Party) bus and seeing God's hand during their Tea Party rallies, the event outside also begins with prayer. At the Ottumwa rally, organizers made sure to thank God first before getting on to Tea Party business.
>
> (…)
>
> All around America the Bible is out and heads are lowered in prayer at these rallies. The prayers are a mix of evangelical language and Tea Party manifesto. In short, it's a Teavangelical prayer.
>
> (…)
>
> The Americans who are praying at these rallies are not doing it for show. It's the real deal. Their love and passion for God and country is with equal zest. While fiscal issues dominate the conversation at these rallies, they don't check their faith at the door.[24]

Just as liberty would not be possible without life, rights such as the TEA Party attempted to restore would not exist without a Creator. Thus, it was impossible for them to have the impact they did without some moral compass to guide them – fortunately, one benefit of our founding documents was their acknowledgment of this fact. This difference created a key distinction between the TEA Party and the secular-based groups that the Left regularly created to serve as a counterweight or foil to the TEA Party; the subjects of my next chapter.

# THE SINCEREST FORM OF FLATTERY

*"The TEA Party will go down in history as a righteous rebellion."* - Mark Levin, January 19, 2017.[1]

While the TEA Party may not have achieved its original goals, its legacy has lived on in unlikely ways.

Imagine, if you will – and I know this will be difficult for most of you reading this book, but try it anyway – that you were a devout Hillary Clinton supporter, or, you were even further to the left and "felt the Bern" throughout the 2016 campaign. Maybe you even voted for Jill Stein of the Green Party, secure in the knowledge that Hillary Clinton would be a sound backstop candidate. For those who fit this description and believed the polls and conventional wisdom that Hillary would be the one to break that glass ceiling, such as former UN ambassador Samantha Power infamously did,[2] consider your utter shock as the results rolled in on Election Night: Ohio is the first surprise call that goes for Trump, then North Carolina and Florida in rapid succession. When Pennsylvania and Wisconsin – a state that had been a Democratic hold since the 1980s! – are called for the GOP, in your panic you realize that the Rust Belt Clinton firewall of states you were assuming was in the bag had collapsed in a heap of rubble. (Eventually even venerable union stronghold Michigan would barely go Trump.) Despite fewer popular votes, in a margin that would grow ever-larger as California received and counted its vast reservoir of popular votes won by Hillary Clinton, that racist, ill-mannered cad Donald Trump was going to become our 45th President.

Sure, there was the half-hearted attempt to shame electors into changing their votes, and it turned out some did – but not in favor of Hillary Clinton. There was (and continues to be, over two years later) significant talk that something had to be done about that antiquated Electoral College.[3] But the real effort was placed into a new political drive which set out to get its revenge on the TEA Party voters who elected Donald Trump by using what they considered the tactics previously used with success against Barack Obama. Thus, the Indivisible movement, also called The Resistance, or #Resist, was born and announced practically the day Donald Trump was inaugurated.

In the early chapters of this book I outlined how long of an incubation process the

TEA Party really had, as its period of genesis could be traced back to the latter stages of the George W. Bush presidency. It only became manifest in the first few weeks of the Obama administration, after his agenda and priority list of legislation were set into motion. Conversely, since few on the Left had even considered the possibility of a Donald Trump presidency and were instead concentrating on how to push Hillary Clinton further into the Marxist camp on various cherished items they held dear, progressives were caught a little bit flat-footed at first. Their shock quickly turned to rage, and rage into a furious pace of action: a massive march that was originally perhaps intended to show support for the Clinton agenda turned into a show of women – many wearing hats shaped like their private parts – that created a sensation of media attention overshadowing the actual Trump inauguration a day earlier.

And while the Republican Party of 2009 was at least willing to allow the presentation of the alternative vision presented by the incoming Obama administration, in 2017 the new Democrat opposition was right there with the protestors. They provided continuous cover for a long-standing and false narrative that the Russians interfered with the 2016 election, with a few Democrats even standing up and screaming that the President was guilty of treason for his Russian connections – charges which weren't conclusively proven despite the fact the Obama administration was secretly conducting wiretapping operations on the Trump campaign, and perhaps had a mole within. (Revelations that dribble out as the months pass suggest a multi-faceted operation on the order of the Watergate coverup, perpetrated by the "scandal-free" Obama administration.)

So Republicans who held townhall meetings in the early days of the Trump administration were greeted by an organized group of opposition citizens who did their best to be disruptive, turned the questioning into an inquisition on impeaching Trump, demanded strict opposition to the Trump agenda, and garnered media coverage which highlighted the protests as opposed to what the elected officials had to say. Yet while these townhall meetings could be loud, they were never seriously threatened with violence. That was a task delivered by anarchist front groups for the Left.

In the spring and summer of 2017, the discord began to turn more violent with the inclusion of the Black Lives Matter (BLM) and Antifa groups, featuring members who vowed to shout down or shut down rhetoric and speakers they deemed too far to the right wing (basically anyone to the right of Josef Stalin.) It all came to a head at a rally in support of keeping a statue of Confederate General Robert E. Lee standing in a Virginia park.

What is now known as Market Street Park[4] in the city of Charlottesville, which is home to the University of Virginia, was once called Robert E. Lee Park. (It was also called Emancipation Park for a year, and the original name change was part of what sparked the unrest.) For over 90 years that park was graced with a statue of its original namesake, but politically ambitious city leadership wanted to tear the statue down despite a state law forbidding it. Leaders of a counter-protest group wishing to preserve the Lee statue called "Unite the Right" had secured a permit to march and hold a rally on August 12, 2017, but the permit was canceled at the last moment. When the "Unite the Right" group, described by the media as mainly white nationalists and supremacists, departed the scene, they were set upon by members of Black Lives Matter and Antifa. Both sides were armed and looking for trouble, and it was trouble they found when a 20-year-old Ohio man who was there to support the "Unite the Right" cause was arrested for the vehicular homicide of a bystander on the opposing side of removing the statues. Heather Heyer was hit by his car as it plowed through a group of people blocking a street and later died from her injuries. In a separate incident that same day, two members of the Virginia State Police were killed in a helicopter crash returning from their surveillance of the protest.

More outrage ensued when President Trump, in a statement delivered that fateful Saturday evening, blamed the violence on "many sides." Left-wingers – and some shaken moderate Republicans – took to social media to condemn the President for including the unnamed Antifa and BLM in the blame for violence, as James Fields, Jr., the driver who fatally struck Heyer, eventually admitted he was there from Ohio to support President Trump and for retaining the Lee statue at its location.

The next few weeks became a frenzy of other protesters, or even city governments themselves, tearing down Confederate and related statues – often in the dead of night. In a sign of how bad this trend was, the state of Maryland removed from their statehouse lawn a statue of Roger Taney, a Maryland native who wasn't a Confederate but was the author of the Supreme Court's *Dred Scott* decision that held slaves were property. This was done with the full support of Maryland Governor Larry Hogan, a Republican who had rejected calls to remove that statue two years earlier in the wake of the Baltimore riots. In another incident, an unknown vandal or group of vandals decapitated a statue of Revolutionary War hero Gen. William Crawford in front of the courthouse of the Ohio county named for him,[5] perhaps under the mistaken belief he was a hero in the War Between the States. (While the perpetrators still have not been found, the Crawford statue was replaced in 2018.)[6] If history is not taught well in schools, one dead white guy tends to look like another.

But the Charlottesville violence was a second chapter to a story opened earlier that summer. On the early morning of June 14, 2017, a group of Republican Congressmen and staffers was practicing for their upcoming charity baseball game against a similar team of Democrats. That practice was interrupted by a lone gunman who had come from Illinois on a mission to stop Republicans in Congress from enacting the Trump agenda; during the incident, Rep. Steve Scalise of Louisiana was seriously wounded while the assailant died in an exchange of gunfire with two Capitol Police officers. The sole reason a police detail was there was the presence of Scalise, who was a part of the House leadership – had it been a practice without any member of leadership present it's possible many of the unarmed members and staffers would have been massacred.

The political leanings of 66-year-old James Hodgkinson were apparent from his social media choices, including belonging to an online group advocating the termination of Republicans. In his final act, Hodgkinson was looking to bring that termination to real life.

This additional violence was not a page in the TEA Party handbook. This isn't to say there weren't violent images and statements made at TEA Party protests and rallies: for example, I attended and covered for my website a gathering in my hometown where our Congressman at the time, Democrat Frank Kratovil, was hung from a noose in effigy.[7] Sensible people in the local TEA Party agreed this counterproductive display served no purpose and was over the top; unfortunately, those in Antifa and BLM don't seem to agree violence should be off limits. To them, the ends of stopping Donald Trump's agenda must be supported by whatever means are necessary.

In trying to compare themselves to the TEA Party, those who consider themselves Indivisibles have a long way to go: for one thing, those in the TEA Party cleaned up after themselves. At the 9/12 Taxpayer March on Washington I attended, there were dozens and dozens of discarded, homemade signs left rather neatly in, or at least near, overflowing trash receptacles. (If anyone reading this book did a yellow sign referencing Joe Biden's three letter word: J-O-B-S, be advised I took it home as a souvenir because it made me laugh out loud. So it didn't contribute to the trash heap.) Left-wing rally attendees didn't keep their surroundings nearly as clean.[8]

However, this most recent activity from activists on the left side of the aisle against what they considered the reactionary elements of the TEA Party is nothing new. Over the decade since the TEA Party gained prominence as a political haven for Constitutional conservatives, there has generally been some sort of center- to far-left purportedly grassroots group placed in response or opposition to them.

First among these opponents was the Coffee Party, which sprang up in early 2010 as the centrist alternative to the perceived extremism of the TEA Party.[9] The Coffee Party's founder, filmmaker Annabel Park, was described by *Newsweek* as "just being exhausted by all-Tea-Party-all-the-time on the news."[10]

As the Venn diagram of the TEA Party expanded from the fiscally conservative and those concerned about the size and scope of government, it began to include (as evidenced in the previous chapter) many who believed that abortion at any stage of pregnancy was wrong and marriage was reserved for one man and one woman – views portrayed by the dominant media as outdated and simply bigoted. Add in those who were passionate about preserving their Second Amendment rights, and indeed the TEA Party was a group bitterly clinging to its guns and religion.

So while the Coffee Party wasn't overt in its support of Barack Obama and his policies, the fact its organizer was a former Obama campaign volunteer[11] should have provided a clue that it would function more or less as an offshoot of the President's Organizing for America online advocacy group. Rather than fealty to the Constitution, the Coffee Party pleaded for a more participatory democracy. As Park wrote:

> In America, we have a democracy, but with vulnerabilities and loopholes.
>
> One loophole is that the most active and organized constituents have disproportionate influence over our government. For instance, corporations can afford to pay thousands of lobbyists to work full-time at doing this. This gives them a disproportionate influence over our government and presents a serious challenge to democracy in America.
>
> This is really at the root of our discontent: our government's relationship to corporate America and this special interest seems altogether unconstitutional.
>
> As the Constitution dictates, we want a government of the people, by the people, for the people. Coffee Party USA is a democracy movement, and our goal is to have the government truly reflect the will of the people.[12]

Forget Park's ignorance of history (the phrase about "government of the people" actually stems from Abraham Lincoln's Gettysburg Address, not the Constitution) and consider the following points.

In the first respect, the two movements seemed to have similar aims, but would go about it in differing ways. Like the TEA Party, the Coffee Party had a list of key issues but they weren't as much to do with taxation or the role of government. Instead, some of them cited in Park's CNN op-ed: "accountability, corporate influence, health care reform, education reform, the economy, immigration reform, filibusters, etc." were being addressed in Congress at the time, with the TEA Party lined up with the conservative opposition. On the other hand, if you looked at a list of the "partners" of the Coffee Party you'd have found a Who's Who of leftist causes.[13]

As you may also recall, one feature of the TEA Party was a resurgence of interest in the Constitution and our founding documents, and it's worth reminding readers that our Founders were, at best, wary of a participatory democracy as advocated by the Coffee Party. To paraphrase Benjamin Franklin, our Founding Fathers had created a republic – if we could keep it.

Similar to the TEA Party, though, the Coffee Party has faded from the limelight. But it's still percolating with an extant website,[14] one which seems to have a little more backing from actual coffee sales as well as a little bit of revisionist history.[15]

On the other hand, while the Coffee Party preaches civility, our current Antifa unrest has its roots in another brief but potent cultural and political uprising called Occupy Wall Street (OWS, or simply Occupy.)

Barely a decade after the financial markets were imperiled by the 9/11 attack, a threat of a different sort began September 17, 2011. A group of protesters took over Zuccotti Park in the Wall Street financial district, squatting day and night on the ¾ acre site (at great expense to local businesses)[16] until the police finally drove them out November 15.[17] While they didn't work in the electoral realm as the TEA Party had done in over 2½ years prior to that point, that two-month stint and its associated and related Occupations around the rest of the nation were credited with instilling the class-envy concept of the "1%" into the political lexicon as well as bringing attention and sympathetic support to a number of other causes within the purview of income inequality, such as a $15 an hour minimum wage for fast-food workers.[18]

In addition – and just in time for the 2012 elections – the Occupy protests galvanized the Left for a number of their other cherished initiatives such as student loan reform, environmental activism including bans on fracking, proposed campaign finance legislation in response to the *Citizens United* decision, and a renewed emphasis on banking and business fiscal regulations to expand on those already included in the Dodd-Frank legislation.

Yet while the Coffee Party was seen as a rather benign, almost farcical counter to the TEA Party, those who helped to lead the TEA Party bristled at comparisons to Occupy. "(T)hose occupying Wall Street and other cities, when they are intelligible, want less of what made America great and more of what is damaging to America: a bigger, more powerful government to come in and take care of them so they don't have to work like the rest of us who pay our bills,"[19] said TPP's Jenny Beth Martin and Mark Meckler.

Added TPP's Michael Prell:

> The Tea Party Patriots have three core principles: fiscal responsibility, free markets, and Constitutionally limited government. By contrast, the Occupy Wall Street protesters are demanding less fiscal responsibility (they want more

government spending), an end to free markets, and the overwhelming majority of OWS demands – from guaranteed wages to free tuition to universal health care and more government control over markets – all call for a radical expansion of the size and scope and power of government to control us, and to take care of us, from cradle to college to grave.

Occupy Wall Street is calling for a declaration of dependence on government; a call for more government control over our lives. It is the direct opposite of the Declaration of Independence that sparked this nation into existence, and it is the direct opposite of the core principles of the modern-day Tea Party movement.[20]

One final take comes from a TEA Party organizer from Fort Wayne, Indiana who happened to be in Washington, D.C. for a TEA Party event and witnessed this:

(As compared to the TEA Party) The Occupy Wall Street movement... is a direct result of union organization and community organization, and is organized and encouraged by leftist activists. The movement is also very well funded.

The biggest contrast to date is the level of violence, arrests and law breaking that shadows the people involved in Occupy.

Recently, I had the opportunity to attend a tea party event in Washington, D.C., at the downtown Convention Center. During the event we were informed that the building had been surrounded by about 500 Occupy D.C. protesters who were attempting to break into the building and were aggressive. As a result of their activity, the building was placed on lockdown.

They were banging on the windows and placing small children in front of the doors to keep those attending the dinner from leaving. I left the ballroom to get a look outside. The building was surrounded by Occupiers, security guards and police. They were chanting, beating on the building and blocking the streets.

Protesters blocked all the exits, and people were finding it difficult to leave the building. Those who managed to exit were attacked with physical violence.

As I walked around the building looking out, I noticed several people being attacked by the protesters and being hit with objects and their fists. At one exit they knocked down an elderly woman and surrounded her. At another exit they attacked people as they exited by allowing them to get halfway or more across the street, then grabbing the last people in the group and hitting them.

This is the kind of action that mobs use to get their point across, not peaceful groups like the tea party movement. The contrast of the groups is very obvious. No tea party group ever left a mess at a rally, attacked people or destroyed property.[21]

Then again, in looking at the political landscape in 2019 it may be argued the brief and mercurial Occupy Wall Street movement was more successful at moving the cultural and political needle to the left than the TEA Party was in moving it to the right, despite the latter's electoral successes. Occupy, however, enjoyed many of the tactical advantages that the TEA Party did not: most helpful to them were a relatively sympathetic media which could use the bullhorn of the nation's largest media markets (as opposed to the myriad small towns and out-of-the-way places in “flyover country” where TEA Party regulars generally chose to call home) to amplify its coverage as well as a governmental administration in a number of the same cities and states that was down with the OWS struggle as fellow far-left travelers. Many of the “sanctuary cities” for illegal aliens also turned a blind eye to their own Occupy groups as long as the protests were kept reasonably peaceful, and they were quick to respond to calls for progressive legislation which could be adopted on a local level, such as the minimum wage hikes.

Compare that to a lack of action on some of the major pieces of national policy and legislation the TEA Party desired – the federal budget is still hopelessly in the red (and will remain so for at least another two years thanks to legislation passed in February, 2018) because no one has the political will to consistently cut spending; meanwhile, eight years later the Trump tax cut finally passed Congress despite being demagogued by people in both parties and passing in a form barely recognizable to its original proponents in the Trump administration. On a still sadder note: even when Republicans were in charge of all branches of government for the first two years of the Trump administration, Obamacare is still the law of the land. (That's a story I'm saving for a little later.)

Now I'll listen to an argument that states a case that things could have been a lot worse for us had the TEA Party never existed as a check and balance to the Obama administration, even though it's impossible to prove such a hypothetical negative. In that respect, the rise of the TEA Party was similar to the situation a decade and a half earlier where Americans elected Bill Clinton over the incumbent George H.W. Bush (a.k.a. “Bush 41.”) Recall that Clinton only won with a plurality of the vote because of the populist Ross Perot running as an independent, and once he was in office Americans did not take kindly to the direction he and fellow Democrats originally wished to proceed, including the prospect of “HillaryCare” socialized medicine. They instead countered it forcefully by embracing the Contract With America and electing a Republican House majority for the first time since the Eisenhower presidency at their first opportunity in 1994.

Any political goodwill for progressive agenda items originally desired by OWS, though, rapidly became extinguished among the masses by its more violent successors in Antifa and Black Lives Matter. Even the best efforts of the news media to spin the events in Charlottesville as brought on exclusively by the white supremacists in attendance failed to pass the smell test, and threats of more violence from these far-left groups if radical change wasn't brought about – such as the impeachment of President Trump and Vice-President Pence – did little to attract the mainstream American or even those who are left-of-center and may otherwise believe in policies these groups advocate. Like most, sensible liberals still think necessary change can be accomplished within our current political system without the implied threats. And don't forget: despite their reputation, a common theme of the TEA Party gatherings was a lack of violence.

The one area where the current Trump "resistance" comes closest to using TEA Party tactics is in the loud and hostile questioning of Republican Congressional members who dare to hold town hall meetings, much akin to the rancor of some similar events hosted by Democrats in 2009-10. It's fine to question the Trump agenda, but the lack of civility in some TEA Party hotbeds is being paid back in spades now. They obviously didn't get the message to "Incite Civility and Reason" the Coffee Party has tried to peddle.

But Antifa and Black Lives Matter aren't the only ones deaf to the clear message of the people. Having seen the failure of the 115th Congress – the first totally Republican-controlled Congress since the end of the 2005-2006 session – to do as they promised and completely repeal the Patient Protection and Affordable Care Act, before I conclude I'll explain how the TEA Party was let down yet again.

In the meantime, though, I want to wrap up this three-chapter departure from TEA Party chronology to consider those who questioned the sincerity of those rank-and-file members who made up the TEA Party. The next chapter looks at the TEA Party through its criticism from the Left, and weighs their arguments to determine whether the contentions were legitimate or not.

# LOOKING FROM ACROSS THE AISLE

*"Eventually, the Republican Party will either moderate or die, but not quickly. The after-effects of the Tea Party disruption will continue to weaken the GOP – and will also bedevil American government and politics for some time to come."* - Theda Skocpol and Vanessa Williamson, *The Tea Party and the Remaking of Republican Conservatism* (2011)

It's not a stretch to say that the opposition to Barack Obama saw him in a far different light than his supporters did. In that same manner, those who didn't see eye to eye with the TEA Party – especially from the Left – generally portrayed it in the most negative terms possible. Borrowing from the *Rules for Radicals* playbook they so often used, progressives didn't hesitate to ridicule the TEA Party, then freeze their target, personalize it, polarize it, and make the TEA Party try to live to the set of rules the Left believed they had. Hypocrisy, Astroturf, and racism were the watchwords assigned by liberals to this new threat to their hegemony.

That's not to say they didn't have something of a case in each of these instances, though. The Left was wrong about a lot of what the TEA Party was about, but at times a small subset of members was all the exception progressives needed to claim they proved the rule.

For example, leftist critics of the TEA Party have always had a field day pointing out what they considered the biggest element of hypocrisy in the movement: grousing about lower taxes and overbearing government while being the beneficiaries of same. Take this example from a Rand Paul rally that featured the firebrand rantings of Sarah Palin, as related by Matt Taibbi of *Rolling Stone*:

> After Palin wraps up, I race to the parking lot in search of departing Medicare-motor-scooter conservatives. I come upon an elderly couple, Janice and David Wheelock, who are fairly itching to share their views.
>
> "I'm anti-spending and anti-government," crows David, as scooter-bound Janice looks on. "The welfare state is out of control."
>
> "OK," I say. "And what do you do for a living?"

"Me?" he says proudly. "Oh, I'm a property appraiser. Have been my whole life."

I frown. "Are either of you on Medicare?"

Silence: Then Janice, a nice enough woman, it seems, slowly raises her hand, offering a faint smile, as if to say, *You got me!*

"Let me get this straight," I say to David. "You've been picking up a check from the government for decades, as a *tax assessor*, and your wife is on Medicare. How can you complain about the welfare state?"

"Well," he says, "there's a lot of people on welfare who don't deserve it. Too many people are living off the government."

"But," I protest, "*you* live off the government. And have been your whole life!"

"Yeah," he says, "but I don't make very much." Vast forests have already been sacrificed to the public debate about the Tea Party: what it is, what it means, where it's going. But after lengthy study of the phenomenon, I've concluded that the whole miserable narrative boils down to one stark fact: They're full of shit. All of them. At the voter level, the Tea Party is a movement that purports to be furious about government spending – only the reality is that the vast majority of its members are former Bush supporters who yawned through two terms of record deficits and spent the past two electoral cycles frothing not about spending but about John Kerry's medals and Barack Obama's Sixties associations. The average Tea Partier is sincerely against government spending – with the exception of the money spent on *them*.[1] (Italics in original.)

I'm not writing this book to teach people about Saul Alinsky, but this passage seemed to my "know enough to be dangerous" eye to be a very textbook usage of his tactics. Yet for a leftist writing this in fall of 2010, it turned out Taibbi wasn't a half-bad prophet:

The Tea Party today is being pitched in the media as this great threat to the GOP; in reality, the Tea Party *is* the GOP. What few elements of the movement aren't yet under the control of the Republican Party soon will be, and even if a few genuine Tea Party candidates sneak through, it's only a matter of time before the uprising as a whole gets castrated, just like every grass-roots movement does in this country. Its leaders will be bought off and sucked into the two-party bureaucracy, where its platform will be whittled down until the only things left are those that the GOP's campaign contributors want anyway: top-bracket tax breaks, free trade and financial deregulation.

The rest of it – the sweeping cuts to federal spending, the clampdown on bailouts, the rollback of *Roe v. Wade* – will die on the vine as one Tea Party leader after another gets seduced by the Republican Party and retrained for the revolutionary cause of voting down taxes for Goldman Sachs executives.[2]

It was a prediction only a cynic could love, but that seems to be the problem with our political system overall, doesn't it? There's no doubt the protests of David and Janice Wheelock – the couple who "don't make very much" – would be replicated in some way, shape, manner, or form by thousands who participated in the TEA Party demanding government spending be slashed but still expecting every dime they were due from Uncle Sam in Social Security and Medicare simply because America "owed" them. After all, they explained, it was the government keeping their account that they had paid into the system for their entire working lives. (Never mind these programs were Ponzi-like systems doomed to fail, but collapsing long after the TEA Party faithful left the scene – leaving their progeny holding the bag and the bills due.) This was the argument of writer Jonathan Chait:

> The image of a mass army of principled constitutionalists agitating to carry out Paul Ryan's domestic-policy vision, while irresistibly useful as conservative propaganda, was a fantasy all along. The backlash against Obamacare did not rest upon any abstract theory about the role of the state. It drew its power from the fear that subsidized (private) insurance would come at the expense of the (single-payer) health care that old people love.[3]

Perhaps this was true for the Baby Boomer generation, but there were enough people who could envision health care done in the style of your local Department of Motor Vehicles to make them think twice. Obamacare also came out just a couple short years after the VA facilities scandal at the former Walter Reed Army Medical Center[4] – not to be confused with the more recent VA waiting list scandal.

Anyway, the Left occasionally swerved into a point: to many TEA Party participants, it was always the invisible "other" who could take the cut, particularly illegal aliens or the younger generation that would have time to set up other means of supporting themselves in their golden years but would also have to pay the freight as the Baby Boomers aged gracefully on the fruits of the labor of those same young workers.

Not so fast, said TEA Party leadership. They were willing to make sacrifices:

> We… travel around the nation and have the privilege of speaking with literally thousands of Tea Party Patriots. Sometimes we are at events with thousands of

> people, and sometimes just sitting around the table in a coffee shop. But wherever we go, we always talk to people about the issue of entitlement spending. We always ask if they are willing to make the personal sacrifices necessary to save the nation. The answer is always a resounding yes.[5]

For more gloom and doom, you could ask William John Cox, who wrote at *Counterpunch* about attendees at the 2011 Tea Party Patriots American Policy Summit:

> More than anything else that can be said, the (Tea Party) Patriots are fearful. They fear the loss of the quality of life they and their parents enjoyed following World War II; however, they also believe that the unions who led the battle for the wages and benefits they received are becoming too powerful. They fear the influx of immigrants and the loss of "American" jobs; however, they overlook that every single one of them is either an immigrant or the descendant of immigrants. They fear the loss of the moral values they were raised with; however, they are quick to deny others the choices they have had the freedom to make.
>
> Those who join the Tea Party Patriots could be your parents, the veteran next door, the Little League coach, or the guy at the hardware store. They are hard-working, conservative, self-sufficient people who are afraid for the future of their families and their way of life. Having been empowered by the rewards of their efforts, they now feel helpless to confront the forces that threaten them. They feel compelled to do something, anything, to defend their beliefs. They are drawn to the Tea Party to meet like-minded patriotic people and to "make a difference."[6]

Now stop and think about this a minute. Cox makes a whole lot of assumptions about what brought about the world we live in now, but fails to consider all of this occurred within a longstanding political system that allowed for it to happen. It was a system that the TEA Party felt was under threat from a President and Congress elected by just a plurality of adult Americans who bought the promise of "fundamental change" without knowing – or even caring about – the actual details. Certainly the TEA Party was skewed toward an older generation, but perhaps it was their wisdom and experience about what worked in the world that drove them to protest. Maybe they even cared about their grandchildren despite the fact the kids weren't down with the more straight-laced morals of the older generation.

The same goes for *Detroit Free Press* columnist Brian Dickerson, who treated his assignment to cover a TEA Party "powwow" in the rural Michigan town of Mt. Pleasant almost like a safari excursion where he had to endure hanging out with the state's redneck population. His conclusions after a lengthy report:

I'm sympathetic to many of the tea party's grievances. Like everyone I've spoken to at the PowWow, I feel profoundly alienated from a political process in which successful candidates in both parties serve at the pleasure of lobbyists and undisclosed mega-donors.

It's the remedies tea party conservatives embrace that make me nervous. I still don't understand how the liberty whose loss they feel so acutely would be enhanced by denying so many outside the devout Christian elect a place at the American table.[7]

The passage becomes even more interesting as years go by and those who are devout Christians actually have lost their liberty to express and live out their beliefs. (While it steps far afield from the TEA Party, a good book to consider on that persecution topic is Erick Erickson and Bill Blankschaen's *You Will Be Made to Care: The War on Faith, Family, and Your Freedom to Believe*.) However, as Taibbi, Cox, Dickerson, and many other critics of the TEA Party have rightly pointed out – perhaps less so in the case of Cox, though, since the causation of the circumstances he brought up wasn't always correlated with the items he chose to assume the TEA Party blamed them on – intellectual consistency wasn't exactly the TEA Party's long suit.

However, that sort of standard of consistency is difficult to attain in a system of government where its continued success depends on the balance of a number of factors: even our Founding Fathers, who defiantly told the world "We hold these truths to be self-evident, that all men are created equal," had to concede that point to assure the completion of the Constitution and placate the factions representing certain regions of the nascent United States who were concerned about their representation in the new republic. Thus, our Constitution originally mandated that certain men were only worth three-fifths of a person and could be bought and sold as property. This fragile contradiction could not long stand, and to finally rectify it brought us to war less than a century later.

As a whole, though, the system of government created by our Constitution and doggedly defended by the TEA Party was the foundation for a republic that's the most wealthy and powerful the world has known – yet one where anyone from the poorest man to the millionaire have the same rights to speak out, contact their representatives, and vote.

This assumed, though, that the TEA Party denizens actually understood the Constitution. One left-tilting pair begged to differ on this point:

Despite their fondness for the Founding Fathers, Tea Party members we met did not make any reference to the intellectual battles and political compromises out of which the Constitution and its subsequent amendments were forged, let alone to the fact the key Founders were Deists, far from any brand of evangelical fundamentalism. Nor did they realize the extent to which some of the positions Tea Partiers now espouse bear a close resemblance to those of the Anti-Federalists – the folks the Founders were countering in their effort to establish sufficient federal authority to ensure a truly *United* States. The Tea Partiers we met did not show any awareness that they are echoing arguments made by the Nullifiers and Secessionists before and during the U.S. Civil War, or that their stress on 'state's rights' is eerily reminiscent of dead-ender white opposition to Civil Rights laws in the 1960s.[8]

Despite that perception – and the lack of indication of the knowledge that the Bill of Rights was added to the Constitution in order to assuage, in part, the concerns of the Anti-Federalists – the point objectors missed was that the TEA Party had a lot of the right ideals even if not every participant supported every plank on the imaginary TEA Party platform. Obviously there's a state of tension between the "role of government" purist who would eliminate all federal entitlement programs as not being Constitutionally valid *vs.* the hypocrite who points out that the federal government made a promise to generations of Americans to take care of them in their old age and that promise should be kept, Constitutional or not.

That struggle of ideas is but one portion of the cat-herding that made it difficult for the TEA Party to have a lasting impact. To the extent the assertion smacks of hypocrisy, there was no shortage of contradictions in the TEA Party. Total fealty to principle would be nice, but in any large group that's impossible – just ask the radical environmentalist progressives what they think of their fellow Democrat Party travelers in the unions, for example.

Corollary to that argument, though, is the political landscape which has been carved out for Americans like Mount Rushmore over the last 150 years, since the demise of the Whig Party before the Civil War. In that span Americans have grudgingly adopted a two-party political system, as dozens of other parties have tried and failed to make a lasting dent in the political process. A few recent examples:

Over the last quarter-century the Reform Party briefly evolved from a vehicle enabling Ross Perot to run for President in 1996 (he ran as a true independent with no party affiliation in 1992) to a third party that scored a significant victory when Jesse Ventura won the 1998 Minnesota gubernatorial race. "Though (the Reform Party) could not be called a true ideological forerunner of the Tea Party movement, it did foreshadow a kind of widespread dissatisfaction with the existing political power structure,"[9] said Michael Patrick Leahy. Evidence of that assertion: Donald Trump briefly sought the Reform Party's Presidential nomination in 2000 before taking advantage of that dissatisfaction as a renegade, populist Republican 15 years later. Party infighting, however, has significantly damaged the Reform Party to a point where it's lost all-important ballot access in most states.

More consistent on the modern-day Presidential ballot are the Libertarian Party and the Green Party. Both were in the news quite a bit in 2016 as former New Mexico Governor and Republican-turned-Libertarian Gary Johnson and Green Party standard-bearer Jill Stein were presented as alternatives to two unpopular major-party presidential candidates. But on Election Day they only combined for 4.3% of the overall vote, and this is for political parties that have been at it since 1971 and 1984, respectively. Their electoral victories have been few and far between, and always at the local or state legislative level.

The minor party that's perhaps closest to the classic TEA Party platform of fiscal responsibility, limited government, and free markets is the Constitution Party, which has been in existence since 1992. But even though 2016 was its high-water mark as far as vote gathering goes, a lack of ballot access in many states doomed it to barely 200,000 votes nationwide – less than 2/10 of 1%. Certainly there are more who support the Constitution, but the long-standing duopoly of parties means compromises have to be made.

Moreover, the brief TEA Party dalliance with third-party candidate Doug Hoffman in the NY-23 race was probably convincing enough to dissuade them from trying to create their own political version of the Tea Party, which would run into the same problems with ballot access that most of these other third parties have faced. Certainly a truly political Tea Party could have the most pure platform, but what good would it do if their candidates couldn't get on the ballot to win elections?

After the Hoffman debacle, the TEA Party quickly figured out this truth:

> To the Tea Party movement, the idea of supporting Republicans was only moderately less distasteful than supporting Democrats. But we knew that if we had "gone rogue" and launched a third-party challenge, we would have split the conservative vote and handed perpetual power to the Democratic Party, at a time when that party's most radical members already had full control over Congress and the presidency.[10]

So it turned out that most TEA Party regulars either maintained their original Republican Party registration or kept their unaffiliated status but voted Republican as they could. "It had been nearly ten years since I had given up on being a Republican and had registered to vote under the party affiliation 'decline to state,' said Mark Meckler of TPP. "In disgust, I had abandoned the politicians who had themselves abandoned the values to which I held true."[11] And because the timing of its rise coincided with the nadir of the Republican Party based on electoral wipeouts in both 2006 and 2008, the TEA Party attracted a host of organizations who hoped to use the energized public for their political ends – as detailed elsewhere in this tome, chief among them were FreedomWorks and Americans for Prosperity. Once inside-the-Beltway lobbyists came on board, it was only a matter of time (read: nanoseconds) before the Astroturf accusations would fly. And once those lobbying groups climbed on board, coming right up their rear would be the Republican Party, because they were in desperate straits.

Thus, the TEA Party endured the criticism of being simply a Republican front group, which was only true to the extent that most who participated in the protests already had their political home in the GOP. Authors Theda Skocpol and Vanessa Williamson studied a number of TEA Party groups for their book *The Tea Party and the Remaking of Republican Conservatism* and observed the following:

> Tea Party supporters overwhelmingly vote for Republicans, especially in general elections where Democrats might otherwise win. But not all of them will call themselves Republicans; they might say they are "Independents" and mean either that they are more conservative than they think the Republican Party is, or, far less commonly, they are center-right people who lean toward the GOP. Labels are complicated by the fact that many Tea Partiers are skeptical, even scornful, of "establishment" Republicans.[12]
>
> (…)
>
> When Tea Partiers are faced at the polls with a choice of Republican versus Democrat, the latter can "fuhgettaboddit." Even when Tea Partiers wish they had better, more conservative alternatives to whatever GOP candidates are on the ballot in general election contests, most are savvy enough voters to know they do not want to help the Democrats. Our interviewees did not think a third party was a good idea, even if they distrusted and disliked their local version of the GOP organizational "establishment," which they usually do.[13]

In other words, the silent majority began to speak out again. Skocpol and Williamson wrote a valuable book in that they studied the makeup of TEA Party supporters and found out what election results confirmed: at its prime the TEA Party was largely made up of inactive Republicans who became excited by the GOP again because, by gosh, there were politicians actually paying attention to THEIR needs. After all, TEA Party denizens saw how Democrats catered and flip-flopped to appease whoever their faction *du jour* was (one day it would be blacks, then the next union members, a day later it was the gay lobby's turn, then environmentalists, then women, Latino voters in turn, and so forth *ad nauseum*) so why not enjoy their day in the sun and demand the change they sought?

On a similar note, the Left often also demands to know why these protests didn't start under George W. Bush – after all, he put the nation trillions of dollars in debt himself and dismantled the capitalist-based system to save the overall economy. The team of Meckler and Martin answer this charge succinctly:

> Only after the government seized control over our banks, our mortgages, our cars, our insurance, and took dead aim at controlling our health – *our very lives* – along with one-sixth of the entire U.S. economy, while going into debt for more money than all of us produce in an entire year – only ***then*** did we rise up in the second American revolution: the modern-day Tea Party movement.[14] (Emphasis in original.)

The TEA Party didn't begin as Astroturf and never was that sort of movement at heart. But those corporate interests sure could collect a lot of money and make certain favored individuals and interests a nice living.

> (T)he 'mass movement' portrayal overlooks the fact that the Tea Party, understood in its entirety, includes media hosts and wealthy political action committees, plus national advocacy groups and self-proclaimed spokespersons – elites that wield many millions of dollars in political contributions and appear all over the media claiming to speak for grassroots activists who certainly have not elected them, and to whom they are not accountable.[15]

It was that portion made up of Astroturf and grifters that turned a lot of people off to the TEA Party in the end.

A look at the Left's criticism of the TEA Party, though, would not be complete without the playing of the race card. One good example I ran across comes from the Institute for Research & Education on Human Rights (IREHR), which claimed the following in a 2015 report it prepared for the NAACP:

> At every opportunity, Tea Party leaders have denied they are "racist." Yet, expressions of the Tea Party's persistent problem with race abound, and have been exhaustively documented. They include the waving of the Confederate battle flag at rallies around the country. Tea Party groups have engaged in the rhetoric of Jim Crow with ceaseless chatter about secession and nullification. Tea Party leaders have minimized of horrors of slavery (like when Ben Carson declared that Obamacare was "the worst thing that has happened since slavery"). Pro-Confederate references to the Civil War as the "War of Northern Aggression" and "the War to Enslave the States," can be heard on Tea Party stages and read on Tea Party websites. A popular Tea Party curriculum on The Making of America even

refers to African-American children as "pickaninnies," claims that the treatment of slaves was "humane," and that "the economic system of slavery chained the slave owners almost as much as the slaves."[16]

The strange thing about this particular passage was that, in a lengthy report with nearly sixty endnotes, not one of those quotes and accusations was ever backed up with its own note. As I have pointed out elsewhere in this volume, it's naive to think that no one with racially hostile feelings was ever attracted to the TEA Party, but as I also noted back in my chapter on slanting the story: when the Left had a perfect opportunity to cash in on Andrew Breitbart's pledge of a $10,000 donation to the United Negro College Fund for proof of racist remarks at an Obamacare protest in 2010, they could not do so.[17] But like so much "investigative reporting" done by the Left on the TEA Party as a whole, the IREHR narrative can be quickly shot full of holes.

First of all, one doesn't have to be proud of their Southern heritage to wave a Confederate battle flag at a rally – even though the instance from which they use the photograph wasn't a TEA Party rally but the 2013 Million Vet March protesting the closing of the World War II Memorial during the government shutdown.[18] After all, what better way is there to equate a cause with racism than with that, ahem, false flag? (It also seems a bit odd that the bearer of said flag was far younger than most of the peers in that march. Again, correlation is not causation, but I'm just sayin'.)

It should also be stated for the record that the IREHR report quoted the black Dr. Ben Carson, but left out the context where he added, "And (Obamacare) is in a way, it is slavery in a way, because it is making all of us subservient to the government, and it was never about health care. It was about control."[19] Put in context, the slavery reference makes more perfect sense. (Carson, by the way, was already in the running for the White House at the time this report came out. Could the writers of the report have been afraid of a conservative black man in the Oval Office to follow our most liberal occupant?)

As a population, the TEA Party wasn't as racially diverse as the general population, but this fact by itself would not make the TEA Party racist. If anything, their goal was a more colorblind society in the vein of Dr. Martin Luther King, and that ran the TEA Party afoul of those who still believed the black race needed special assistance to get by (and would reward those benefactors with their votes.) It only took about a year for the NAACP to get the message from their allies in the mainstream media that condemnation was in order, and once the message was received the NAACP was docile enough to comply. "(T)he NAACP says, a number of Tea Party members think that issues of importance to African Americans get too much attention," wrote CNN's Shannon Travis.[20] But, one may ask, how can quotas and set-asides for a particular race or gender be squared up with the declaration that "all men are created equal?" The TEA Party advocated equality of opportunity because no government can guarantee equality of outcome, even at the point of a rifle.

Is it possible the racist element of society saw the TEA Party as a lifeline because it was the only group actively opposing the policies of our first black president? If you look at it through the lens of growing a white nationalist movement, the TEA Party was probably not the right place to go because it was mainly a population that was already set in their ways. Certainly they would complain about the excesses brought on by some pieces of the civil rights movement, such as affirmative action quotas for hiring and advancement, but the Generation X members of the TEA Party also raised arguably the most colorblind generation our nation has known with the Millennials.

Not only that, many within the TEA Party were hypersensitive to the charge of racism, so much so that they were often called upon to police their own ranks:

> The Tea Party needs evangelicals not just from a numbers perspective to affect change but the movement would be well served if evangelicals rose to the occasion to state unequivocally that any hint of racism will not be tolerated at these rallies or otherwise. Granted, evangelicals can't play hall monitor at all the rallies, but the hint of racism speaks to the larger need of evangelicals using their moderating influence to help shoo away the extreme elements of certain Tea Party members.[21]

So the "racist" argument basically came down to opposition of policies that were put in place by a black president as well as the standard TEA Partier reaction to criminal activities resulting in the deaths of black men: neither Trayvon Robinson, who George Zimmerman shot in self-defense in a Florida incident, nor Ferguson, Missouri resident Michael Brown, killed in the street by a white police officer after Brown attempted to disarm him, elicited a great deal of sympathy from TEA Party regulars. In contrast, they especially came down on the side of Ferguson police officer Darren Wilson.

Coupled with their opposition to illegal immigration, the strong law-and-order stand of the TEA Party easily explains their reverence for the Constitution as the ultimate in American legal authority, second only to the absolute authority of the Bible. Since the Left tends to believe in a "living" Constitution and often refers to the Bible as a work of fiction or folklore, it's no wonder they don't get the TEA Party.

While it's not exclusive to those who followed the TEA Party by any means, those who were adherents are more likely to appreciate the closing sentences of this chapter as a final criticism of the Left.

Fifty-six men signed the Declaration of Independence, and in doing so pledged their lives, their fortunes, and their sacred honor to the cause. Fortunately or not, the creators of the TEA Party had to endure no violent revolution; then again their rewards were nowhere near as great either – instead of a nation which has managed to survive for nearly 250 years, they had a political season that faded into the rubric of a corrupt political party then morphed into their backing for Donald Trump – a guy who said the right things, even if the planning and follow-through left something to be desired.

# ONBOARD THE TRUMP TRAIN

*"I don't march with the tea party. But I'll tell you what, they have a good point, because when you see the kind of money that this country is – to use a horrible expression, Larry, I know you've never heard this – but that this country is pissing away, I can understand where they're coming from."* - Donald Trump, *Larry King Live*, April 15, 2009.

*"When Donald Trump was blustering about Obama's birth certificate, he got a chuckle and an 'Atta boy' from some Tea Partiers, but no one seemed to take him seriously as a presidential contender."* - Theda Skocpol and Vanessa Williamson, *The Tea Party and the Remaking of Republican Conservatism* (2011)

It took Donald Trump awhile to embrace the TEA Party, but once they became politically useful to him he was all-in, and many millions responded.

While he wasn't brash enough to march with the TEA Party at first, perhaps it was because Donald Trump was more willing to give Barack Obama a chance to enact his agenda. In the same interview with Larry King that I used as the pull quote to open this chapter, Trump praised Obama as doing the best he could with the situation:

> Well, I really like him. I think that he's working very hard. He's trying to rebuild our reputation throughout the world. I mean, we really have lost a lot of reputation in the world. The previous administration was a total disaster, a total catastrophe.
>
> And, you know, the world looks at us differently than they used to. And I think he's trying to restore our reputation within the world. And he was handed a pretty bad deck of cards. I mean, he was given a pretty tough situation.
>
> And I'm not saying I agree with everything he's doing. I do agree with what they're doing with the banks. Whether they fund them or nationalize them, it doesn't matter, but you have to keep the banks going.[1]

Yet as the Obama presidency progressed, and Trump considered another bid for the Oval Office – he hinted at the task[2] as early as 1987 and briefly made a run on the Reform Party ticket in 2000 before reconsidering a few months later (despite winning Reform Party primaries in Michigan and California)[3] [4] because he felt that party couldn't provide enough support – his tactic to gain more media attention for the 2012 campaign was that of bringing up Barack Obama's birth certificate, beginning with a March, 2011 interview with the ABC morning show *Good Morning America* from Trump Force One.[5]

Because Trump led off with the discredited "birther" issue, the so-called political experts and handicappers were the first to dismiss his chances for 2012. Journalist Christopher Byron wrote on the CNN website that "Trump has been playacting as a presidential contender for roughly the last 25 years, and behind each faux candidacy has been his desire to promote a specific moneymaking opportunity for himself."[6] Byron went on to point out several instances where Trump dropped such hints, from promoting his book *The Art of the Deal*, to his *Celebrity Apprentice* TV show, and a Presidential run being "a great way to raise the rents."

Even his future opponents were skeptical: "I don't know if Donald Trump wants to be President," said Chris Christie to ABC's Diane Sawyer. "I'll believe it when I see it." Yet at the same time, the lead of the story was Trump's surging to second place in 2012 GOP polling.[7] And Trump insisted he wasn't fooling around this time: "If I need $600 million, I can put up $600 million myself. That's a huge advantage over the other candidates."[8]

But if there's anything we have learned about Donald Trump, it's that he is a very shrewd observer. One lesson likely learned from the events of 2011 was the impact the free media of the 24/7 news cycle could have on a potential White House run. Coming from the entertainment world, his audacious remarks – which seemed crazy from the perspective of political conventional wisdom – made as much of a splash on tabloid entertainment news sources such as *Inside Edition*[9] or *Entertainment Weekly*[10] as they did on the mainstream media. And surely he noticed, too, that when he was on one network, it became news on all the networks: who else would get plenty of CBS coverage for appearing on a Fox program?[11]

Observing all this as well was an audience which included a large segment of TEA Party supporters and sympathizers. Trump's coming-out party, as it were, with the TEA Party came in April, 2011 when he co-hosted a Tax Day Tea Party held by the South Florida Tea Party in Boca Raton. Introduced by then-Congressman Allen West, Trump held court for over 40 minutes in a stump speech (due to The Donald's celebrity status, it was a local TEA Party rally nationally covered by C-SPAN)[12] to a crowd described by local leader Everett Wilkinson as very supportive: "In every poll the Tea Party had, Donald Trump came out number one," he told CNN.[13] And Trump expressed his appreciation of the TEA Party as well, telling them they "made Washington start thinking."

Another sign that Trump was thinking and learning about politics through observation was his assertion to ABC's George Stephanopoulos that, "The problem with running as an Independent is that if I don't win, it assures Barack Obama gets back in as President. Because I'm a very conservative guy. And I would I think take 99.9% of the votes away from the Republican Party, which I don't want to do."[14] It was the same lesson the TEA Party learned the hard way with Doug Hoffman in 2009.

Trump's flirtation with a 2012 bid, however, lasted only a couple months until Byron's CNN premise came true: indeed it was time to insure *Celebrity Apprentice* would be on NBC's fall schedule and that he would be the host. Moreover, the abortive run was hard on the thin-skinned Trump, who told a New Hampshire audience, "Nobody said it was going to be easy, but I had no idea I would get hammered in the way I've been hammered the past few weeks."[15] Once again, the experts crowed, Donald Trump had "strung the country along."[16]

While it's certain he has supporters who will swear up and down they figured this out all along – a former political colleague of mine brashly told our Central Committee that she thought Donald Trump should have run for President as far back as 1993, when she met him – no one could have known for sure that Trump would prove himself to be right when he predicted, "I maintain the strong conviction that if I were to run, I would be able to win the primary and ultimately, the general election."[17]

With all these false starts in his past, it was natural to be a little skeptical of Donald Trump's intentions when he came down the escalator at Trump Tower to announce his latest Presidential bid on June 16, 2015. At that time, Trump joined a Republican field crowded with 11 seeking the nomination and among that group were a number of hopefuls already considered to be aligned with the TEA Party: Senators Ted Cruz of Texas and Rand Paul of Kentucky were chief contenders among the conservative and libertarian-minded, while evangelicals favored Dr. Ben Carson, 2008 candidate Mike Huckabee, and 2012 hopeful Rick Santorum.

Out of all the candidates, Trump seemed on the conventional wisdom surface to be one of the least attractive to those disaffected members of the TEA Party as he held a number of political positions that were anathema to rank-and-file members of various stripes: evangelicals didn't like his lengthy pro-choice stance,[18] Second Amendment types weren't sure about his feelings on gun control,[19] fiscal conservatives fretted that he wanted to leave entitlements alone,[20] and everyone was on edge about a New York liberal who was friends with likely Democratic nominee Hillary Clinton.[21] (So friendly, in fact, that some saw Donald Trump's bid as a ploy to insure a Hillary Clinton presidency.)[22] Trump's one saving grace was a hardline position on immigration – a subject that put onetime TEA Party darling Senator Marco Rubio on the outs with the mainstream of conservatives as part of the "Gang of Eight" in 2013 – but several other candidates were basically on the same page insofar as border security and avoiding amnesty.

In the words of "national Republican political strategist and media consultant" Rick Wilson:

> Trump has been unforgivably wrong on every single issue in the conservative portfolio, and his current road-to-Damascus conversions on abortion, guns, taxes, religion, and immigration all have the air of the man up for parole promising that he's changed his ways.[23]

In those respects Donald Trump was wrong for the conservatives politically, but remember once again that he had the one thing other candidates didn't: celebrity.

The average TEA Partier isn't all that much different than the average American: they are more or less in tune with popular culture, so having the familiarity with an audience who watched the various incarnations of *The Apprentice* he hosted and could easily picture Donald Trump as the guy telling those in the Beltway swamp "you're fired!" gave him a tremendous advantage. That celebrity factor also insured that, when it came to the ranks of Presidential candidates who were usually known only in their home state and perhaps among the tiny percentage of people who were political junkies nationwide, Trump would get the largest number of eyeballs in news coverage. To an even greater extent than his 2012 run, in short order once his 2016 campaign got underway Trump became the nightly lead story, sucking the air out from the other GOP efforts.

Subsequent events eventually revealed two key differences in Trump's 2012 and 2016 runs. Because C*elebrity Apprentice* had faded in popularity and at the time was not in a set position on the NBC schedule – the show did not air at all in the 2013-14 season and failed to secure good ratings in its return as a mid-season replacement in 2014-15 – it mattered less to Trump when the network opted to "re-evaluate" his position once he declared a run despite greenlighting another season earlier in 2015.[24]

That re-evaluation turned into a dismissal once Trump launched into his initial issue-based salvo. While the "birther" issue played to a certain segment of the voting public, it was more of a sideshow than a major issue on Americans' minds by the time Trump decided to give his 2012 run a go in the spring of 2011. On the other hand, the Obama administration's unpopular unilateral declaration of deferred action for both illegal aliens who had arrived as children and illegal alien parents who had had children who qualified for birthright citizenship (DACA and DAPA, respectively, which had the potential to grant *de facto* amnesty to 4 million undocumented immigrants)[25] allowed Trump to make illegal immigration and border security his keystone campaign plank. Trump's brash language on the matter alienated the Hispanic lobby, which prevailed on NBC to cut ties with the *Celebrity Apprentice* host and cancel the upcoming broadcasts of both the Miss USA and Miss Universe pageants, which were jointly owned by Trump and NBC/Universal.[26] But it made him a lot of fans where it counted, and Trump knew he could portray himself as a fighter against a liberal mainstream media conglomerate with maximum bravado:

> If NBC is so weak and so foolish to not understand the serious illegal immigration problem in the United States, coupled with the horrendous and unfair trade deals we are making with Mexico, then their contract violating closure of Miss Universe/Miss USA will be determined in court. Furthermore, they will stand behind lying Brian Williams, but won't stand behind people that tell it like it is, as unpleasant as that may be.[27]

In one fell swoop, Donald Trump had set himself up as a leader on an important issue and a victim of political correctness by having his shows canceled by a major network. His campaign quickly climbed up the GOP presidential polls.

Moreover, with TEA Partiers organizing and operating under the belief they were the political outsiders in an era when everything was being handed down by fiat from the pen of Barack Obama, thousands of faceless bureaucrats, and a reckless Supreme Court, the idea of the ultimate political outsider and a man who carried the image of having succeeded “bigly” in the business world seemed to be just the type of guy to go into our nation's capital, kick ass, and take names. (Remember, in that regard he was already popular in 2012 – part of a business-oriented outsider phenomenon that also, to a smaller scale, explained the popularity of Herman Cain with the TEA Party that year.) Granted, immigration was a hot-button issue, but policy didn't matter as much as attitude, particularly when you compared Trump to the cold and calculating persona of Barack Obama – a personality somewhat at odds with his image among those in flyover country that he was a beta male at best.

So as summer turned to fall and Trump remained at the top of the GOP polls – aside from a brief surge from Ben Carson, Trump consistently led the Republican nominee polls after the summer of 2015 – those whose political fortunes were tied to the TEA Party had to make a choice. It was an invocation of the Buckley Rule: was Donald Trump really the most conservative candidate who could win? After poll upon standing-room rally upon being lead story on the news each night, many of the TEA Party insiders cast their lot with Trump in the belief he could be their meal ticket. One was Tea Party Patriots co-founder and later TPX head Amy Kremer, who joined up with what was then known as TrumPAC in January 2016. (The group would later become the Great America PAC, intended to “lengthen...Trump's coattails in races across America.”)[28] Later Kremer would co-found the Women for Trump PAC, as moss was not allowed to grow under her feet.[29]

Standing across the great divide of the TEA Party were Trump skeptics, led by fellow TPP co-founder Jenny Beth Martin. At CPAC 2016 Martin made withering remarks about Donald Trump's campaign as a litany of conservative skepticism:

> Donald Trump took a look at the political environment when he decided to run for President, and said to himself, "Self, that Tea Party is the thing for me!" So he took on one of the biggest issues that drives the Tea Party today, and did his best to make it his own. Since then, we've heard him say over and over again, "I love the Tea Party!" And he's done his best to cloak himself in the garb of the Tea Party, taking on the Establishment.
>
> (…)
>
> But we need to speak some hard truths this morning. Because one of the candidates I just talked about isn't really Tea Party at all. I know Donald Trump says he loves the Tea Party – but that's not what it takes to be Tea Party.
>
> If you want to be Tea Party, you have to love our country and you have to love our Constitution. And you have to be willing to fight for them above your own interests and put our freedom above your own interests.
>
> Let me ask you a question – have you ever heard Donald Trump talk about the Constitution? I haven't. Donald Trump stole a line from Ronald Reagan – he says he wants to make America great again.
>
> Well, I'm going to borrow a line from Ronald Reagan – trust, but verify. And here's what I have verified: Many of Donald Trump's critics say he's inconsistent.
>
> (…)
>
> Yes, he is inconsistent – if all you look at is the flip-flops on the issue positions. But if you look at his motivation for taking those positions, you'll see that there is, in fact, a remarkable consistency – it's the consistency of serving his own interests!
>
> Because you can always count on this: On any given issue, at any given time, Donald Trump will take the position that serves his interest as he perceives it at the time.
>
> (…)
>
> Donald Trump is about love of himself. But the Tea Party is about love of

country, and love of our Constitution.

> I know you're angry, and upset. I am, too. And I know Donald Trump is tapping into that anger. It's a smart campaign strategy, because he makes it seem like he shares our frustrations, like he cares about fighting on our behalf. And when he says he wants to "make America great again," we cheer – because we all believe America is great, and we appreciate what sounds like love of country on his part. It's a seductive pitch, and I have several friends and colleagues who support him, even as I speak.
>
> Here's what I think: Donald Trump loves himself first, last, and in between. He loves himself more than the country. He loves himself more than the Constitution. He does not love you or me. He does not love the Tea Party. Donald Trump has no business thinking he's Tea Party, and every Tea Party supporter who truly loves the Constitution should take that into account when casting their vote.
>
> And why should you vote for Donald Trump, anyway? If you're Tea Party, you've got a much better candidate to support – Ted Cruz![30]

Furthermore, among those who were fervent about the purity of conservative principles in general (and, perhaps, by extension, those of the TEA Party in particular) there was a sentiment that the Trump campaign was the end of the TEA Party as we knew it. Taking to the space of *Politico*, Rich Lowry, editor at the venerable conservative outlet (and eventual bastion of #NeverTrump thought) *National Review,* explained:

> If the grass-roots movement that (Bernie) Sanders has built will pressure Democrats all the way to the Philadelphia convention and beyond, Trump has arguably done more to pull the country's politics leftward. He has, for now, managed to do what the Democrats and the media have been attempting for most of the Obama era: **to kill off the tea party as a national force**.
>
> By dividing it, eclipsing it and making its animating concerns of limited government and constitutionalism into after-thoughts, Trump has neutered a heretofore potent vehicle against Big Government. With or without Sanders, the Democrats were going to drift in a more progressive direction. It was far from inevitable, though, that the Republican Party would de-emphasize its opposition to growth in the size of government. That is entirely the doing of Trump.[31] (Emphasis mine.)

Yet, as I proclaimed in the last chapter, many of those who claimed TEA Party membership were concerned about two things: keeping their share of the goodies and sticking it to the Man in Washington. To that group of loyal voters, Donald Trump's tough talk was music to their ears.

So it wasn't the smoothest of rides for the Trump campaign, but as the remaining contenders stayed in the race believing that they should be the person who the rest of the Republican Party should coalesce around to defeat Trump they handed The Donald more and more victories by plurality once the votes began to be cast and delegates awarded. By the end of February, 2016 several key players who began in Iowa with high hopes were out: former candidates Mike Huckabee and Rick Santorum were the first to go in the wake of the Iowa caucuses, followed by the disappointing campaign of Rand Paul. A week later after disheartening New Hampshire primary results they were joined on the sidelines by Carly Fiorina, Chris Christie, and the nonentity campaign of Jim Gilmore, with Jeb Bush throwing in the towel on February 20 after the South Carolina primary. Bush, ironically, was the first candidate Trump upstaged: Trump's announcement came the day after Jeb! formalized his entry.

This left Trump in the race with four others going into Super Tuesday on March 1: Ben Carson, whose campaign was basically on fumes at that point, and the much stronger positions of Ted Cruz, Marco Rubio, and Ohio Governor John Kasich, whose campaign occupied the lane on the moderate Republican side of the track. As the primaries shifted to a mode of winner-take-all, the four-way opposition split insured Trump could win based on name and media recognition, often pulling less than 40 percent of the vote but getting 100 percent of the all-important delegates. (With the exception of a race no candidate appeared for in the Northern Mariana Islands – thus, almost strictly a contest based on name recognition – Trump didn't break 50 percent in a race outside his home state until the April 26 "Acela primary" in Connecticut, Delaware, Maryland, Pennsylvania, and Rhode Island. By that time it was a three-man race, as Rubio and Carson had long since withdrawn.)

While the TEA Party was all but finished as a political entity by this time, its name besmirched by the constant bombardment of media hit pieces (and conversely, a conservative "information silo"[32] that simply preached to the choir without attracting a lot of new viewers), a lack of love from the establishment Republican Party, and the perception that the movement had finally run its course, there were still a number of voters and activists who once belonged there looking for a leader. And while a significant part of the TEA Party's problem in the campaigns of 2010 and – especially – 2012 was the lack of a strong, forceful leader that the rank-and-file could look up to, Donald Trump's populism was just what the doctor ordered for those former TEA Party supporters.[33]

So why Trump, and not some of the others? TEA Party denizens had been burned too many times by establishment Republican promises, even if they came out of the mouths of onetime TEA Party heroes like Marco Rubio or Ted Cruz. Rubio lost most of his TEA Party support when he backed the "Gang of Eight" immigration deal; however, many TEA Party members in Florida didn't trust him to begin with. "I wonder if he was ever listening or it was just a ploy to get votes…He says all the right things to the audience he needs, and we in Florida are no longer his audience. His new audience is national voters who might elect him president,"[34] according to Lisa Becker, a TEA Party leader with a unique group called The Sisterhood of Mommy Patriots who told this to *The Daily Beast*. This was after Becker described herself as a "big fan" of Rubio before he was elected.

There was also a sad sense of what could have been. "If Marco Rubio had kept his promise to Florida voters and had gone (to the Senate) to oppose amnesty… Donald Trump wouldn't even be in the race. It would be Marco Rubio up there, with the rest of the field trying to knock him out," said Jack Oliver, legislative director of a group called Floridians for Immigration Enforcement.[35]

Conversely, Cruz was a TEA Party favorite but one that the faithful thought may have been a better fit where he was, or, in a dream conservative administration, the newest member of the Supreme Court. Perhaps Cruz's biggest sin, though, was simply running in a year when much of his potential support base said, in the words of American Majority founder Ned Ryun, "Cruz people feel they can work within the status quo, Trump people say screw the status quo, we're sick of it."[36] After years of being kicked in the teeth by the political establishment, those who were TEA Party said enough was enough.

Their non-politician choice could have been Dr. Ben Carson, another long-tern recipient of a TEA Party draft movement since he criticized Barack Obama at the 2013 National Prayer Breakfast, with the President in attendance.[37] While establishment Republicans blanched at Carson's comments, such as when he said he couldn't support a Muslim for President, TEA Party leaders understood the sentiment perfectly.[38] But concerns over Carson's leadership ability and lack of business acumen eventually relegated his support to the more evangelical corners of the TEA Party. Perhaps Carson would be a great Surgeon General, they said, but he wasn't quite the candidate they wanted as President. (Carson eventually instead took the job of HUD Secretary, appointed by President Trump and confirmed in 2017.)

So despite their misgivings and perhaps a dose of the Reagan 80% rule – if your political ally advocates for 80 percent of what you stand for, you don't sweat the other 20 percent – many TEA Party participants gravitated from a movement without a leader to a leader without a movement; at least not the one the TEA Party was originally intended to be. Donald Trump was that leader, a man who said the right things and was unsullied by being inside the Beltway.

Yet to those looking at the TEA Party from the outside, Donald Trump was still an enigma; a square peg in a round hole. He certainly threw the race for a loop, as Molly Ball noted in *The Atlantic*:

> This combination of Tea Party and establishment sensibilities explains why his rivals couldn't stop Trump. They were stuck in the old mindset. Jeb Bush planned to run against a Tea Party candidate – someone like Cruz. Cruz thought he'd be up against an establishment candidate – someone like Bush. The two sides couldn't agree on why Trump was bad: Did he have to be stopped because unlike Cruz, he wasn't a true conservative, or because he would set back Bush's efforts to reform and broaden the party?[39]

To be sure, establishment conservatives looked at Trump with horror, convinced he was a liberal Trojan horse bent on destroying the GOP. Even TPX's Sal Russo believed, in a *Washington Examiner* interview headlined "Tea Party sours on Donald Trump":

> Trump's message lacks the substantive seriousness and positive, uplifting vision required to turn anti-establishment agitators, like President Ronald Reagan, into winners at the ballot box."[40]

Yet the Left correctly deduced Donald Trump was the TEA Party's "very own" presidential candidate. Why?

> (P)erhaps the simplest explanation is the best: He relishes telling other people to go to hell. That's essentially what the Tea Party movement is all about. The Tea Party has no constructive agenda, just a desire to frustrate whatever Democratic and Republican leaders are trying to accomplish. It's anti-government, anti-politician, and anti-media.
>
> So if Trump gets in a verbal scrape with a debate moderator or an elected official, he's a stand-in for Tea Party activists against the establishment. When he all but extends his middle finger to establishment types, he's reminding his supporters that he isn't of Washington. And when he comes under attack, they come under attack. That makes it very hard for his rivals to undermine him with his base.[41]

While a lot of the TEA Party rank-and-file was solidly in Trump's corner, though, some leaders were still seeking more ideological purity. One of those was Bill Pascoe, a Ted Cruz supporter purportedly representing the Tea Party Patriots, who expressed to NPR after a GOP primary debate the frustration other candidates had with Trump and the factor that flummoxed them so:

> It seems to me that one of the things that's been going on for many months is that the critique against Donald Trump has been that he's inconsistent. And we saw some of that last night. We saw, in fact, as you just mentioned, the Fox News moderators talking about his flip-flops and making him watch video of his flip-flops. So the argument has been that he's inconsistent.
>
> (…)
>
> The fact that he is, in fact, remarkably consistent. You just have to know what to look for. He's inconsistent if you look at his flip-flops on the issues, but he's remarkably consistent if you go to the motivation for his flip-flops. The motivation is always the same, and that is that at any given time on any given issue, Donald Trump can be counted on to take the position that serves his own interests at that time.[42]

So let me remind you again of Jenny Beth Martin at CPAC 2016 – or, even better, of what Rick Wilson said, but adding his very next statement:

> Trump has been unforgivably wrong on every single issue in the conservative portfolio, and his current road-to-Damascus conversions on abortion, guns, taxes, religion, and immigration all have the air of the man up for parole promising that he's changed his ways. **But his supporters simply don't care. His appeal to them isn't so much ideological as it is nihilistic.**[43] (Emphasis mine.)

Indeed, there was always a segment of the TEA Party that wanted to burn everything down. Perhaps once upon a time in the early days most of the others had the naive belief that they could change the system, but once again the broken promises were too much for them. More among this group moved into this camp once the establishment managed to con enough voters into nominating Mitt Romney in 2012, while the bitter clingers may have hung on until 2014, seething as TEA Party favorites for Senate seats were crushed by the establishment. Analyzing these dead-enders, conservative pundit Erick Erickson saw the support of Trump as their measure of revenge.

> Drastic measures meant Trump. The conservatives, like Paul, Rubio and Cruz, could not be trusted because they were of Washington. That they had opposed Washington to varying degrees made no difference. The angry and paranoid concluded they were infected by establishmentarianism.[44]

But many who were in the TEA Party were simply looking for a winner, and Donald Trump exemplified that attitude. Amy Kremer was one of those Trump supporters.

> (A) growing number of former tea party activists see (Donald Trump) as their new hope, noting that Republicans have failed to repeal Obamacare, stop illegal immigration or scale back Obama's domestic spending programs.
>
> "We've given the Republican Party a chance," said Amy Kremer, a founding tea party leader who now backs Trump. "They would have never taken the House without the tea party. We gave them the Senate. What have they accomplished? They haven't accomplished a damn thing."[45]

Michigan TEA Party organizer Joan Fabiano remarked on further attractive elements Trump provided. Part of his appeal was being self-funded, but the issues he ran on in 2016 lined up well with the TEA Party. "People were ready for America First," Fabiano told me.[46] My reading of her description: Trump was a blue-collar billionaire outsider, if there was such a thing.

Texas TEA Party leader (and later Congressional candidate) Katrina Pearson was another Trump fan. Pearson actually supported Ted Cruz for his Senate seat and was backing him for president – until she met Donald Trump. Eventually she turned her backing to Trump, telling *Politico,* "Cruz would be a good president, but I think right now with all the hyperpartisanship in the country, I think Trump would be the better person to transition out of Obama. It would be a softer transition for some on the left. It would be a harder transition for some on the right."[47]

Michael Johns, a unique early TEA Party leader in that he had experience inside the Beltway as (among other tasks) a speechwriter for President George H.W. Bush and policy analyst for the Heritage Foundation, was also a Trump backer. He explained why after speaking at a controversial appearance[48] at Cornell University in February, 2018:

> I defended Trump since very early on. First, I find it difficult that insider problems can be resolved by insiders. So the fact that he was an outsider was appealing. Second, he very clearly identified key issues that Republicans usually never touched, like trade agreement and illegal immigration, into tenants of his candidacy.[49]

I'll return to Johns' remarks in the next chapter since they were uttered in the midst of Trump's tenure in office, but suffice it to say that if insiders were split – Johns, Kremer, and Sarah Palin for Trump, Jenny Beth Martin and Christine O'Donnell for Ted Cruz – imagine what those looking in saw and felt. "The shifting alliances leave the impression the tea party is no longer a coalition joined by a common refrain – Taxed Enough Already – but silos of think-tank wonks, big-business conservatives and angry white voters who don't speak the same language,"[50] wrote Lisa Mascaro of the *Los Angeles Times*.

As the race went on and contenders withdrew, the divide between Cruz and Trump deepened and became a Republican cold war, intensifying further after the departure of Marco Rubio.

> Trump has... split the Tea Party, perhaps irrevocably. The populist and free-market absolutist forces that came together to form the Tea Party turned severely at odds with one another, and daily fierce debates on Tea Party websites and on talk radio rage between supporters of Cruz and supporters of Trump. Cruz supporters argued in terms of fidelity to conservative principles: "Real conservatives have a message for the Trump campaign. We are conservatives first and then Republicans. We are Republicans because the party is allegedly the conservative party."[51]

Meanwhile, the pundits argued whether it should be John Kasich or Ted Cruz who should drop out to make it a two-man race in order to stop Trump. Still fiddling while Rome burned.

That divide, which showed its initial fissures when Trump took the lead in the primary race, spread to all quarters of the conservative political world. Quoting Wilson again:

> Every day, their enemies list grows longer: George Will, Megyn Kelly, Fox News, Glenn Beck, Charles Krauthammer, Karl Rove, Roger Ailes. All are marked and targeted by the Troll Party. I feel like I'm in good company, and frankly I'm proud to be included on their hit list.[52]

Glenn Beck is a good example of this "enemies list." You may recall in the days of the TEA Party's formation Beck was an early cheerleader and promoter, but after a number of members of the group jumped on board the Trump Train, Beck was their fiercest critic.

> I don't think these are Tea Party people who are following him. Some of them may be, but I think these – I mean, you can't – if you were a Tea Party person, then you were lying. You were lying. It was about Barack Obama being black. It was about him being a Democrat, because this guy is offering you many of the same things, as shallow as the same way.[53]

Beck soon found he had few remaining friends in the TEA Party. "Glenn Beck was not a part of the Tea Party movement. He took advantage of it, as many did, to catapult his career,"[54] said Tea Party Nation founder Judson Phillips.

Once the GOP nomination was secured by Trump – despite a last-ditch effort to "Free the Delegates"[55] – those on the winning side called on the losers to join them. But a segment of the TEA Party and other Republican voters remained resolutely #NeverTrump, in particular complaining about his lack of fundraising[56] and "ground game" organization. Included on this list were a number of familiar names: former Presidential opponents Sen. Lindsay Graham and Ron Paul, libertarian-leaning Congressman Justin Amash of Michigan, TEA Party favorite Sen. Ben Sasse of Nebraska, former FreedomWorks leaders Matt Kibbe and Brendan Steinhauser, and media personalities Glenn Beck, Steve Deace, Erick Erickson, and, for most of the campaign, Mark Levin – although Levin changed his mind just before the election.[57]

But even as they lit into the #NeverTrumpers for forgetting the Supreme Court or being a vote for Hillary Clinton, it was up to the ragged remnants of the TEA Party to bring him the prize, and they were up to the task.[58] TEA Party faith in Trump was justified when the Tea Party Patriots Citizens Fund endorsed him in late September,[59] also promising to work on Senate races in Florida (Rubio), North Carolina (Richard Burr), Ohio (Rob Portman), and Pennsylvania (Pat Toomey). In that group, they went 5-for-5 as Trump won all those states and all four Senators stayed on.

After the Trump triumph the Tea Party Patriots – conveniently forgetting that their leadership accused Trump of being insincere and strongly backed his top primary opponent – were glad to claim credit and assure us they were still a viable force:

> In addition to defeating the Big Government philosophy, another significant collateral "win" from this election is that it effectively mutes the Washington Establishment's oft-repeated allegation that the tea party movement is dead.
>
> The myth that the Tea Party movement has run its course and is on the decline is a convenient narrative, and a clever technique to dismiss and sideline an effective political opponent. After all, no one needs to take seriously a dormant or dead movement.
>
> This election, however, is definitive proof not only of our ability to engage in political races and help the candidates win, but also affirms the broad popularity of our message and agenda.[60]

In recent years, the term "silo mentality" has become a buzzword, but it's one that seems quite apt at describing TEA Party support for Donald Trump. Let's go back to the beginning and again remind you the origins of the TEA Party were libertarian, in opposition to higher taxes and excessive government spending. At that point it didn't have a lot of adherents but those who followed the nascent movement were fiscal conservatives very interested in Constitutional government, or at the very least not passing on trillions of dollars in debt to their grandchildren.

As the number of TEA Parties grew and more people became interested in them, many also adopted the reflexive qualities of being in a Republican-based movement. Some of the new people were in a sinister but small subset of racists, while many more exhibited an unwillingness to believe (or shift away from) certain sources of news. In a manner of speaking that relates to the overall mentality, they were in an information silo.[61]

Reporting on the Obamacare bill was a good example of this, although it's hard to assign complete blame on average people not attuned to politics when the legislative sausage-making process created a bill that was larger than most big-city phone books. (Readers of a certain age will immediately relate; those under 30 will have to trust me on this one.) So many concepts, such as the "public option" and so-called "death panels," went in and out of the bill and/or were proposed as amendments so quickly it was hard to keep track.

And then there were the tricks the Democrats used to pass the bill without risking a GOP filibuster once Scott Brown was elected to the Senate. For example, Obamacare supporters used a common Congressional ruse of what I call "hollowing out" a previously-passed House bill with a complete replacement by the Senate, then passing it and sending the revised bill back to the House for a vote. This technique gets around the Constitutional prohibition from spending bills originating in the Senate as they are only allowed to originate in the House. It's why the key Obamacare vote on Christmas Eve 2009 was in the Senate but the final bill came to President Obama from the House after passage the next March, after the Senate had placed reconciliation rules on the bill to pass it without the possibility of a filibuster.

Can a layman keep up with all that, let alone all the other bills Congress was considering? Since the answer was no, Joe Sixpack had to find sources he could trust, and having a similar worldview to his was a quick way of building trust. Unfortunately, those who created "fake news" understood this, too.

It bears mentioning that the protest movements on the other side of the aisle felt similarly disaffected by their small-d democratic process. While the powers-that-be in the Democrat Party already had a way to game their system through the use of superdelegates who weren't bound to state election results, they had decided as early as 2009 that, come 2016, it was going to be Hillary's turn – because it should have been Hillary's chance to break the so-called White House "glass ceiling" in 2008 before this "mainstream African-American who is articulate and bright and clean"[62] upstart named Barack Obama jumped the line. So no others needed apply for 2016, and except for Bernie Sanders they probably shouldn't have because they got zero traction in the race.

But that Sanders guy was a Pied Piper to a segment of voters otherwise disinterested in the Democrats and more enamored by the anarchists of Antifa, Black Lives Matter, and the remnants of Occupy Wall Street and various other haunts. Had the mainstream media been Republican-leaning instead of in the tank for Democrats in general and Hillary in particular, that segment of frustrated progressives may have carried Sanders over the top just as the TEA Party irregulars pushed Donald Trump past a group of talented, conservative Republicans who didn't have Trump's celebrity or reputation as unafraid to speak his mind even when politically imprudent.

Yet the press that promoted the Hillary vs. Trump matchup (in the case of Trump, with $2 billion in unearned media assistance in the Republican primaries[63] that expanded to $5 billion by Election Day)[64] as, in their interests, being both good for ratings and the best way to get Hillary elected – as Trump was the loosest of cannons – completely miscalculated the effect of the remnants of the TEA Party which, as they often assured us, was dead. This turned out to be a fatal mistake when you consider the Sanders progressives who were thrown under the bus by the mainstream Democrat Party and in their spite stayed home or voted for Green Party candidate Jill Stein.[65] (Stein's votes could have flipped Michigan, Pennsylvania, and Wisconsin into Clinton's column as the Green Party candidate outperformed Trump's victory margin in each of those jurisdictions. This would have allowed Clinton to eke out a narrow Electoral College win.)

Moreover, take a look at the states in the so-called Clinton firewall that collapsed, particularly Florida, Michigan, Ohio, Pennsylvania, and especially battle-tested Wisconsin, and you'll find surprising strength in their respective TEA Parties.[66] Four of the five states had Republican governors as well, with Pennsylvania the exception (although they elected a GOP governor in 2010.) It turned out Trump exceeded his polling numbers in most of those states: in October all but Ohio were polling for Hillary.

Yet the signs were there. Looking at the respective primaries, Trump ran close behind Hillary in each of those states, except in Ohio where he defeated her outright (but lost to favorite son John Kasich.) Again with the exception of Pennsylvania, more Republicans than Democrats came out to the primary in each state, all of which had Democratic and Republican primaries simultaneously. Consider as well that Obama carried all five in 2012, so these people weren't as fired up about Mitt Romney.

Also worth pointing out: the polling that favored Hillary all along spawned the conventional wisdom that Donald Trump would lose, perhaps even in a Goldwater-style landslide. Even more promising was the idea they would finally be rid of this pesky TEA Party:

> Nevertheless, even if organization, resources, and strong networks keep its various parts active for some time to come, it is hard to see the Tea Party as such hanging together for many more years. The 'Tea Party' label has become more ho-hum. Elites that find the label for electoral or policy struggles will downplay it during the general presidential contest in 2012. The greater limitation for the Tea Party is the age of its participants. Grassroots Tea Partiers are mostly older people whose activism will of necessity wane in coming years. GOP supporters and Fox viewers, too, are disproportionately from the ranks of older white Americans. Both the Tea Party grass roots, and key institutions surrounding it, must find ways to appeal to younger cohorts of Americans, who are more racially diverse, or their decline is assured.[67]

Even better, the leftist experts cheered that Trump's loss would force the Republican Party to "moderate or die."[68] Just like in the aftermath of 2012, though, some pundits believed there would be a pony hidden beneath all the manure: one *RedState* blogger believed the purge of populists from the GOP in the wake of a Hillary win (had things happened that way) may have benefited conservatism in the end:

> Perhaps the only silver lining in Trump's likely defeat is that the Republican Party and conservatism will move back to a more constitutionalist footing. We gave populism a chance and it failed besides giving us a flawed candidate.[69]

But when Trump didn't lose, it was noted (by researcher Elizabeth A. Yates, writing in the *Washington Post*) that, while he wasn't the ideal TEA Party president he at least played for the right team:

> Trump is not a tea party president, but many tea party activists see his election as an opportunity to pursue an agenda unfettered by the establishment that has blocked their advances. "This was a great election," explained one activist, "because it's going to separate the herd," eliminating "progressives" from the Republican Party.[70]

What it didn't appear to do was make a dent in the core issues of the TEA Party, as their diehard pro-Constitution remnants may look back in four to eight years and curse the Trump administration as a missed opportunity to truly rightsize government.

In the end, it took one of Trump's vanquished opponents a couple years to figure out his appeal. I have all the respect in the world for former Louisiana Governor Bobby Jindal, and after a year of a Trump presidency he analyzed it this way:

> Many Trump voters are unapologetic social conservatives who reject secularism and multiculturalism while embracing patriotism. At the same time,

> they are economic populists. They want to cut federal funding for Planned Parenthood, but don't share Paul Ryan's eagerness to limit the growth of their Social Security and Medicare benefits. They don't view Mr. Trump's break from Republican orthodoxy on legal immigration and free trade as problematic. They cheer his denunciation of kneeling football players.
>
> These voters suspect, with not inconsiderable evidence, that the GOP's leaders have less in common with them than with the cultural elite. In their lifetimes, they have watched both parties, all three branches of government, and the popular culture move from embracing many of their core values to, at best, tolerating them.[71]

In fact, these were the TEA Party refugees who elevated Donald Trump to the highest office in the land (over Governor Jindal, among others.) But as it turned out, a significant part of the problem in the era of Trump was the Republican Congress the TEA Party helped to elect in 2010, 2012, and 2014. My next chapter moves forward to the Trump presidency and its failure to do what had been promised for seven years to TEA Party faithful: repeal Obamacare.

# OBAMACARE ENTRENCHED

*"If Republicans cannot repeal Obamacare now, they're going to have to call hospice because their majority is not long for this world."* Tony Perkins, Family Research Council, July 19, 2017.

On November 9, 2016, the world was a little brighter for those who opposed the Patient Protection and Affordable Care Act, better known to the world as Obamacare. After six long years of struggle, the pieces for its repeal were finally in place: the House was still in Republican hands as it had been since 2010, the Senate stayed in the GOP's grasp after their 2014 takeover, and at long last Barack Hussein Obama would be on his way out of the White House, which was now to be occupied by a man who had promised to repeal Obamacare, President-elect Donald J. Trump.

But, as I've said previously in this volume, governing is the hard part. And it's even more difficult when you are elected as the electoral loser (with the exception, of course, of winning the all-important Electoral College vote) as well as having to deal with a partisan mainstream media hellbent on making your one term as ineffective as possible. Before the Trump term began these forces were pulling out all the stops to neutralize the President and the Congress, the majority of whom ran for years on the pledge to repeal Obamacare.

However, the door to disappointment was opened well before Trump's election. Despite the GOP's solemn vow to rid us of the Affordable Care Act, at several stops along the line to eliminating Obamacare we began to hear those two dreaded words, "and replace." It started out as the talk of moderate and establishment Republicans, but by the time the 2016 campaign was in full swing Donald Trump was among those uttering the two-word phrase that pains.

And there was a lot of pain and heartburn endured by the TEA Party when it came to Obamacare. Despite the fact the TEA Party derived much of its early impetus from Barack Obama's attempts at stimulating the economy through a Keynesian fiscal solution on steroids, it came of age in the summer of 2009 as the people's opposition to socialized medicine. As onetime TEA Party Express spokesman Mark Williams noted, "Obamacare was the fiscal issue that was the final straw for Americans. We had stood by for generations while citizens' rights have been eroded, our melting pot culture fractured and radicalized and we citizens economically enslaved."[1]

Perhaps the TEA Party's first victory was helping to stave off the "public option," a prized Democratic addition to Obamacare which would have set up a government-funded health insurer to undercut private plans – after all, who has deeper pockets than the government that can raise whatever taxes they want? However, after independent Senator Joseph Lieberman, who caucused with the Democrats, threatened to join Republicans and be the 41st vote in a filibuster if the public option was not removed from the bill, the idea was scrapped.[2]

Granted, that was a minor victory, a skirmish won in a war that was ultimately lost when Democrats passed the PPACA in March, 2010. But the second-biggest heartbreak was when the Supreme Court used tortured logic to "rule against the American people"[3] and determine Obamacare wasn't unconstitutional because its penalty for non-compliance was a tax. "In this case, however, it is reasonable to construe what Congress has done as increasing taxes on those who have a certain amount of income, but choose to go without health insurance. Such legislation is within Congress's power to tax," wrote Chief Justice John Roberts in the 5-4 decision on *National Federation of Independent Business v. Sebelius.*[4]

The wake of that decision also brought an early usage of the term "repeal and replace." A news release from the Tea Party Patriots talks about Senator John Cornyn's use of the term to a local news radio station, quoting Cornyn as saying, "We've got to repeal (Obamacare) and replace it with a patient-centered bill, not a government takeover."[5] And it was already a question[6] whether Mitt Romney, who originated the idea of a governmental mandate for individuals to carry health insurance when he green-lighted the Massachusetts plan in 2006,[7] would do away with Obamacare or just tinker around its edges to make it a more efficient big-government entitlement.

But when Romney fell in defeat to Barack Obama, even the election of a Republican-controlled Senate in 2014 couldn't put a dent in the program. However, a few legislative maneuvers passed by the GOP curtailed critical portions of the original bill, with possibly the most important one addressing the open-ended fiscal temptation of "risk corridors."

Risk corridors were, as intended, an accounting trick of sorts where profitable insurers were supposed to support a federal fund which would then be divvied out to their less-successful peers. Instead of subsidizing this with federal money as originally envisioned over the three-year life of the program, though, Congress managed to pass a provision that required the risk corridors to be a zero-sum game within the insurance industry, taking taxpayers off the hook but leaving the risk corridor fund billions of dollars short.[8] To the left, it was example #1 of Republicans "sabotaging" the Affordable Care Act.

As we now know after Obamacare's full 2014 implementation, it's done little to increase the number of insured – save for a massive expansion in the group depending on Medicaid around the nation due to relaxed income eligibility requirements – and those who buy insurance on the individual market have often had to endure double-digit percentage increases in their premiums as well as rapidly appreciating deductibles and co-pays. Those who remain on employer-based plans have fared little better as employers pass more of their increased costs to their workers.

In short, Obamacare was a mess, and people were expecting the newly-elected Donald Trump to jump in with both feet to address the issue.

But knowing that Trump was elected with only the second-best plurality, and secure in their place among the bitter enemies he made along the way by his brash and uncompromising rhetoric, those opposing Trump made their displeasure known very quickly. I've previously pointed out these progressives who called themselves the “Indivisible” movement (or just “the Resistance”)[9] openly admitted they were borrowing tactics, particularly when it came to townhall meetings, used by the TEA Party eight years earlier.[10] As Ezra Levin, one of the Indivisible leaders, told Dave Gilson of *Mother Jones*:

> We point to a two-pronged strategy that made the tea party successful. One, you have to be local. You have to focus on your local members of Congress. Looking around at all these great groups that have popped up, we've seen people say, “Hey, contact the committee chair. Contact the leadership or this member of Congress.” What we knew from our time on the Hill is that members of Congress care about reelection most of all. And that means they care about their constituents. So you have to be a constituent to make your voice heard.
>
> The second strategy that the tea party smartly embraced was one of being almost entirely defensive. They consciously decided not to figure out which of their really abominable conservative policy priorities to prioritize. Instead, anything that came out of the Obama White House they were against. What they recognized is that when you've lost the White House and the House of Representatives and the Senate, you're not setting the agenda anymore.[11]

And Levin recognized that Obamacare repeal would be among their first priorities:

> Their goal is to quickly pass as much bad legislation and regulatory changes as possible because they know their ideas aren't popular and they know they don't represent the vast majority of the country.
>
> (…)

> Obama had a mandate for change and Trump clearly does not. The Democrats had much larger majorities in Congress when Obama first took office. Our position now is actually stronger—though it's hard to imagine. But it's only stronger if people act. If people don't get as engaged as the tea party was, we're going to lose.[12]

Bear in mind, of course, another thing the Left has that the TEA Party did not is a sympathetic mainstream media. However, because of that information silo Ezra Levin and company didn't understand the mood of ordinary Americans, with the *prima facie* evidence of Donald Trump being elected in part as a reaction to the policies of the last eight years and how they devastated the heartland of this nation. If those average Americans were happy with the situation, Donald Trump wouldn't have won state after state thought to be safely in Democratic hands.

Yet this new political wave worked in a manner completely backwards from the TEA Party: they began with the large-scale protest of the Women's March that drew as many as a half-million participants in Washington, D.C.[13] as well as hundreds of thousands more globally – events that had no shortage of network news coverage.[14] From there they reversed field to smaller, local protests which were attempts to garner more local news coverage.[15] (Perhaps this was a sign their original protests were Astroturf?)

This may be a time, though, for me to remind you they did not change that part about harassing members of Congress at townhall meetings.[16] [17] They just did it to Republicans instead of Democrats.

Nor did the Indivisibles miss out on the TEA Party aspect of the "leaders" trying to cash in:

> The Indivisible Project's founders, married couple Leah Greenberg and Ezra Levin, didn't think they were starting a mass protest movement.
>
> (…)
>
> Within a couple of months Greenberg and Levin had both quit their jobs to head up the new movement full-time.[18]

I'm curious to find out how many left-wing scribes are going to go through the finances of this effort, which had "hired 16 other staff members with funding from donations"[19] by May, 2017 and by the following October was boasting "a mostly Washington-based staff of about 40 people, with more than 6,000 volunteer chapters across the country… (which) has raised nearly $6 million since its start,"[20] with a fine-toothed comb. Wait, are those crickets I hear?

Fortunately, enterprising Capital Research Center journalist Matt Middleton has documented some of the Astroturf ties[21] of this so-called "grassroots" movement, which are far more extensive than those from which the TEA Party ever benefited.

What this so-called resistance accomplished, though, was unlike what the TEA Party did – or maybe came about in reaction to what longtime members of Congress remembered from the 2010 election. (One other key lesson learned by Indivisible: they skipped the third-party flirtation tried by the TEA Party in 2009 and set their sights straight away on radicalizing the Democrats.)[22]

Despite a number of great ideas[23] about alternatives to Obamacare which could have been enacted – or just the straight-out repeal sponsored by Sen. Rand Paul[24] – in the spring of 2017 Congress led off with a weak, watered-down repeal and replacement package that was hardly worth the effort. Conservatives panned it for not going far enough – two cases in point, from outside of Congress as well as within: writer David Harsanyi groused about the "watered-down repeal effort that offered states some meager level of federalism in the form of block grants";[25] meanwhile, Senator Paul Tweeted that, "Keeping 90% of Obamacare is not ok and it's not what we ran on. Conservatives should say no."[26] Meanwhile the Left (and the media, but again I repeat myself) howled about anyone touching their sacred cow.

And the pressure worked to an extent, although the Tax Cuts and Jobs Act passed late in 2017 eliminated one key Obamacare provision: penalties enforced by the Internal Revenue Service as a "shared responsibility payment." (In the later bipartisan budget deal, the so-called "death panels" – which never were actually created – also became a thing of the past.)

While the Trump administration and Congressional Republicans couldn't stitch together a coalition large enough to fully repeal Obamacare, one victory that was perhaps TEA Party-influenced was the passage of the aforementioned Tax Cuts and Jobs Act. It was a measure that, just like Ronald Reagan's and George W. Bush's were previously, will forever be referred to as the Trump tax cuts. Yet even that fell short of initial expectations, as the original goals of cutting seven income brackets to three or four and eliminating a number of deductions were chipped away to a barely simpler tax package – but a significant reduction in the corporate tax rate, which may be its longer-lasting legacy.

In the midst of that fight, however, came yet another electoral battle that showed the confluence of the ragtag remnants of the TEA Party, the Republican establishment, and a press that always seems to be willing to spread dirt about Republicans yet be silent about the foibles of Democrats until they become too obvious to ignore.

When Senator Jeff Sessions was selected by the Trump administration to be Attorney General, his temporary replacement was Alabama's own Attorney General, Luther Strange. Chosen by then-Alabama Governor Robert Bentley, Strange's selection was seen by critics as a way to reward one of Bentley's political friends as he had called for impeachment procedures against Governor Bentley to be delayed. (Two months after the February, 2017 appointment of Strange, Bentley pleaded guilty to misdemeanor charges related to the coverup of an extramarital affair and resigned.)

While Strange was appointed to the Senate, he was not there intending to be a caretaker as some placed in this position have pledged to be in order to avoid a nasty political fight. Instead, Luther fully intended to run for the seat permanently, but, like a field of clover attracts bees, the race drew several other Republican aspirants: most prominent among them were Congressman Mo Brooks – the choice of former TPP/TPX leader Amy Kremer and her newest group, Women for Trump[27] – and former Judge Roy Moore. The popular jurist, who had twice been ousted from the Alabama Supreme Court – once over a monument depicting the Ten Commandments and the second time over refusing to enforce the Supreme Court's *Obergefell* decision legalizing same-sex marriage (which was not legal in Alabama prior to the SCOTUS ruling) – upset Strange in the primary and again in the runoff election.

Moore's victory was considered a setback for the Beltway establishment, particularly the "lackluster leadership styles" of Senate Majority Leader Mitch McConnell and Speaker of the House Paul Ryan, whose support was with Strange.[28] As Congressional leaders, they were the ones being blamed for the lack of legislative accomplishment in the early months of the Trump presidency. "If Moore 'threatens' a GOP majority in the Senate, it is a meaningless one," wrote George Neumayr at *The American Spectator*. "The rank-and-file is supposed to be terrified at the prospect of losing a 'majority' led by the likes of (moderate Maine Senator) Susan Collins?"[29] But with Alabama as solid of a Republican state as one can find – its 28-point margin for Trump was the largest among the states in the old Confederacy – after his primary win it looked like a *fait accompli* that Judge Moore would soon be Senator Moore.

All that changed on November 9, a month out from the December 12 special election. In that morning's edition the *Washington Post* pulled out its own October surprise: scandalous decades-old allegations against Moore that included the molestation of a 14-year-old girl that Moore (then a 32-year-old bachelor) was dating.[30] A total of four primary accusers stepped forward to reveal to the *Post* something the paper assured us was not a secret in Alabama – "a *Post* reporter heard that Moore allegedly had sought relationships with teenage girls"[31] – despite the fact Moore had run for office several times before.

Within hours, the calls for Moore to drop out were being screamed from inside the Beltway[32] and the Republican Party was at war with itself. Establishment types were convinced by the stories of the accusers and considered Moore – whose brand of God-fearing conservatism was looked at with horror by Republicans always concerned about the women's vote – as fatally damaged goods. Conversely, many who considered themselves TEA Party faithful were sure they had seen this movie before, but run backwards as the media covered up stories which could have been fatal to the electoral chances of Democrats. (In an earlier chapter I alluded to an example of this: what if the *Post* had been as diligent in debunking the "it was caused by a video" excuse given for the Benghazi massacre? Chances are we would be considering the second term of President Romney as a mixed bag for the TEA Party.)

As the election date drew closer, though, the Andrew Breitbart assertion that culture was upstream of politics was once again being proven true. The deepening Hollywood scandal of sexual harassment and abuse centered on movie producer Harvey Weinstein spread itself into the political world and led to change in Congress on both sides: Arizona Rep. Trent Franks, a Republican, resigned thanks to allegations he was offering female staffers in his office cash payments to be a surrogate mother for his wife, who could not bear children; meanwhile, on the Democrat side both Senator Al Franken of Minnesota and long-standing Rep. John Conyers of Michigan left thanks to harassment allegations. At the time of his resignation, Conyers was the House member with the longest seniority, first elected in the Goldwater massacre of 1964.

The Franken case was intriguing because it also thought to provide convenient cover for Roy Moore in dealing with his accusers. While Moore's accusation was more serious, nearly forty years had passed since then and it was not indicative of a known pattern of abuse, as Moore has been married for more than 30 years. (Moore's wife, though, is 14 years his junior and he has known her since she was a teenager.) On the other hand, Franken's accuser alleged the incident was but a decade or so old and others also stepped forward to accuse Franken of similar, more recent acts. (This despite the fact Franken also has a long-standing marriage of over 40 years.)

Given the source of the accusations and their timing, some observers saw the Moore case as a Democratic ploy. Dov Fischer at *The American Spectator*:

> No Democrat is pushing Franken out because Democrats know how many Senate seats it takes to pass or preserve Obamacare. To keep taxes high. To prevent conservatives from naming federal judges and Supreme Court justices. To keep the border porous. So Al is staying put – *on the Senate Judiciary Committee, yet.*
>
> That is how Democrats do it. They make Republicans feel guilty. They con

> Christians and religious Catholics and observant Jews into feeling that, somehow, there is a religious or moral imperative to abandon a critical United States Senate seat. Then they cynically scoop it up, cobbling together Congressional majorities built on the hands and in the trousers of their House icons and their Senate royalty like Al Franken, Ted Kennedy, Chris Dodd, and other gems. All backed by a quarter-century iconization of Bill Clinton and Hillary, who only now – finally – are being thrown under the bus as the Donna Braziles, Kirsten Gillibrands, and others belatedly race to dissociate from them because, now that the Clintons finally are dead in Democrat politics, the survivors who fed off their teets for years rush to tell us that they just never knew about Juanita Broaddrick, Paula Corbin Jones, Kathleen Willey, Monica Lewinsky… or the young rape victim over whom Hillary giggled when describing how she got the rapist off.[33] (Italics in original.)

As the drumbeat went on and Moore seemed closer to victory, recovering in the polls after an initial drop in support, Democratic Senators eventually prevailed on Franken to leave. On December 7, five days before the Alabama election, Franken announced he would leave "in the coming weeks."[34] (Eventually Franken left on January 2, 2018; Tina Smith was sworn in to replace him a day later.)

The second angle pursued by those wishing Moore had left, though, was that of putting more clouds in an already gloomy outlook for the 2018 midterms. Democrats, they claimed, would be happy to have the issue left on the table. "If you're running in 2018 (as a Republican), Roy Moore's going to be your new best friend," Senator Lindsey Graham told *Politico*.[35]

And there was wailing and gnashing of teeth about the effects TEA Party-style politics were having on the political discourse in general. *RedState*'s Joe Cunningham:

> Many in conservative media, from reporters to editors to pundits, choose to overlook the evidence (against Moore) and feed these conspiracy theories and defend the indefensible. Where once we accused the Democrats of having a wagon-circling echo chamber, we now copy their tactics.
>
> And, I readily admit that the atmosphere that created Trump and Moore is on me. That in my zealous attacks on certain Republicans in Washington, I fed the masses that were looking for someone to buck it all. I do not like Mitch McConnell, and wish that Matt Bevin had won that Kentucky primary. But, in my anger over McConnell's rule of the Senate, I stoked certain flames.[36]

In the end, the *Washington Post* managed to cobble yet another Senate seat, and the Democrats snatched victory from the jaws of defeat by the slimmest of margins:

their candidate Doug Jones won with a plurality of the vote. His 21,924 vote victory was by fewer than the number of write-in votes, many of which were cast for a last-minute Republican challenger.[37]

For all its bluster, though, the Alabama Senate seat and a handful of other electoral results (particularly in Virginia) were pretty much all the so-called Resistance had to show for Trump's first year. "The Resistance is a try-hard, embarrassing, ineffectual adult temper tantrum that has nothing to show for all the stupidity it forced on everyone,"[38] wrote *RedState*'s Brandon Morse. If anything, though, the threat of Indivisible proved the Republican establishment was a batch of sunshine patriots who wilted when their time came to make their promises a reality.

But the Democrats' house is split much as the TEA Party eventually rent the Republican Party – radical leftists who supported Bernie Sanders are working just as hard to pull the Democrat Party farther from the mainstream to the left as the early TEA Party did to push the nation toward a Constitutional, limited government direction. "Many in Sanders's legions of supporters criticized the mainstream Democratic Party for not being left-wing enough, and – with the phrase "democratic socialism" in their minds – some were drawn what they see as the natural heir to their campaign: the Democratic Socialists of America (DSA)," explained Chace Paulson of the Capital Research Center.[39]

Also just like the TEA Party and their deepest fears of Barack Obama, there are those on the far left who believe the Democrats aren't going far enough to stop Donald Trump. "The Democratic base needs to know there are members of Congress who are willing to stand up against this president,"[40] said Rep. Steve Cohen, who introduced articles of impeachment against Trump in November, 2017.[41]

And while establishment Democrats vowed to listen to voter concerns[42] – admittedly, more than the Republicans did with the TEA Party – surely their goal is to bring the disaffected voters into their fold like the GOP did eight years earlier. This tactic of paying attention to what the district wants and not to shifting political winds worked exceptionally well in the March, 2018 PA-18 special election, where Democrat Conor Lamb narrowly prevailed in a district Trump won with a 22-point margin 17 months earlier by localizing the election and not focusing on the President. Instead, Lamb pointed to issues like access to health care, fighting opioid abuse, fracking, and investing in infrastructure to promote union labor.[43]

On the other hand, Trump supporters like national TEA Party leader Michael Johns can passionately and rather truthfully point to areas of success, too – speaking before an audience at Cornell University Johns proclaimed an impressive list of Trump accomplishments in several areas: employment, economic growth, debt, taxes, poverty, regulatory reform, health care, immigration, and trade among them.[44] I'll grant that many of these were aims of the TEA Party but Trump's means of accomplishing them haven't always been the remedies prescribed by the Constitution.

As one who was elected to Congress as part of the TEA Party wave in 2010, Idaho's Rep. Raul Labrador summed up the entire effect of the TEA Party inside the Beltway in his waning months in office:

> Armed with what they felt were clear mandates from their voters, Labrador and his fellow Tea Party freshmen came to transform Congress itself – to stop Washington's spending binge and to return the Republican Party to its small-government foundations.
>
> (…)
>
> "I thought it was a revolution. I thought we were going to completely change the way that Washington worked," Labrador says. "Within one week – I'm not exaggerating – I saw a large majority of my class saying, essentially, 'Whatever you need us to do, we will do.' And I was sick inside."[45]

I'm sick inside, too, because in my political naivete – I still have something of a Polyannish view of politics despite being active as a local party official for a couple decades – I thought we elected TEA Party representatives to help in "draining the swamp." By that token, perhaps a President such as the ideologically impure but politically fearless Donald Trump was necessary.

To conclude this book, I need to take a look at one last election. For the TEA Party it took four election cycles (2010 through 2016) to put themselves in a position where some of their policies could be enacted. Would the "blue wave" prophesied by supporters of various factors of the Democrat Party actually crash ashore in the 2018 midterms and wipe out everything for which the TEA Party had labored so hard and sacrificed so much?

# ENDGAME: THE 2018 MIDTERM ELECTIONS

*"Let's make sure we show up wherever we have to show up! And if you see anybody from that Cabinet in a restaurant, in a department store, at a gasoline station, you get out and you create a crowd! And you push back on them! And you tell them they're not welcome anymore, anywhere."* – Rep. Maxine Waters (D – California) at a pro-immigration protest in Los Angeles, June 23, 2018.

As 2017 came to a close it seemed the Democratic Party was ascendant. In the last chapter I detailed the surprising results of the Alabama special election where Democrat Doug Jones – with a huge wet kiss from the *Washington Post* – snatched a Senate seat away from the GOP and reduced their majority to a bare 51-49 Senate advantage. While it was the first time the Democrats had succeeded in winning a previously Republican seat in a special election – previous attempts in Kansas, Georgia, South Carolina, Montana, and Utah had fallen shy of victory – anti-Trump "Resistance" Democrats (the "Indivisible" crowd) pronounced 2018 as the year of the "Blue Wave" that would restore Congressional control to their side and enable them to impeach Donald Trump.

Besides the Alabama special election, their evidence came from off-year elections in Virginia and New Jersey: while the governor's seat in Virginia was a Democrat hold as Lieutenant Governor Ralph Northam succeeded former Clinton Administration official and DNC Chair Terry McAuliffe, their bigger excitement was coming literally one person's vote short of eradicating a once-formidable 66-34 GOP advantage in the Virginia House of Delegates. The final contested seat, in House District 94, was won when the name of GOP incumbent David Yancey was drawn from a bowl containing two canisters with slips of paper: one with Yancey's name and one with the name of his Democrat challenger Shelley Simonds.[1] The pair had split two previous recounts, with Yancey winning at first and Simonds carrying the second by one vote – however, a state court ruled an uncounted ballot with both names circled but a slash through Simonds' name was intended as a vote for Yancey, meaning the two were tied with 11,608 votes apiece. Had Simonds' name been drawn, the Virginia House of Delegates would have been split 50-50, ending nearly two decades of GOP control – still, the 15-seat swing was a major boost to Democratic hopes for two reasons: many of the districts Democrats captured were the suburban districts where the proverbial "soccer moms" live, and most of their first-time winners were female candidates. The roster of Democrats even included the first openly transgender person elected and seated in a state legislative capacity in the nation.[2]

Although the Democrats also won in New Jersey and made modest gains in their legislature, their news wasn't as exciting because few expected any Republican attempting to follow the deeply unpopular, scandal-ridden, and term-limited Governor Chris Christie to succeed. But it was a Democrat sweep, and given how the 2009 election that put both those states' governorships in the GOP column (Christie in New Jersey and former Governor Bob McDonnell in Virginia, where governors are limited to one four-year term) was painted as a precursor to the 2010 midterms by TEA Party groups, the Resistance optimism seemed to be justified. One month later, Doug Jones won the open Senate seat in Alabama (akin to the Scott Brown win for the "Kennedy seat" in Massachusetts in January, 2010 even down to the fact both represented the longtime minority party in their respective states) and the narrative of a Blue Wave for 2018 was set.

The first House incumbents to lose, however, were defeated in their party primaries. Republicans in North Carolina were first, ousting three-term incumbent Rep. Robert Pittenger. While Pittenger was an incumbent, he never enjoyed smooth electoral sailing from his own party, defeating primary challengers to both gain office in 2012 and stay there in 2014 and 2016. This time he lost a rematch with 2016 primary opponent Mark Harris.[3]

Pittenger, who had formed a bipartisan and centrist Congressional caucus with fellow freshman members[4] after his 2012 election, also angered TEA Party activists shortly after his election[5] for not supporting a government shutdown to defund Obamacare and never really got back in their good graces as the TEA Party regularly supported his opposition.[6] In a rare moment of agreement, Mark Harris secured the endorsement of the Tea Party Express[7] and Tea Party Patriots Citizens Fund[8] PAC for the 2018 election and won the primary by a scant 828 votes after losing in 2016 (without the TEA Party endorsements) by just 134 votes.[9]

Those close votes weren't finished yet for Harris: he squeaked out a 998-vote win in November in what was considered an R+8 district.[10] However, weeks after the race, the Democrat-controlled North Carolina State Board of Elections entertained allegations that absentee ballots were being collected illegally (a practice known as "ballot harvesting") in minority-dominated areas, refusing to certify the results.[11] After their investigation, in February the NCBOE ordered a new election in the Ninth District, with neither Harris nor Pittenger among the ten participating in a May primary on the GOP side; however, 2018 Democrat nominee Dan McCready was the lone one from his party to file for the special election slated to be held in September – unless a GOP runoff is necessary.[12] In that case, voters from that district will have to wait for November, 2019 to seat a Congressman.

The TEA Party also rolled snake eyes with their choice of incumbent South Carolina Republican Rep. Mark Sanford.[13] A longtime TEA Party darling,[14] Sanford was defeated by state Rep. Katie Arrington, who barely avoided a runoff against the incumbent by securing 50.6% of the vote. Arrington credited her win to an eleventh-hour Tweet of support[15] from President Trump that was critical of Sanford.[16] [17] In October Arrington finally got the TEA Party nod from the TPX,[18] but it wasn't enough as she lost the race by 1.4% to Democrat Joe Cunningham, doubling South Carolina's Democratic delegation.[19]

Yet while the 2018 Republican primary campaign started off with those two upsets, remaining elections held fewer surprises for them. The Pittenger and Sanford upsets may have raised a few eyebrows, but from a conservative, TEA Party perspective little was really changed in the Republican ranks as one upset pushed the party a little bit rightward while the other tugged it back in a populist direction thanks to the Trump support.

Conversely, the Democratic upsets left little doubt as to the direction of their party.

It began with the New York primary June 26, a date which turned out to be a momentous day in the ranks of the far-left progressive wing of the Democratic Party. It was expected that 10-term incumbent Rep. Joe Crowley would win a rare contested primary in NY-14 over 28-year-old upstart Alexandria Ocasio-Cortez, but the young Latina would use a "ruthlessly efficient grassroots"[20] to defeat the longtime Congressman, rumored to be an *heir apparent* to Minority Leader (and former Speaker) Nancy Pelosi should the Democrats regain control of the House later in the fall. Instead of the possibility of New York City representatives running both houses of Congress with Crowley joining Sen. Chuck Schumer in a leadership role, voters selected the challenger and it wasn't even close: Ocasio-Cortez blew Crowley out by 14 points.[21] Ironically, New York's arcane election laws gave Crowley a second chance as he refused to vacate his spot on the Working Families Party ballot line but he quickly made it clear he wouldn't actively campaign to retain the seat.[22] [23] (Still, Crowley picked up over 6% of the November vote on his ballot line – losing to the GOP candidate by just 7 percent.)[24]

Ocasio-Cortez's improbable upset was huge, and it managed to upstage another victory that June day by a fellow Bernie Sanders acolyte: former NAACP head Ben Jealous handily won Maryland's Democratic gubernatorial primary, pacing a nine-person field crowded with well-known and perennial candidates alike with a shocking 39.6 percent of the vote.[25]

Two months later, Massachusetts 7th Congressional District voters tossed out yet another 10-term incumbent: Rep. Michael Capuano was defeated in favor of Boston city councilor Ayanna Pressley. While Pressley admitted she and Capuano were both well left-of-center,[26] she staked her race on the need for "a new, more assertive style" against Donald Trump and Republicans.[27] "(Capuano and I) might vote the same way, but we will lead differently," Pressley told a group of supporters. "These times require and this district deserves bold, activist leadership."[28]

It should also be noted that both Crowley and Capuano are white males who were both defeated by women of color in districts that are majority-minority. But those Congressional primary wins, along with Democratic gubernatorial primary victories by progressive favorites Jealous, Tallahassee Mayor Andrew Gillum in Florida, and House Minority Leader Stacey Abrams in Georgia – all of whom are minorities – buoyed hopes among the Resistance crowd that they could provide a counterpunch to the Trump White House and set him up for defeat in 2020. In short, they saw the 2018 campaign as the flip side to the TEA Party wave election in 2010 – with an exception I'll get to in due course.

While the similarities to 2010 were there in the primary election results, the overall condition of the nation was far different eight years later. Donald Trump's 2016 election immediately boosted people's economic perception[29] [30] and, thanks in large part to tax reform passed in 2017, their optimism was eventually borne out with exceptionally low unemployment – as in more jobs available than people to fill them[31] – and regular GDP growth seldom seen during the Obama years. And despite left-wing rhetoric to the contrary about companies using their tax cuts simply to repurchase their stock,[32] people were generally all right with the Trump tax cuts as they also led to increased hiring, employee bonuses, and billions of dollars in capital improvements among American businesses.[33]

Moreover, economic gains were just the beginning: Trump's administration was taking a chain saw to the regulatory state, cutting down over 20 regulations for each new one and creating a *Federal Register* that hadn't been so skinny in nearly 25 years – one-third smaller than the last Obama rendition at the end of 2016.[34] Add to that a proposed new trade deal with Canada and Mexico to supplant the hated NAFTA[35] and a reversal in diplomatic tone to an America-first policy that included backing out of Obama-era pacts like the Iran nuclear deal and Paris Climate Agreement, and it was no wonder Trump's popularity was inching up despite the oppressively negative press about him.

Yet as the primary season came to a close in mid-September – mere weeks before early voting began in some states for the November 6 decision date – there was still the conventional wisdom of an electoral Blue Wave. The Left remained buoyed by its unity in hatred of Donald Trump and all things Republican while the GOP struggled to find a cohesive message and voice. However, in the space of a few gripping weeks as the center of a news (and personal) maelstrom, Supreme Court nominee Brett Kavanaugh altered this political equation.

As the 2017-18 Supreme Court session came to a close, Justice Anthony Kennedy surprised the nation by announcing his retirement after three decades on the nation's highest court. Yet perhaps they shouldn't have been: at 81 years of age, he was the second-oldest justice on the court and the final Ronald Reagan appointee to serve.

Kennedy's retirement put the Democrats in a panic, as he was considered the swing voter of the Supreme Court. The Left was still smarting from having a SCOTUS seat "stolen" from them in 2016: after the sudden passing of Justice Antonin Scalia in February of that year, the Republican-controlled Senate refused to hold hearings for prospective appointee Merrick Garland, citing a 1992 precedent commonly known as the "Biden Rule" where vacancies in the high court were to be filled by the winner of that year's Presidential election after taking office. Instead of Garland being the third and final Obama appointee, Neil Gorsuch was elevated from the Denver-based Tenth Circuit Court of Appeals in April, 2017 as Donald Trump's first selection.

So it really didn't matter who Trump selected for the post: the radical Left had press releases and signs[36] ready for opposing anyone (including "XX")[37] who was reasonably believed to be on Trump's short list. Their chief misgiving about the conservative Brett Kavanaugh was how he would throw the Supreme Court out of its long-standing "balance" – as fate would have it, Barack Obama joined his most recent predecessors George W. Bush and Bill Clinton in selecting two new justices who replaced departing members with a common political philosophy. In their eight years in office apiece, Obama and Clinton each got to replace two of the more activist jurists while Bush selected two new members as reinforcements on the conservative side. Conversely, George H.W. Bush could have pulled the Supreme Court significantly to the right with his two picks to replace activist judges, but misfired with his initial choice, David Souter. However, Clarence Thomas has been effective on the conservative side. (It was in the wake of the Thomas selection when then-Senator Joe Biden made his "Biden Rule" pronouncement during the 1992 campaign.)[38]

Had Garland made it through confirmation, the Supreme Court would certainly have been an even more activist court than it has proven to be over most of the last half-century – fortunately, Senate Majority Leader Mitch McConnell's gamble paid off, and less than 18 months into his term Donald Trump was already getting his second SCOTUS pick.

The process of replacing Kennedy became easier thanks to changes the

Democrats had made during the Obama era when they still ran the Senate – in part as a reaction to the demands for strict originalist fealty uttered by Republican Senators either elected with TEA Party support or fearful of a primary challenge from that new wing of the GOP. Thanks to former Senate Majority Leader Harry Reid, the once-formidable challenge of amassing a 60-vote supermajority to end a filibuster to thwart the appointment of judges deemed unfit for office on political grounds was scrapped – Reid's Democrats revised the Senate rules midstream to allow for a simple majority to end debate on appellate and district court nominees. Called the "nuclear option," McConnell extended Reid's precedent to Supreme Court nominees once Trump was in office and Democrats threatened to filibuster Gorsuch's nomination.[39]

Because of that, it appeared for most of the Kavanaugh nomination process that he would be confirmed, with the only question being how many endangered Democrat senators from states that voted for Donald Trump would follow in line and run the affirmative vote to 55 or more. But a July letter from California-based professor of psychology Christine Blasey Ford would throw the process into a tailspin. In Ford's letter, originally delivered to Rep. Anna Eshoo and passed along to Sen. Dianne Feinstein, she accused Kavanaugh of sexual assault stemming from an incident that occurred sometime in the mid-1980's, although later in testimony Ford would peg the timing as the "summer of 1982."[40]

Stammering Republicans immediately halted the march to confirmation, bending to Democrat and media demands that the accuser have her day in court, as it were. Pushing the nominating process beyond the October 1 opening date for the 2018-19 Supreme Court term, Senate Judiciary Committee Chairman Charles Grassley ordered a supplemental hearing on the Kavanaugh nomination, with only Ford and Kavanaugh as witnesses. It would be a contest of "he said, she said," and the partisan lines deepened[41] as outgoing GOP Sen. Jeff Flake brokered a deal between the two sides to delay a Judiciary Committee vote in order for the FBI to conduct yet another investigation of Kavanaugh and the allegations.

With a narrow 11-10 vote to advance Kavanaugh's confirmation out of committee, a 51-49 cloture vote,[42] and a bruising 50-48 Senate vote[43] to confirm Justice Kavanaugh, there was no question the country was divided. But Republicans and conservatives were galvanized by Kavanaugh's ad-libbed opening remarks, where he told the Senate Judiciary Committee: "This confirmation process has become a national disgrace."

"I will not be intimidated by withdrawing from this process. Your coordinated and well-funded effort to destroy my good name and destroy my family will not drive me out," Kavanaugh added defiantly. "You may defeat me in the final vote, but you'll never get me to quit. Ever."[44]

If Kavanaugh's riveting opening statement wasn't enough, Senator Lindsey Graham – previously considered a lightweight RINO by many in the TEA Party,[45] who openly recruited primary opponents when he ran for re-election in 2014 – threw down this shocker:

When you see Sotomayor and Kagan, tell them that Lindsey said hello because I voted for them. I would never do to them what you've done to this guy. This is the most unethical sham since I've been in politics. And if you really wanted to know the truth, you sure as hell wouldn't have done what you've done to this guy.

Are you a gang rapist?

(Kavanaugh: No.)

I cannot imagine what you and your family have gone through.

Boy, you all want power. God, I hope you never get it. I hope the American people can see through this sham. That you knew about it and you held it. You had no intention of protecting Dr. Ford; none.

She's as much of a victim as you are. God, I hate to say it because these have been my friends. But let me tell you, when it comes to this, you're looking for a fair process? You came to the wrong town at the wrong time, my friend.[46]

The Kavanaugh confirmation battle came to a close in early October, and its effects were immediate: what was once a 10-point "enthusiasm gap" between Democrat and Republican voters in July melted away to a statistically-even 2-point swing in the aftermath of the Kavanaugh saga, which ended with the swearing in of the newest Supreme Court Justice moved inside amidst protests outside on the steps of the Supreme Court.[47]

Yet there would be further October surprises on the way to this midterm. On October 22, the first of what would be over a dozen improvised explosive devices was found at the estate of left-wing philanthropist George Soros, with more, addressed to other prominent Democrats including Hillary Clinton and Barack Obama, discovered over that week. All had the return address of former DNC Chair Rep. Debbie Wasserman-Schultz, whose name was misspelled in the return addresses as "Shultz." The misspelling became a prominent clue in identifying the culprit.

Of course, many of those loyal to the TEA Party movement smelled a "false flag" rat, even as some of the mainstream conservative outlets dubbed those skeptics as conspiracy theorists on the order of the disgraced Alex Jones.[48] As just one prominent example, filmmaker (*2016: Obama's America*) and author Dinesh D'Souza Tweeted,

"Fake sexual assault victims. Fake refugees. Now fake mail bombs. We are all learning how the media left are masters of distortion, deflection & deception."[49] This attitude of disbelief became more entrenched when the perpetrator of this clumsy scheme was caught just four days later thanks to a fingerprint match on one of the envelopes,[50] apprehended in an AutoZone parking lot with his van, a vehicle festooned with pro-Trump, anti-media stickers. Cesar Sayoc, a longtime felon once jailed after pleading guilty to a charge of making bomb threats, was the alleged culprit. (He was indicted days after the November election on 30 counts, including using weapons of mass destruction,[51] eventually pleading guilty in March, 2019 to a 65-count accusation.)[52]

But the evidence was just too obvious and Sayoc too much of a patsy for some. Rush Limbaugh, on the afternoon of the arrest:

> This guy's van. Cesar Sayoc's van. He lives in a van down by the river. This van, every window has stickers, decals, bumper stickers! There are so many of 'em, you can't see out these windows. The first reaction I had when I first heard – when I first was told and believed it – that this was the guy's van, my first reaction, "How in the world does a van like that in south Florida not get defaced?"
>
> Do you realize how…? There are a lot of Democrats down in south Florida. There are a lot of people that hate Donald Trump down here. This guy driving that van? That van would have tomatoes all over it and rotten eggs. Swastikas would have been painted on it. Any number of things would have been done to deface this. There is no way that you could hide in that van. There is no way that you could remain obscure, invisible. It's just the exact opposite!
>
> (…)
>
> Very little of it looks faded, meaning it doesn't look like it's been there very long. Certainly, this guy's van is parked outside; he's been driving around in this thing. We have inclement weather here in south Florida. There's been some rain. But it's a hot, baking, wet sun. And even if these stickers are plastered on the insides of the windows, there would be some fading of this stuff.[53]

Needless to say, there were still a lot of skeptical people, even after the arrest was made and Sayoc dubbed the "MAGA bomber." While some relished the chance to say, "told you so,"[54] unfortunately that story was quickly swept off the front pages by a tragic mass shooting the day after Sayoc's capture.

On October 27, a Pittsburgh synagogue[55] became a crime scene – eleven murders quickly blamed on President Trump despite the fact the anti-Semitic assailant, Robert

Bowers, believed Trump was too much influenced by Jews himself. (Among the reasons: Trump's son-in-law Jared Kushner, who also serves as a Trump adviser, is a practicing Jew and his wife Ivanka Trump adopted the faith nearly a decade ago.) Politicizing the event also meant mass protests of Trump's visit a few days later.[56]

Simmering in the background while all this was happening was an event hundreds of miles outside the United States. Eventually nicknamed the "caravasion,"[57] it began as a band of asylum-seekers left Honduras and Guatemala in October. While it was rumored that the migrants were getting enough travel assistance to reach the border in time for an election-eve showdown, the Trump response of Operation Faithful Patriot – sending military troops in to assist the Border Patrol with non-lethal activities such as building tent cities to house those claiming asylum until their cases could be heard and staffing command-and-control facilities[58] – was thought by the Left to be too heavy-handed,[59] even as the caravan refused Mexico's offer of jobs and asylum in order to cross into America.[60] Their charge was that Trump's reaction was a political stunt in order to drive up voter turnout among border hawks.

All this, then, served as a lead-in to the final balloting on November 6. But a quick electoral review may be in order.

In 2010, the first national election governed by the TEA Party, voters were stoked by anger on the Republican side and they allowed a massive 63-seat swing in the House. This was countered in 2012 by a cooling of interest from TEA Party members, who had to be begged and cajoled to turn out to support GOP nominee Mitt Romney.

In 2014, the TEA Party's second midterm, voter participation slacked even further despite the fact Republicans finally won back the Senate, albeit with a more "establishment" group of candidates than the TEA Party may have liked. But they resurrected themselves by enough of an extent to shock the political world and lift Donald Trump to an Electoral College victory over the heavily favored Hillary Clinton.

In electoral terms, that 2016 election may have been the zenith and last hurrah of the TEA Party. Anger was again a key motivator in 2018, and it was anger toward a President once again. But turnout in the 2018 midterm smashed records dating back to 1966, a midterm where Democrats lost a significant part of their staggering House and Senate majorities but still prevailed to lead for another 14 years in the Senate (until Reagan's election in 1980) and 14 more House terms, until the 1994 Gingrich revolution.

In 2018, much of what the TEA Party gained in 2010 was lost by the Republican Party that adopted them: 40 seats and the majority in the House, over 300 state legislative seats, governorships in Kansas, Maine, Michigan, New Mexico, and (most importantly, based on his prominence in the movement) Scott Walker's defeat in Wisconsin as he sought a third term. In essence, this "blue wave" wasn't quite as successful on a federal level as many predicted, but it may have finally eroded away the base of local support the TEA Party could always provide.

The 2018 midterms also showed to just what lengths the Democrats would go in pursuing electoral success, as Georgia's Stacey Abrams refused to concede her governor's race and claimed her opponent, Secretary of State Brian Kemp, suppressed thousands of votes, making his victory illegitimate. "If Stacey Abrams doesn't win in Georgia, they stole it. I say that publicly, it's clear," said Ohio Senator Sherrod Brown.[61]

But the Abrams race was a sideshow compared to the saga in Florida, where three separate statewide races ended on election night with razor-thin margins for Republicans in the lead: Ron DeSantis for Governor over the aforementioned Bernie Sanders disciple Andrew Gillum, outgoing Governor Rick Scott over incumbent Senator Bill Nelson, and Matt Caldwell in the lead for Agriculture Commissioner over Democrat Nikki Fried. However, two counties were having issues reporting their final results, and (of course) they were the Democrat stronghold counties Broward and Palm Beach. Palm Beach County admitted they could not complete a machine recount of three separate races in time to overturn their November 6 results,[62] but Broward County defiantly demanded more time to do its recounts and found a judge[63] to allow them to do so. If they were looking to steal an election for Gillum and Nelson, though, the increasing amount of public scrutiny as time passed from Election Day was making it impossible.

So while DeSantis and Scott were finally declared winners a week and a half later, the election night lead for Caldwell disappeared in Broward County, leaving Fried as the only Democrat to flip the initial results.[64]

But Florida wasn't the only place where Democrats found more votes after the election was ostensibly over. A loss of House seats that looked as if it would fall in the mid-30s on election night for the GOP stretched to the forty mark as absentee, provisional, and mail-in ballots were collected and counted – California was particularly brutal in this regard as three seats originally thought to be GOP holds flipped once the stragglers were counted;[65] meanwhile, even in deep red Utah Republican Rep. Mia Love eventually lost a lead she had held with 96% of the vote in to her Democrat challenger.[66] (Other similar flips were recorded in New Jersey and New Mexico.)[67] At that point, the trend was obvious: "Nine of the previous 10 House races that had been called by The Associated Press flipped to the Democrats after Gil Cisneros defeated Republican Young Kim in California's 39th District," wrote Griffin Connolly at *Roll Call*. There are two stated reasons for the anomaly in

California: one is that absentee, provisional, and mail-in ballots are counted in the order in which they were received, and the other is a change in the law allowing anyone (rather than the voter or a family member) to drop off absentee ballots. The latter practice drew Republican charges of "ballot harvesting,"[68] and frankly it was suspicious because Democrats would have known the margin to overcome on election night.

On the other hand no Republican overcame a similar deficit to win a race, and as noted earlier the NC-9 where the Republican led on election night was not certified due to questions on absentee ballots. A similar 1984 controversy was decided on a nearly party-line vote[69] in the House of Representatives, which has the final say and switched to Democratic control after the 2018 midterms. In this case, the seat remains vacant pending the 2019 special election.

Another factor in the midterms made 2020 prospects even worse for Trump: a number of key states he won in 2016 now have Democrat control in two key offices: governor and Secretary of State. The latter office is important because that person generally serves as the chief election officer.[70] Michigan, Pennsylvania, and Wisconsin fall into that category, although Trump won Pennsylvania in 2016 despite that handicap. Arizona, another state Trump won, kept their GOP governor but elected a Democrat as Secretary of State and flipped a Senate seat as part of a Democrat trend in that border state. Losing two or three of those four states could spell defeat for Trump.

We obviously can't know at this writing who Donald Trump's Democrat opponent will be next year, particularly as over a dozen serious candidates were already in the race when I finished this book, but we can look back at the TEA Party experience in 2012. Will the Democrats overplay their hand once again as they did in governor's races in Florida, Georgia and Maryland and nominate a candidate suitable only for the progressives? There was none of that fear among analysts in the immediate wake of the election, but once Democrats began entering the 2020 Presidential race, some began to ponder this possibility.[71] On the flip side, it can also be asked whether the Democrats will repeat their 2016 campaign and nominate someone who doesn't appeal to the far left? That would be akin to the difficulty the TEA Party leadership had in getting their rank-and-file excited about voting for Mitt Romney as opposed to just casting a ballot against Barack Obama.

One thing buoying the hopes of the TEA Party opposition is demographics, as the Left often crows about its dominance with voters under 35.[72] Voters under 30 went Democrat by a 67%-32% margin in the 2018 midterms, and while youth aren't the best of voters they will come out for the right candidate – the previous best for Democrats in that demographic was the initial Obama election in 2008. Eventually, though, youth has to be served: just as many of us on the back side of middle-aged fondly recall the Reagan years, today's youth will gain a nostalgia about Obama as the first black President, a guy who was considered "hip" and "cool" by those celebrities who matter and who hate Donald Trump.

After all, while the seasoned citizens who made up a significant percentage of the TEA Party were the best voters, their numbers were long ago eclipsed by younger generations of voters and in the 2018 midterms enough of those meddling kids were motivated to push the TEA Party aside for one final time. Given the fact that Congress will be split between the parties and President Trump has re-election on his mind, it's doubtful the frenetic pace of reform he attempted in his first two years will be maintained; moreover, the guy who wrote *The Art of the Deal* will now have different adversaries with different agendas and goals to fulfill that may whet other parts of his populist appetite.

It was a nearly decade-long run. Behold, then, the rise and fall of the TEA Party.

Yet the movement still has a lot of unfinished business requiring our attention. In my epilogue I answer the question: what's next on the agenda?

# EPILOGUE: SO WHAT COMES NEXT?

*"Give me four years to teach the children and the seed I have sown will never be uprooted."* - quote attributed to Vladimir Lenin (1870-1924).

As I reach the end of this book, it's the judgment of this author that the rise and fall of the TEA Party coincided with the amount of influence the mainstream political parties had on it. A significant part of its initial appeal was the fact the TEA Party was at first issue-based and not wed to a particular political party. Rick Santelli did not go out and rant that he was hosting a TEA Party that summer and planning to allow the Republican Party to infiltrate his gathering that fall, but as time went along that's what happened. As political party influence grew, the fortunes of the TEA Party sank because it became perceived as just another special interest group.

At heart, it was supposed to be a grassroots effort. As an exercise while researching this book, I asked early TEA Party leaders what the movement did wrong (and right.) Perhaps the most poignant answer came from a man who fell from grace in the movement, Mark Williams:

> Inasmuch as it was never a thing, like as in an actual party, group, or even gospel, I'm not sure how to answer (this question) except to point out that it sprung organically among Americans who used people like me – without entirely trusting us, thank God – yet understanding that something was happening. I am a HUGE fan of the Buffalo Springfield song (*For What It's Worth*) to this day and still listen, and relate to the words – I lived them. The "Tea Party" was America working as she was designed to work. Our official apparatus had wandered far, far beyond their Constitutional prison and citizens responded, *en masse* and peacefully. Even in the face of physical attacks, these people still believed and took a stand.
>
> I think that we did it ALL Right (in every sense of the word) and absolutely nothing wrong. We just did and made whatever sacrifices that Americans have to do every couple of generations.[1]

Speaking of generational sacrifices, consider the original Tea Party: the one which occurred in Boston on December 16, 1773. Armchair historians tend to agree that the incident was an "act of American colonial defiance,"[2] the start of the "violent part of the Revolution,"[3] and a "defining event in American history."[4] Foreshadowing the more recent version, it even had its own huckster:

> Samuel Adams, who was a professional agitator, probably did not actually plan or aid the effort to dump the tea, but he immediately saw the propaganda value of the protest, and began working to publicize and defend this act of political protest. Adams argued that the Tea Party was not the act of a crazed mob, but arose out as the only response available to the colonists who were defending their reasonable principles and that they took this action as only remaining option the people had to defend their constitutional rights.[5]

The original Tea Party was a shot across the bow to the Crown, setting forth a chain of events on both sides of the Atlantic that would lead to war barely sixteen months later and our eventual declaration of independence before three years had passed.

At first, the TEA Party (vintage 2009) was indeed wed to a greater understanding of the Constitution and the benefits of limited government, as well as an opportunity for citizens to speak out. As Eric Eisenhammer, another Sacramento TEA Party leader, told me, "I think the grassroots nature of the Tea Party movement, where anybody could be a leader, was… a strength in that it empowered citizens to fight for their rights and make a difference."[6] There was a significant helping of libertarian influence which may have strangled the TEA Party in the crib as a political movement had they continued in that direction given the America we currently live in, but this was only because they were missing a key element – one I will get to momentarily.

As the TEA Party grew, however, it attracted a segment of the electorate that advocated for items directly contradictory to the movement's original stated mission. Limiting government was fine – but only on these newcomers' terms. I spent an earlier chapter discussing these incidents of hypocrisy, so I'll not rehash them here – suffice to say that the TEA Party got itself distracted and spread too thin, chasing its tail too often on the political processes it didn't understand enough of and ignoring the hard work of building on its coalition. Remember, polling never showed it gaining acceptance of more than about 1/3 of the population.

The political process that it never really cared for was what consumed the modern TEA Party in the end. My best attempt at an analogy to the 1773 version would be to imagine how things would have turned out if George Washington, John Adams, Thomas Jefferson, *et. al.* had somehow turned the political system in such a way that they went to serve in the House of Commons. While all were men of character, the big "what-if" question is what if they had been co-opted by the power and prestige they gained while in Parliament and not among the colonists? Would America have missed its opportunity, turning out to be more of a basket case like other former British colonies?

So if you consider the Boston Tea Party (1773 version) as Tea Party 1.0 and its 2009 revival as version 2.0, the TEA Party 3.0 beta starting today has to be thought of as a multi-generational process. Lesson one is to understand that the American political system is, by its nature, full of inertia.

First case in point: in the federal system, it normally either takes a 3/5 majority of a legislative body or a special set of rules to get anything done, and since the occasions are rare where one political party or another has that 3/5 degree of control any change is either going to involve some level of compromise or be, at least at first, temporary by nature.

In the next instance it should always be remembered that, in the eyes of the bureaucrat, to solve a problem is to put himself out of a job. If someone announced a cure for cancer tomorrow, surely the naysayers would come out and call the bearer of the news crazy – but we would likely find those naysayers are all the doctors, clinicians, and pharmaceutical companies which were immediately placed at risk of losing all of their lucrative treatments in favor of a simpler (and likely cheaper) solution.

I also like the description penned by Dick Armey and Matt Kibbe – back when they were on speaking terms:

> Whereas individuals in the real world have to live with the consequences of their decisions (unless they get a bailout), government does not because it can always get more money from the taxpayer. The only check on its growth is the ire of the citizenry. Government is also staffed by people who do not worry; they have the ultimate in job security. When a government program fails, the advocates of big government inevitably claim it failed because it was underfunded, not because it was a bad program.[7]

Two other points to keep in mind: the power to tax is the power to destroy and absolute power corrupts absolutely. Consider how much effort is spent lobbying Congress and IRS bureaucrats to adjust the tax code to benefit or penalize certain interests: for one example, Americans have millions of dollars redistributed to those who buy electric cars. Before GM got out of the production of both of these cars in 2018-19, the electric-hybrid Chevy Volt could easily cost twice as much as the conventionally-powered car which shared its chassis platform, the Chevy Cruze. So in order to entice buyers, the Volt had the sweetener of a $7,500 tax credit attached to it – a tax credit the rest of us who preferred a good old-fashioned gasoline-powered car like the Cruze paid for. Imagine the vast number of carveouts, exceptions, and interpretations that someone in power – elected or unelected – can hand out, and it's no wonder that our bloated government attracts rent-seekers like ticks latch onto dogs.

Once the politicians elected by the TEA Party came into power, we were often disappointed to find they weren't a whole lot different than the people they replaced:

> (W)e fell into what I call the "Benevolent Despot" trap. If we just elected the right people to public office, they would do the right thing regardless of the political consequences. We have all slipped into this way of thinking, waiting for the perfect leader to take charge and drive the right reforms of big government from the top down.[8]

This, in a nutshell, is why people often believe there's not a dime's worth of difference between the two dominant political parties. We elect and eject different people every few years but get the same old results. Haven't they told us that's the definition of insanity? I know it's driven me to the brink.

So in order for TEA Party 3.0 to succeed – and it would be a tall order, indeed – it has to transcend politics. I believe its focus has to be on a generation that won't be able to vote for several years. Proverbs 22:6 says it well: "Train up a child in the way he should go: and when he is old, he will not depart from it."[9] It will take the honesty of a George Washington, the moral fiber to resist the temptation absolute power would bring, and the self-sacrifice and altruism to consider that the generations before had become accustomed to the plethora of extra-Constitutional entitlements in place and would be allowed to receive benefits their peers might not as that system is phased out.

Children need to learn that what the Constitution really means, and that our political system has gone well beyond that which was intended. A piece by W. James Antle III, written in the wake of the defeat of the Obamacare repeal, illustrates the point well:

> In practice, the American people want a much bigger federal government than the Constitution currently authorizes.
>
> Not long ago, a conservative wag quipped that if a president actually tried to enforce the Constitution's limits on federal power, he or she would be impeached.
>
> But even if Republicans find a way to give Obamacare a haircut, part of a new "skinny" welfare state, it will more closely resemble past free-market corrections of liberalism's excesses than a serious constitutional conservative challenge to

liberalism.

> That doesn't bode well for the Tea Party project of rolling back major liberal initiatives. The point of voting Republican will remain to make the inexorable growth of the welfare state as slow and painful as possible, a political posture that may be attractive to neither libertarian-leaning conservatives nor the populists drawn to Trump in the last presidential election.[10]

Because of the prevailing attitude of the American people, there has to be an understanding that change like the TEA Party desired isn't going to be political in nature at first – or maybe at all – but instead has to start out as educational, cultural, and spiritual. If you take the philosophy that "politics is downstream of culture" to heart, then the idea has to be that of changing the culture to suit the politics desired, and the best place to start in that process is with enlightening the young.

While the group that undertakes this may or may not be known as a TEA Party, the first issue those who care about America should work on is school choice. In order to be able to teach children properly, it may be necessary to take things into one's own hands – yet too many places have a stranglehold on the children by virtue of a subpar public educational system that fails to teach children the benefits of freedom, liberty, and limited Constitutional government. Moreover, there's a lack of opportunity for parents to teach them properly due to economics or state laws that work too much in favor of a single public educational system. After the obvious first step of removing federal influence on education by eliminating the Department of Education and restoring its power to the states closer to where it belongs, we can further break that chain by lobbying the several states to allow educational money to follow the child regardless of whichever public or private option parents demand – including homeschooling. Once that precedent is set, other chains may be worked off as well.

Hand-in-hand with that is the hard work of restoring traditional American mores and standards. Being born in 1964, some people would consider me a Baby Boomer and others would peg me as part of Generation X, which is my preference. In either case, though, our time as the direct drivers of culture is pretty much spent – the key demographic that advertisers and popular culture now shoot for is closely bracketed (here in 2019) by the two children I've helped to raise – one turned 35 last fall and the other just celebrated her 19th birthday in January. There are troubling signs that it will be a generation that's leaning to be far more socialist[11] than any other prior one, and we in the Baby Boom and Generation X have ourselves to blame because those of us who believe in American ideals and Constitutional government didn't take the time and effort to train the Millennials in the way they should go.

As an example of how we need to address culture, I finished the initial draft of this epilogue days after the 2018 presentation of the Grammy Awards took place. The seminal event of that telecast wasn't a showstopping performance by a famous musician, but was instead Hillary Clinton reading excerpts from a book bashing Donald Trump.[12] President Trump was also the basis of criticism for his stance on immigration and alleged racism; in return, the 2018 Grammy show plummeted to its lowest ratings on record for the 18-to-49 demographic.[13] The slide has been reflected in other Hollywood award shows that have aired over the past several seasons.

On the surface that may appear to be a good sign, but given some of the other cultural rot Americans seem to partake in these days, that ratings decline simply means we're not into Tinseltown navel-gazing. This isn't to say that all of us should be whatever slang word is now the proper term for being less than socially acceptable to the youth, but why not seek out and consume entertainment that promotes traditional values, liberty, and portrays our nation in a positive light as a beacon of freedom for the world? Surely there are entertainers out there who do this, so it's up to my readers to find them. The larger of a market created, the better chance that people will wish to get in on it.

*RedState* commentator Kira Davis explained this point:

> While we've been raising politicians and policy wonks, the left has been raising programmers and technology geeks. Now those people own the very technology that has changed our society the most, and we are just depending on their good will to be allowed to speak on those platforms.
>
> (…)
>
> If we want to preserve the avenues for conservative voices to reach the mainstream then we have to be more proactive in filling those jobs that serve the mainstream. It is great to encourage your children to be independent thinkers who share conservative values, but don't get stuck there.[14]

Finally, I devoted an entire chapter to the idea of God and man in the TEA Party because it was such a divisive topic in the last rendition. Remember, TEA Party 2.0 was initially led by those who tried at first to keep social issues out of it. But once that cat was out of the bag, libertarians eventually left when they felt the TEA Party was being taken over by those who wished to steer the movement into social issues.

Yet America was founded in the afterglow of the Great Awakening and shortly after its birth enjoyed the Second Great Awakening – both periods of significant religious revival. It's been close to a century since the last major religious revival in America, although there was an uptick in spiritual growth in the 1970s that led to the formation of the Moral Majority and a number of similar groups. One possible reason for this lengthy absence: politics from the pulpit is discouraged by the threat of the IRS withdrawing tax-exempt status from churches if they delve into politics thanks to the Johnson Amendment (named after President Lyndon Johnson, who sponsored this prohibition in 1954 as a member of Congress.) The Johnson Amendment is a favorite whipping boy of conservative politicians, but the last great opportunity to repeal it came and went when the Tax Cuts and Jobs Act passed in 2017 – a late draft of the bill repealed Johnson, but the final bill struck the repeal and preserved it.[15]

Even with the Johnson Amendment in place, though, there's no prohibition on preaching to matters of culture or praying for revival: among many others, the Reverend Billy Graham knew this:

> My heart aches for America and its deceived people. The wonderful news is that our Lord is a God of mercy, and He responds to repentance. In Jonah's day, Nineveh was the lone world superpower – wealthy, unconcerned, and self-centered. When the Prophet Jonah finally traveled to Nineveh and proclaimed God's warning, people heard and repented.
>
> I believe the same thing can happen once again, this time in our nation.[16]

I will confide in you that it's also my earnest prayer this nation enjoys a revival.

I believe in my heart those are the key steps to accomplishing in TEA Party version 3.0 what we tried and failed to do in the second go-round, for reasons I've written close to 100,000 words spelling out.

My literary journey through the TEA Party is coming to a close, but the time is now to begin planning out the next one – the one which, Good Lord willing, Americans both now and into future generations will make into a success. To my newfound reader friends: I thank you for sticking with me to the end of this book to learn the lessons of a political movement begun with the best of intentions. Like I said at the end of my introduction, may it be only a short time before the TEA Party rises from the ashes of history because we need it more than ever.

# ENDNOTES

## INTRODUCTION

1 http://www.freedomworks.org/content/taxpayer-march-washington-scheduled-september-12-2009

2 http://michellemalkin.com/2009/09/12/celebrating-the-912-rallies/

3 http://talkingpointsmemo.com/dc/freedomworks-cuts-estimate-for-crowd-at-its-9-12-rally-by-one-half

4 http://abcnews.go.com/Politics/tea-party-protesters-march-washington/story?id=8557120

5 http://articles.baltimoresun.com/1991-02-17/news/1991048114_1_eastern-shore-william-donald-schaefer-governor

6 http://monoblogue.us/2009/04/15/pictures-from-salisburys-tea-party/

7 http://monoblogue.us/2009/02/19/the-next-guy-on-the-unemployment-line/

8 http://monoblogue.us/2009/03/02/steele-vs-limbaugh/

9 http://monoblogue.us/2009/03/07/quirky-but-appropriate/

10 http://monoblogue.us/2009/04/08/a-retro-protest/

11 http://www.npr.org/templates/story/story.php?storyId=103901536

12 http://abcnews.go.com/Politics/donald-trump-walks-back-tax-plan-negotiated/story?id=38959168

13 http://www.businessinsider.com/donald-trumps-tax-plan-i-win-2015-9

14 http://www.wsj.com/articles/donald-trump-says-his-past-politics-were-transactional-1438213199

15 http://abcnews.go.com/Politics/donald-trump-hell-protect-constitutions-article-xii/story?id=40422352

16 http://www.mediaite.com/tv/donald-trump-rails-against-cutting-social-security-medicare-during-gop-summit/

17 https://www.indivisibleguide.com/guide/

18 http://www.latimes.com/local/lanow/la-me-ln-berkeley-protests-20170827-story.html

19 http://www.teapartytribune.com/2016/01/30/the-tea-party-then-and-now/

20 http://www.nationalreview.com/corner/429994/trump-april-15-2009-i-dont-march-tea-party

# ORIGINS AND INFLUENCES

1 http://www.newsbusters.org/blogs/nb/tom-blumer/2009/02/19/rant-ages-cnbcs-rick-santelli-goes-studio-hosts-invoke-mob-rule

2 http://transcripts.cnn.com/TRANSCRIPTS/0812/16/ldt.01.html

3 To be exact, Clinton noted, "(T)he current administration (of George H.W. Bush) has compiled the worst economic record in 50 years." http://www.ibiblio.org/nii/econ-posit.html

4 Dick Armey and Matt Kibbe, *Give Us Liberty: A Tea Party Manifesto* (New York: William Morrow, 2010) p. 5. "We made life difficult for the establishment old bulls in the party because we thought they were too complacent. The Republican leadership was always having to apologize to the Democrats for us."

5 http://economix.blogs.nytimes.com/2008/12/01/december-2007-the-date-the-recession-officially-began/

6 http://usatoday30.usatoday.com/money/perfi/taxes/2008-04-25-tax-rebate-checks_N.htm

7 http://www.nber.org/digest/mar09/w14753.html

8 https://www.cbo.gov/publication/43662

9 Armey and Kibbe, p. 62-63.

10 http://www.inquisitr.com/14704/obama-speech-january-8-2009-video-transcript/

11 *Ibid.*

12 *Ibid.*

13 https://www.gpo.gov/fdsys/pkg/PLAW-111publ5/html/PLAW-111publ5.htm

14 http://www.huffingtonpost.com/2011/12/28/ron-paul-voting-record_n_1173255.html

15 http://clerk.house.gov/evs/2004/roll304.xml

16 https://web.archive.org/web/20160828234249/http://www.ronpaul.com/on-the-issues/civil-rights-act/

17 http://www.4president.org/speeches/2008/ronpaul2008announcement.htm

18 http://thecaucus.blogs.nytimes.com/2007/11/05/paul-supporters-raise-27-in-a-day/

19 https://www.nolanchart.com/article460-ron-pauls-tea-party-html

20 http://www.politico.com/story/2007/12/ron-paul-becomes-6-million-man-007421

21 https://web.archive.org/web/20090418190507/http://www.ronpaul.com/2009-04-15/nationwide-tax-protests-party-like-its-2007/

22 Joan Fabiano, a Michigan-based leader of the TEA Party, recalled it differently: "The whole thing started on Twitter," she said. While Libertarians "had events called Tea Parties," the credit should go to the TCOT group, which will be explained further as I go on. Notes from telephone conversation with Joan Fabiano, February 25, 2018.

23 http://memory.loc.gov/cgi-bin/ampage?collId=lljc&fileName=002/lljc002.db&recNum=154&itemLink=r?ammem/hlaw:@field(DOCID+@lit(jc00254))%230020155&linkText=1

24 https://oll.libertyfund.org/titles/adams-revolutionary-writings#lfAdams_label_023

25 https://www.loc.gov/resource/rbpe.34604500/

26 http://founders.archives.gov/?q=stamp%20act%20franklin&s=1511311111&r=176

27 http://press-pubs.uchicago.edu/founders/documents/v1ch14s10.html

28 https://docs.google.com/document/d/1hThywy7Gmfpxj4ypwZeU4M5GZzcn1nW4Dpk285lBaFw/edit

29 The text of the Articles can be found here. Notice that, while many of the aspects of this government would be maintained in the Constitution to come, one significant difference is the lack of separation of powers.

https://www.ourdocuments.gov/print_friendly.php?flash=false&page=transcript&doc=3&title=Transcript+of+Articles+of+Confederation+%281777%29

30 Rep. Paul testified that, "the special privileges granted to Fannie and Freddie have distorted the housing market by allowing them to attract capital they could not attract under pure market conditions. As a result, capital is diverted from its most productive use into housing. This reduces the efficacy of the entire market and thus reduces the standard of living of all Americans." https://www.lewrockwell.com/1970/01/ron-paul/fannie-and-freddie/

31 https://mises.org/library/mises-and-austrian-economics-personal-view

32 A reasonable summary of the argument can be found at https://mises.org/library/economics-taxation.

33 Even worse, it's a quarterly toll for many in the entrepreneurial class.

34 https://fee.org/articles/supply-side-economics-and-austrian-economics/

35 One of my favorite literary works because it rings very true. If you have not read it, *Atlas Shrugged* should be the next book you buy (assuming you bought this book, of course.)

36 Michael Patrick Leahy: *Covenant of Liberty: The Ideological Origins of the Tea Party Movement* (New York: Broadside Books, 2012) p. 217.

## TRULY ORGANIZING FOR AMERICA

1 The story of Rakovich is told from a FreedomWorks point of view in the Dick Armey and Matt Kibbe book, *Give Us Liberty: A Tea Party Manifesto* (New York: William Morrow, 2010)

2 https://web.archive.org/web/20120505223349/http://redistributingknowledge.blogspot.com/2009/01/conservatives-coming-out-of-closet-so.html

3 http://redistributingknowledge.blogspot.com/2009/02/day-is-here-protesterama.html Since my original research in 2017, this page has been taken private and is not archived.

4 https://www.realclearpolitics.com/articles/2011/11/11/rise_of_the_tea_party_112035.html

5 Sending tea bags wasn't an original or new idea. It has been recycled from time to

time – here's an example from 1989. http://articles.sun-sentinel.com/1989-02-08/news/8901080135_1_tea-bags-roy-fox-lee-fowler

6 http://content.time.com/time/specials/packages/article/0,28804,2096654_2096653_2096665,00.html

7 http://independentpoliticalreport.com/2009/01/boston-tea-party-calls-for-bailout-tea-party/

8 https://www.theguardian.com/world/2010/oct/05/us-midterm-elections-2010-tea-party-movement

9 Reporter and author David Brody also notes financial expert Dave Ramsey "proclaimed, 'It's time for a Tea Party" in Brody's book *Teavangelicals,* cited elsewhere in this volume.

10 http://michellemalkin.com/2009/02/09/stop-the-stimulus-protest-in-ft-myers-fl-tomorrow/

11 http://readmylipsticknetwork.blogspot.com/2009/02/stimulus-protest-tomorrow-fort-myers-fl.html

12 http://michellemalkin.com/2009/02/16/from-the-boston-tea-party-to-your-neighborhood-pork-protest/

13 http://michellemalkin.com/2009/02/17/yes-we-care-porkulus-protesters-holler-back/

14 http://archive.azcentral.com/community/mesa/articles/2009/02/18/20090218prez-protest0218.html

15 http://michellemalkin.com/2009/02/19/gimme-gimme-gimme-more-scenes-from-the-anti-obama-backlash/ Malkin had a little snark as well: noting Santelli's remarks (as a "CNBC host") calling for a tea party for the first time, she pithily added "We've been doing it all week."

16 http://www.huffingtonpost.com/alex-brantzawadzki/a-time-for-tea-a-tea-part_b_538963.html As you can see in subsequent notes, though, the timeline is inaccurate on a few items. I love the first line of the story, though: "It would take a book or three to provide a comprehensive documentation of every aspect of the origins of the Tea Party movement." Here you go.

17 Not only did the Illinois Libertarian Party chair at the time, Dave Brady, claim "in December of 2008 the LP Illinois formulated the Boston Tea Party Chicago concept...Santelli got wind of this and went public on the floor of the Chicago Stock (*sic*) Exchange" (see http://independentpoliticalreport.com/2009/04/libertarian-party-of-illinois-we-

gave-rick-santelli-the-idea-for-the-tax-day-tea-parties/) but a WHOIS search of the Chicagoteaparty.com domain confirms it was created in August, 2008.

18 http://michaelpatrickleahy.blogspot.com/2009/02/tcot-and-online-conservatives-launch.html I slightly edited this from the original.

19 http://web.archive.org/web/20090226220005/ http://www.nationwidechicagoteaparty.com/ According to the domain's WHOIS information, it expired in February, 2017.

20 Archived at http://web.archive.org/web/20090223100929/http://www.taxpayer teaparty.com/. Americans for Prosperity was linked at the bottom of the page, which opens by shouting “Rick Santelli was dead right!”

21 https://www.theguardian.com/world/2009/sep/18/republicans-internet-barack-obama

22 http://michellemalkin.com/2009/02/26/lets-get-this-tea-party-started/

23 Mark Meckler and Jenny Beth Martin: *Tea Party Patriots: The Second American Revolution* (New York: Henry Holt and Company, 2012) p. 9.

24 Notes from telephone conversation with Gary Aminoff. January 28, 2018.

25 https://janeqrepublican.wordpress.com/2009/02/27/asheville-area-tea-party-a-rainy-day-success/

26 Notes from telephone conversation with Joan Fabiano, February 25, 2018.

27 Social media conversation with Eric Eisenhammer, January 28, 2018.

28 I found a number of “Chicago Tea Party” videos with a simple Bing search of “tea party february 27 2009” under the “Videos” tab. They made for an interesting day of watching.

29 http://www.cbsnews.com/news/obama-unveils-75b-mortgage-relief-plan/

30 http://www.cbsnews.com/news/obama-signs-stimulus-plan-into-law/

31 Meckler and Martin, p. 5.

32 Paraphrased from Michael Patrick Leahy: *Covenant of Liberty: The Ideological Origins of the Tea Party Movement* (New York: Broadside Books, 2012) p. 233.

33 https://youtu.be/BgkZoDFmAFw

34 https://youtu.be/Lk-dksW1RKY

35 http://apackof2-theworldaccordingtome.blogspot.com/2009/02/over-300-at-lansing-mi-tea-party.html As I spoke with Fabiano, I learned about her blogsite. She has photos of the Lansing rally, although the site hasn't been updated since 2012.

36 Meckler and Martin, p. 19-20.

37 https://youtu.be/1vKr95e5aIE

38 Leahy, p. 229.

39 https://scrosnoe.wordpress.com/2009/04/10/grassroots-teaparty-efforts-and-you/

40 *Ibid.*

41 https://youtu.be/jvalWg2F7d8?t=2m9s

42 https://web.archive.org/web/20090418190507/http://www.ronpaul.com/2009-04-15/nationwide-tax-protests-party-like-its-2007/ The original Tate statement was not available on the Campaign for Liberty site.

43 http://www.nytimes.com/2009/04/16/us/politics/16taxday.html

44 https://youtu.be/4Wc4kQM3L24 – Greensburg, Pennsylvania.

45 https://youtu.be/DibuXZ86pfM – Montecello, Arkansas.

46 https://youtu.be/8M6pjl11WbQ – Millersburg, Ohio. All three videos have background music and everything.

47 Just like the February 27 iteration, a Bing video search of “tax day tea party april 15 2009” unlocked a host of videos from gatherings big and small. And I'm sure this only scratches the surface.

48 http://monoblogue.us/2009/04/15/pictures-from-salisburys-tea-party/

49 https://youtu.be/3CxS1MpB8fU?t=1m55s

50 https://web.archive.org/web/20090412113406/http://www.atlantateaparty.net/2009/03/sean-hannity-to-broadcast-live-from.html

51 https://youtu.be/-t_rCdR5Ti4?t=2m27s

52 Theda Skocpol and Vanessa Williamson: *The Tea Party and the Remaking of Republican Conservatism* (Oxford: Oxford University Press, 2011) p. 136-137.

53 https://thedanashow.wordpress.com/2009/04/17/retrospect/

54 http://www.newsbusters.org/blogs/nb/brent-baker/2009/04/16/abc-cbs-and-nbc-try-discredit-tea-party-protests

55 https://obamawhitehouse.archives.gov/video/Real-Tax-Cuts-Making-a-Real-Difference This is the video, as the original statement was archived in 2017 after I began this chapter.

56 https://obamawhitehouse.archives.gov/the-press-office/briefing-white-house-press-secretary-robert-gibbs-41509

57 https://obamawhitehouse.archives.gov/video/Town-Hall-in-Arnold-Missouri#transcript

58 https://web.archive.org/web/20090520231158/ http://www.nationwidechicagoteaparty.com/May1President.pdf

59 http://www.prwatch.org/spin/2009/04/8334/freedomworks-behind-tax-day-tea-party-protests

60 https://thinkprogress.org/spontaneous-uprising-corporate-lobbyists-helping-to-orchestrate-radical-anti-obama-tea-party-dabd014bbfb#.ekcu06ppq

61 https://janeqrepublican.wordpress.com/2009/04/16/asheville-tax-day-tea-party-amazing-success/

62 https://thedanashow.wordpress.com/2009/03/03/i-wish-i-were-funded-by-billionaires/

63 http://mediamatters.org/research/2009/04/08/report-fair-and-balanced-fox-news-aggressively/149009

64 http://www.urbandictionary.com/define.php?term=teabagging

65 http://www.huffingtonpost.com/2009/04/09/rachel-maddow-ana-marie-c_n_185445.html

66 Unfortunately, my website's archiving of photos doesn't extend to this post.

67 https://capitalresearch.org/article/the-tea-party-movement-leftist-attacks-fail-to-stop-its-growing-influence/

68 http://www.freedomworks.org/content/taxpayer-march-washington-scheduled-september-12-2009

69 https://web.archive.org/web/20180309055128/http://www. teapartyfortlauderdale .com/ After the death of its founder, they dropped the TEA Party moniker but planned to continue the weekly meetings.

70 E-mail exchange with Ralph Reagan, January 1, 2018.

# UPRISING: A CALL FOR LEADERSHIP

1 http://hennessysview.com/2014/02/20/5-years-ago-today-tea-party-born-phone-call/

2 https://web.archive.org/web/20181106214214/http://www.michaelpatrickleahy.com/teapartyfounders.html

3 *Ibid.*

4 http://michaelpatrickleahy.blogspot.com/2009/02/tcot-and-online-conservatives-launch.html

5 http://web.archive.org/web/20090225023816/http://www.topconservativesontwitter.org/ Archived page from February 25, 2009.

6 http://web.archive.org/web/20090226031827/http://www.tcotreport.com/ Archived page from February 26, 2009.

7 http://www.newsbusters.org/blogs/nb/jeff-poor/2010/02/08/how-conservatives-found-twitter-and-evolution-tcot-according-tea-party

8 https://www.cnet.com/news/barack-obama-dominates-twitter/

9 http://www.nytimes.com/2008/11/10/business/media/10carr.html

10 Michael Patrick Leahy: *Covenant of Liberty: The Ideological Origins of the Tea Party Movement* (New York: Broadside Books, 2012) p. 4-5.

11 The "official" #dontgo account made its last Tweet March 4, 2009. https://twitter.com/dontgomovement

12 http://www.nytimes.com/2010/02/19/us/19cncodom.html

13 https://web.archive.org/web/20180426053354/https://ericodom.com/ The article in question was from December, 2017 and buried on the archived front page.

14 http://www.redstate.com/erick/2010/08/24/charlatans-and-the-horse-they-rode-in-on/

15 Melissa Deckman, *Tea Party Women: Mama Grizzlies, Grassroots Leaders, and the Changing Face of the American Right* (New York: New York University Press,

2016) p. 57.

16 http://www.pr.com/press-release/139912

17 http://jeffrey-feldman.typepad.com/frameshop/2009/02/tea-party-republicans.html

18 http://www.nytimes.com/2009/04/13/opinion/13krugman.html

19 Theda Skocpol and Vanessa Williamson: *The Tea Party and the Remaking of Republican Conservatism* (Oxford: Oxford University Press, 2011) p. 9.

20 Leahy, p. 235.

21 http://www.wsj.com/news/articles/SB10001424052702304173704575578332725182228

22 http://www.nationwidechicagoteaparty.com/ was still available when I accessed it September 17. 2017; however, by May, 2018 the site was gone.

23 Mark Meckler and Jenny Beth Martin: *Tea Party Patriots: The Second American Revolution* (New York: Henry Holt and Company, 2012) p. 18.

24 http://www.thelibertypapers.org/2009/04/09/telling-tea-party-truth/

25 http://www.ipwatchdog.com/2010/11/08/trademark-collective-marks-trademarking-the-tea-party/id=13187/

26 https://www2.gwu.edu/~action/2008/interestg08/stopobamatour.html

27 It was once at this address: https://www.youtube.com/watch?v=bBoJDXW-ly0 Since I began this book, it's been removed.

28 Social media conversation with Mark Williams, January 26, 2018. I lightly edited this for clarity.

29 http://www.politico.com/story/2010/04/gop-operatives-crash-the-tea-party-035785

30 https://web.archive.org/web/20100417015142/https://www.politico.com/static/PPM154_teapartyexpress041709.html It turned out they pretty much followed the outline to a T.

31 http://dailycaller.com/2013/02/12/inside-the-tea-party-patriots-plan-to-launch-a-super-pac/

32 http://www.brendansteinhauser.com/blog/5th-year-anniversary-of-the-91209-taxpayer-march-on-washington

33 https://twitter.com/912DC The Twitter handle has been dormant since September 25, 2009.

34 https://www.facebook.com/91209-Tea-Party-March-on-Washington-95179126183/ This was regularly updated through the 2010 edition of 9/12. There was also a 912dc.org website but it was inaccessible via internet archive.

35 http://web.archive.org/web/20020913052026/http://www.usteaparty.com/

36 https://www.c-span.org/video/?288868-1/freedomworks-rally It's a fun three hours of watching, and in my case it's not just reliving the memories but actually being able to listen to some of the speakers! Just try hearing someone from hundreds of yards away while you're taking photos for your own personal website.

37 http://www.motherjones.com/mojo/2011/11/tea-party-goes-trial

38 http://web.archive.org/web/20091011001921/http://washingtonindependent.com/63299/tea-party-activists-reject-pac-backed-tea-party-express While the *Washington Independent* site is apparently history, the internet is forever.

39 http://www.nytimes.com/2010/09/19/us/politics/19russo.html

40 https://philrusso.wordpress.com/2009/11/02/the-tea-party-express-fruad/

41 https://philrusso.wordpress.com/2009/12/17/tea-party-express-fraud-exposed/

42 Skocpol and Williamson, p. 112.

43 http://www.redstate.com/erick/2010/08/24/charlatans-and-the-horse-they-rode-in-on/

44 Full disclosure: the author penned occasional op-ed columns for a subsidiary group to ALG called Liberty Features Syndicate from 2009-10.

45 Compare this archived version of the American Liberty Tour website from November 29, 2009 (http://web.archive.org/web/20091129104053/http://americanlibertytour.com/) to an earlier one from September (http://web.archive.org/web/20090927173911/http://americanlibertytour.com/). There was an issue with following the TPX too soon through some stops.

46 https://thecaucus.blogs.nytimes.com/2010/02/06/notes-from-the-tea-party-convention/. Kate Zernike repeated the information in her later book on the TEA Party, *Boiling Mad: Inside Tea Party America* (2010).

47 http://talkingpointsmemo.com/muckraker/the-tea-party-movement-is-about-to-be-hijacked-activists-slam-plan-for-convention

48 http://www.redstate.com/diary/Erick/2010/01/11/im-afraid-sarah-palin-might-be-ruining-herself-unintentionally/

49 http://www.washingtonpost.com/wp-dyn/content/article/2010/01/28/AR2010012803565.html

50 http://www.foxnews.com/politics/2010/03/25/wealthy-donor-sues-tea-party-convention-organizer-palins-fee.html

51 http://www.huffingtonpost.com/2012/08/13/tennessee-tea-party-las-vegas-hotel_n_1772497.html

# WHAT CAN BROWN DO FOR US?

1 While there were only 58 elected Democrats, the two Senate independents – former Democratic VP candidate Joe Lieberman of Connecticut and eventual 2016/2020 Presidential candidate (as a Democrat) Bernie Sanders of Vermont – caucused with the Democrats. So for practical purposes they had their 60 votes.

2 http://articles.latimes.com/2009/aug/21/nation/na-kennedy21

3 http://articles.latimes.com/2009/sep/25/nation/na-kennedy-seat25

4 That election was held on March 31 to replace Rep. Kirsten Gillibrand, who was elevated to the Senate to replace former Senator Hillary Clinton. Democrat Scott Murphy edged out Republican Jim Tedisco in a close race – a 401 vote margin out of 160,940 cast. One could only speculate the result if the race were held concurrently with the NY-23 race.

5 http://www.syracuse.com/news/index.ssf/2009/08/democrats_nominate_bill_owens.html. Owens, the eventual winner, served out the remainder of the term and was re-elected twice before declining another term in 2014.

6 http://swingstateproject.com/diary/5072/amazing-political-history-of-ny23

7 McHugh's ACU lifetime score by 2008 was 71.55, placing him fifth out of the six Republicans representing New York in the House at the time. http://acuratings.conservative.org/acu-federal-legislative-ratings/?year1=2008&chamber=12&state1=45&sortable=1

8 http://www.politico.com/story/2009/10/gop-pick-sparks-revolt-on-right-028071

9 http://www.watertowndailytimes.com/article/20090928/BLOGS09/909289984/BLOGS09

10 http://thehill.com/blogs/blog-briefing-room/news/63455-gingrich-endorses-scozzafava-in-ny-23-race

11 http://www.politico.com/story/2009/10/ny-23-race-an-early-2012-test-028760?o=0

12 http://www.politico.com/story/2009/10/top-republicans-jump-ship-in-ny-23-028671 Of that group, only Bachmann, Pawlenty, and Santorum ran in 2012.

13 http://www.politico.com/story/2009/10/palin-backs-hoffman-in-ny-23-028641

14 http://www.politico.com/story/2009/10/scozzafava-bows-out-of-ny-23-race-028970?o=0 An unnamed Democrat quoted in the story conceded, "If we don't get her on board (for Owens) we lose."

15 http://www.foxnews.com/politics/2009/11/01/scozzafava-endorses-democrat-dropping-ny-congressional-race.html

16 http://www.syracuse.com/news/index.ssf/2009/11/its_not_over_recanvassing_shows_ny23_race.html

17 http://www.elections.ny.gov/NYSBOE/Elections/2009/Special/23rdCDSpecialVoteResults.pdf Scozzafava's vote was also significant as she represented both the Republican and Independent parties, and her total vote was over twice the difference between Hoffman and Owens, who won with a plurality, not the majority.

18 http://www.washingtontimes.com/news/2009/nov/04/tea-partiers-hone-skills-in-ny-house-race/

19 http://www.foxnews.com/opinion/2009/11/04/lloyd-green-new-york-congressional-district-victory.html

20 http://www.weeklystandard.com/scozzafava-spoils-doug-hoffmans-run/article/271401

21 http://www.politico.com/story/2009/11/conservatives-on-ny-23-we-didnt-lose-029161

22 *Ibid.*

23 *Ibid.*

24 http://www.politico.com/story/2009/10/calif-race-in-new-yorks-shadow-028710?o=0

25 http://teapartyexpressblog.blogspot.com/2009/10/wow-huge-crowd-turns-out-in-walnut.html

26 http://elections.cdn.sos.ca.gov/special-elections/2009-cd10/final-official-results-cd10-primary.pdf

27 *Ibid.*

28 http://www.eastbaytimes.com/2010/12/02/harmer-still-not-ready-to-concede/

29 http://clerk.house.gov/evs/2009/roll887.xml

30 https://caliblues.wordpress.com/2009/10/31/the-real-story-behind-newt-dedes-breakup/

31 Unlike other states where names appear on the ballot once, candidates in New York can show up multiple times as well. As you'll read much later, this also had potential to affect a key 2018 New York race.

32 http://www.weeklystandard.com/scozzafava-spoils-doug-hoffmans-run/article/271401

33 https://caliblues.wordpress.com/2009/11/02/hoffmanscozzafava-let-the-spin-begin/

34 https://research.bshor.com/2010/01/15/scott-brown-is-a-more-liberal-republican-than-dede-scozzafava/

35 http://www.huffingtonpost.com/2009/12/08/massachusetts-senate-prim_n_379365.html

36 https://groups.google.com/forum/#!topic/alt.politics.bush/W7S9DdmuDmM However, Brown still had a better chance than Donald Trump in 2016 and we know how that went.

37 http://rightardia.blogspot.com/2010/01/coakley-to-win-massachuesets-special.html You know, it's funny reading those on the Left who consider themselves so smart – sort of like Wile E. Coyote.

38 http://independentpoliticalreport.com/2010/01/carla-howell-and-michael-cloud-endorsement-of-joe-kennedy-warning-to-tea-party-activists-supporting-scott-brown/

39 http://monoblogue.us/2010/01/20/freezin-for-a-reason/ I posted this right after the Brown election. One of our 2010 U.S. Senate candidates, Dr. Eric Wargotz (who won the GOP nomination but lost in the general election) went up to Massachusetts to serve as a Brown volunteer.

40 http://canadafreepress.com/article/tea-party-express-endorsement-of-republican-scott-brown-for-u.s.-senate-in- Accessed February 4, 2017. This is a republication of an e-mail appeal purportedly sent by TPX.

41 http://www.washingtonpost.com/wp-srv/politics/campaign/2010/spending/MA-S1.html

42 http://web.archive.org/web/20110911081508/http://www.publicpolicypolling.com/pdf/ PPP_Release_MA_45398436.pdf

43 http://bluemassgroup.com/2010/01/extreme-right-wing-tea-party-group-endorses-scott-brown/

44 http://teapartyexpressblog.blogspot.com/2010/01/scott-brown-campaign-shhh-secret-we-can.html

45 http://www.foxnews.com/politics/2010/01/17/health-care-line-obama-heads-massachusetts.html

46 *Ibid.*

47 http://web.archive.org/web/20110223181605/http://www.examiner.com/american-politics-in-vancouver/scott-brown-rejects-tea-party-says-it-s-not-productive-to-criticize-obama This is a relatively short but reasonable indictment of the Brown record. Original no longer available.

# THE STORY SLANTED

1 http://jeffrey-feldman.typepad.com/frameshop/2009/02/tea-party-republicans.html

2 The *Playboy* link is no longer available (see note 5 below), but the story is retold here: http://exiledonline.com/exposing-the-familiar-rightwing-pr-machine-is-cnbcs-rick-santelli-sucking-koch/

3 *Ibid.*

4 https://web.archive.org/web/20150211165202/http://www.libertynews.com /2011/08/ the-tea-party-conspirators-and-the-real-story-behind-the-tea-party-movement/

5 https://www.theatlantic.com/business/archive/2009/03/playboy-dips-a-toe-into-investigative-journalism/4770/ The Ames/Levine piece was only up for a matter of days, apparently solely as an online feature. No wonder so few read *Playboy* for the articles, right?

6 https://thinkprogress.org/spontaneous-uprising-corporate-lobbyists-helping-to-orchestrate-radical-anti-obama-tea-party-dabd014bbfb#.ytlhnvt2w

7 http://www.nytimes.com/2009/04/13/opinion/13krugman.html

8 http://talkingpointsmemo.com/dc/freedomworks-long-history-of-teabagging

9 https://thinkprogress.org/pelosi-tea-parties-are-part-of-an-astroturf-campaign-by-some-of-the-wealthiest-people-in-america-ad5d6c86cd95

10 https://web.archive.org/web/20140518052456/http://seattleweekly.com/home/939482-129/civics101

11 http://old.seattletimes.com/html/opinion/2009139525_opina29ramsey.html

12 http://www.lizmair.com/blog.php?Index=452

13 http://www.prwatch.org/news/2010/04/9012/will-real-tea-party-movement-please-stand Surprise, surprise: they also mention the Koch brothers.

14 https://www.newyorker.com/magazine/2010/02/01/the-movement

15 Theda Skocpol and Vanessa Williamson: *The Tea Party and the Remaking of Republican Conservatism* (Oxford: Oxford University Press, 2011) p. 150.

16 http://www.huffingtonpost.com/eric-zuesse/final-proof-the-tea-party_b_4136722.html

17 http://talkingpointsmemo.com/dc/freedomworks-long-history-of-teabagging Note how quickly the "teabagging" term took hold, since MSNBC host Rachel Maddow had only made that analogy days before.

18 https://thinkprogress.org/pressed-on-freedomworks-connections-to-tea-parties-dick-armey-lashes-out-at-tp-as-juvenile-delinquen-f128e42c6b72#.x1y5mvbyd

19 http://www.politico.com/story/2009/08/the-summer-of-astroturf-026312?o=0

20 http://talkingpointsmemo.com/dc/tea-baggers-team-with-freedom-works-to-target-blue-dogs-in-anti-health-care-push Another daily double: Astroturf and "tea baggers."

21 http://blogs.discovermagazine.com/intersection/2010/10/26/the-tea-party-and-astroturfing/#.WJqZBIWcGM9

22 A transcript is found at http://www.newsbusters.org/blogs/nb/noel-sheppard/2009/04/16/garofalo-tea-party-goers-are-racists-who-hate-black-president. Also worth noting: earlier in the exchange Olbermann gleefully uses a number of sexually suggestive double entendres in the vein of "teabagging" regarding the TEA Party.

23 https://web.archive.org/web/20090922211755/http://www.cnn.com/2009/POLITICS/ 09/17/obama.witchdoctor.teaparty/

24 http://reason.com/archives/2009/11/16/are-tea-parties-racist1 Walsh goes on to bemoan the fact he made what was considered by the Left a "racist slip" of comparing something President Obama said in a speech to a Snoop Dogg lyric.

25 http://littlegreenfootballs.com/article/34267_Disgusting_Racist_of_the_Day

26 http://littlegreenfootballs.com/article/34686_No_Racism_at_the_Tea_Party

27 http://littlegreenfootballs.com/article/33765_White_Supremacists_Plan_to_Rec This refers to the original Anti-Defamation League article which is no longer in their archives.

28 http://www.huffingtonpost.com/2011/12/28/ron-paul-voting-record_n_1173255.html

29 https://www.facebook.com/notes/tea-party-patriots/breaking-health-care-news-code-red-red-alert/355928423822

30 http://www.mcclatchydc.com/news/politics-government/article24577300.html

31 https://www.youtube.com/watch?v=6fdaPZx1cpU

32 http://www.politico.com/story/2010/03/dems-say-protesters-used-n-word-034747#ixzz0ilzDfX0I

33 http://michellemalkin.com/2010/03/26/andrew-breitbart-offers-10000-to-united-negro-college-fund/

34 https://thedanashow.wordpress.com/2010/03/20/video-debunks-lib-accusations-that-slurs-were-shouted/

35 Social media conversation with Eric Eisenhammer, January 28, 2018.

36 http://www.huffingtonpost.com/2009/09/15/tea-party-leader-melts-do_n_286933.html

37 https://www.theatlantic.com/politics/archive/2010/06/mark-williams-steps-aside-as-chairman-of-tea-party-express/58402/ In this story he was the "controversial, anti-Islamist chairman of TEA Party Express" Mark Williams.

38 http://legalinsurrection.com/2010/07/naacp-passes-tea-party-is-racism-resolution/

39 http://www.huffingtonpost.com/2010/07/14/mark-williams-tea-party-express-naacp-racist_n_646989.html

40 https://web.archive.org/web/20100719211349/http://www.rolandsmartin.com/blog/index.php/2010/07/16/mark-williams-letter-to-lincoln-from-the-coloreds/

41 http://www.politico.com/story/2010/07/tea-party-federation-boots-williams-039909

42 https://www.theguardian.com/world/2010/oct/28/tea-party-infighting

43 https://web.archive.org/web/20100903203008/http://articles.cnn.com/2010-07-18/politics/tea.party.imbroglio_1_national-tea-party-federation-naacp-resolution-racist-elements?_s=PM:POLITICS

44 Social media conversation with Mark Williams, January 26, 2018. I lightly edited this for clarity but chose to retain the expletive.

45 https://nationalcenter.org/2009/09/16/press-release-statement-of-deneen-borelli-on-allegations-of-racism-against-critics-of-obama-policies/

46 https://katpierson.wordpress.com/2010/07/13/i-condemn-the-naacp/

47 Jonathan Wakefield: *Saving America: A Christian Perspective Of The Tea Party Movement* (Houston: Crossover Publications, 2012) p. 155-162.

48 https://www.youtube.com/watch?v=zTXBOgPCh9w

49 http://www.weeklystandard.com/eye-witness-to-st.-louis-scuffle-seiu-representative-punched-him-in-the-face.-updated-w-gladney-quotes/article/240840

50 http://www.thegatewaypundit.com/2011/07/gladney-trial-defense-claims-gladney-was-selling-obama-in-white-face-pins-ergo-they-beat-his-a-on-pavement/

51 http://www.thesmokinggun.com/documents/crime/plane-crash-suspects-online-diatribe

52 https://web.archive.org/web/20100222223048/http://www.rightpundits.com/?p=5608

53 http://www.redstate.com/diary/ladylibertas/2010/02/20/austin-tea-party-leaders-speak-with-lady-libertas-about-joseph-stack/

54 http://www.newsmax.com/Headline/austin-attack-media-tea/2010/02/18/id/350266/

55 https://www.huffingtonpost.com/2012/07/20/brian-ross-tea-party-colorado-shooting_n_1689471.html

56 https://www.usatoday.com/story/news/politics/onpolitics/2017/08/15/lawmakers-

slam-trumps-latest-defense-charlottesville-response/570573001/

57 http://www.cnn.com/2017/08/12/politics/trump-statement-alt-right-protests/index.html

58 Angle, Sharron. *Right Angle: One Woman's Journey to Reclaim the Constitution*, (Bloomington, Indiana: Author House, 2011). p. 214-215.

59 http://www.huffingtonpost.com/alex-brantzawadzki/anatomy-of-the-tea-party_b_380567.html This is just one example, covering the Tea Party Patriots. They had a series of investigations on the TEA Party, but seemed less curious about the Obama administration.

60 http://ew.com/article/2010/03/31/david-letterman-pam-stout-tea-party/

61 Just a few examples, in order of release:

*Boiling Mad: Inside Tea Party America*, by New York Times reporter Kate Zernicke

*The Whites of Their Eyes: The Tea Party's Revolution and the Battle Over American History* by Jill Lepore, a staff writer at The New Yorker

*Crashing the Tea Party: Mass Media and the Campaign to Remake American Politics* by Paul Street (author of Barack Obama and the Future of American Politics) and Anthony R. DiMaggio

*The Tea Party and the Remaking of Republican Conservatism* by Theda Skocpol and Vanessa Williamson. Skocpol is a Harvard professor and past president of the American Political Science Association, while Williamson is a doctoral candidate at that institution as well as former policy director for the left-leaning Iraq and Afghanistan Veterans of America.

*The Tea Party: A Brief History* by historian and academic Ronald P. Formisano

*Steep: The Precipitous Rise of the Tea Party* by Lawrence Rosenthal and Christine Trost, at the time both of the Center for Comparative Study of Right-Wing Movements. It is now known as the Berkeley Center for Right-Wing Studies, part of the University of California.

62 https://newrepublic.com/article/78138/teaism-tea-party- This review was for *Boiling Mad.*

63 https://www.pbs.org/newshour/politics/tea-party-how-big-is-it-and-where-is-it-based

64 Skocpol and Williamson, p. 142.

65 https://caliblues.wordpress.com/2009/10/31/the-real-story-behind-newt-dedes-breakup/

# BACKLASH FROM THE BELTWAY

1 https://www.senate.gov/history/partydiv.htm

2 http://www.huffingtonpost.com/2009/04/28/arlen-specter-switching-p_n_192298.html

3 http://www.nbcnews.com/id/31778598/ns/politics-capitol_hill/t/after-long-wait-franken-sworn-senator/#.WKfjt4WcGM8 Franken had fewer votes on election night, but absentee ballots counted during a controversial recount process pushed him ahead. He won by 312 votes out of nearly 2.9 million cast.

4 http://www.huffingtonpost.com/joseph-bafumi/a-forecast-of-the-2010-ho_b_697051.html

5 https://web.archive.org/web/20100918094638/http://www.npr.org/elections2010/scorecard/

6 https://www.cbsnews.com/news/did-the-tea-party-cost-republicans-the-senate/

7 http://www.nbcnews.com/id/40044181/ns/politics-decision_2010/t/complaints-tea-party-hurt-gops-senate-hopes/#.WcBiRsiGOM9

8 http://www.politifact.com/truth-o-meter/statements/2010/oct/14/joe-manchin/joe-manchin-attacks-john-raese-wife-registered-vot/

9 http://www.politico.com/story/2010/10/gop-ad-casting-call-hicky-wva-look-043254

10 http://www.politico.com/story/2010/10/john-raese-thinks-were-hicks-043363

11 https://www.cbsnews.com/news/democrat-joe-manchin-takes-dead-aim-at-health-care-cap-and-trade/

12 http://www.huffingtonpost.com/2010/10/11/joe-manchin-ad-dead-aim_n_758457.html

13 https://www.youtube.com/watch?v=xIJORBRpOPM

14 http://www.politico.com/story/2010/10/nugent-to-stump-for-raese-044128

15 http://blogs.denverpost.com/thespot/2010/04/13/norton-petitions-onto-gop-ballot/8376/

16 http://www.sandiegouniontribune.com/sdut-years-later-politicians-tripping-over-

trackers-2010aug08-story.html

17 http://www.politico.com/story/2010/08/can-he-buck-the-system-041023

18 *Ibid.*

19 http://www.slate.com/articles/news_and_politics/politics/2010/12/the_ghost_of_gaffes_past.html

20 https://www.cbsnews.com/news/gop-rivals-jane-norton-ken-buck-fight-over-high-heels-and-manhood/

21 http://www.nbcnews.com/id/39674828/ns/meet_the_press-transcripts/t/meet-press-transcript-oct/#.WcHIAsiGOM8

22 http://www.huffingtonpost.com/2010/10/17/colorado-senate-debate-ken-buck-gay-alcoholism_n_765670.html

23 https://www.mediaite.com/online/ken-buck-on-mtp-homosexuality-is-a-choice-similar-to-alcoholism/

24 http://www.denverpost.com/2010/10/14/michael-bennet-for-u-s-senate/ As you'll note, *The Denver Post* endorsed Bennet.

25 http://www.coloradopols.com/diary/14525/video-cameras-playing-journalists-role-on-campaign-trail#sthash.lRbsSfS8.dpbs

26 http://www.denverpost.com/2013/08/09/ken-buck-embarks-on-u-s-senate-run-despite-2010-baggage/ Once you get baggage in the eyes of the Left you'll always carry it.

27 http://www.rollcall.com/rothenblog/why-ken-buck-has-the-inside-track-in-colorado-4th-district/

28 https://www.cbsnews.com/news/sue-lowden-stands-by-chicken-health-care-barter-plan/

29 http://swampland.time.com/2010/07/08/sharron-angles-latest-gaffe/

30 http://www.huffingtonpost.com/2010/07/08/sharron-angles-advice-for_n_639294.html

31 https://www.cbsnews.com/news/sharron-angle-tells-hispanic-students-they-look-asian-argues-immigration-ad-not-about-southern-border/

32 http://www.washingtontimes.com/news/2010/aug/16/a-race-of-he-who-gaffes-last-in-nevada/

33 https://lasvegasweekly.com/news/2010/aug/19/incredibly-true-bizarre-story-scott-ashjian-and-35/

34 http://www.nevadaappeal.com/news/opinion/chuck-muth-scott-ashjian-tea-party-crasher/

35 http://www.lasvegasnow.com/news/iteam-nevada-tea-party-candidate-faces-liens-fines-and-lawsuits/77621945

36 https://www.reviewjournal.com/news/tea-party-of-nevada-head-ditches-ashjian-backs-angle/

37 http://dailycaller.com/2011/01/18/sen-harry-reids-turnout-machine/

38 http://www.delawareonline.com/story/news/politics/2016/09/16/crowded-primary-elections/90415558/ After Castle was first elected to the Delaware House, he quickly moved up to their Senate for eight years before serving as lieutenant governor for a term, then governor for just short of two terms – he resigned a few weeks early to join the House. As of the 2010 election, Castle had spent 40 of the previous 44 years in political office, with the other four in private law practice.

39 http://acuratings.conservative.org/acu-federal-legislative-ratings/?year1=2009&chamber=11&state1=21&sortable=1 Castle's 2010 rating was just 38, which would have dragged his lifetime score even closer to 50.

40 https://elections.delaware.gov/archive/elect10/elect10_Primary/html/stwoff_kns.shtml

41 https://elections.delaware.gov/archive/elect08/elect08_general_election/html/elect08_gen_KWNS.shtml

42 https://www.csmonitor.com/USA/Elections/From-the-Wires/2010/0913/Christine-O-Donnell-roiling-Delaware-s-GOP-establishment

43 http://www.nytimes.com/2010/09/11/opinion/11collins.html

44 http://www.teapartyexpress.org/date/2010/09 The site has a link to both ads, which are still available for viewing. There's nothing special or groundbreaking about them.

45 https://www.politico.com/story/2010/09/rove-odonnell-said-nutty-things-042205

46 http://www.npr.org/sections/thetwo-way/2010/10/05/130353168/-i-m-not-a-witch-republican-senate-candidate-christine-o-donnell-says-in-new-ad

47 https://elections.delaware.gov/archive/elect10/elect10_General/html/stwoff_kns.shtml Unfortunately for O'Donnell, the county she lost cast over 60%

of the ballots – New Castle County includes the city of Wilmington and is home to a majority of Delaware's population and voters.

48 https://www.voanews.com/a/republicans-credit-tea-party-for-gains-in-midterm-election-106803248/129910.html

49 This 2011 autobiography was self-published through the Author House imprint.

50 Sharron Angle: *Right Angle: One Woman's Journey to Reclaim the Constitution*, (Bloomington, Indiana: Author House, 2011). p. xi.

51 *Right Angle*, p. 11.

52 *Right Angle*, p. 31.

53 Christine O'Donnell: *Trouble Maker: Let's Do What It Takes To Make America Great Again* (New York: St. Martin's Press, 2011).

54 *Trouble Maker*, p. 258. Considering the state party has won only one statewide race since (down-ballot for treasurer, a seat lost four years later) this philosophy may still hold true.

55 http://www.nytimes.com/2010/10/19/us/politics/19taxes.html. The "Making Work Pay" credit generally came in the form of less backup withholding – see https://www.irs.gov/newsroom/the-making-work-pay-tax-credit – but sometimes required the addition of another tax form, Schedule M – see https://www.irs.gov/newsroom/claim-the-making-work-pay-tax-credit-on-your-tax-return-with-schedule-m.

56 https://www.urban.org/research/publication/social-security-and-medicare-lifetime-benefits-and-taxes/view/full_report

## THE FLEETING TASTE OF SUCCESS

1 http://reason.com/archives/2010/04/13/the-son-also-rises/

2 http://content.time.com/time/nation/article/0,8599,1990183,00.html

3 http://www.foxnews.com/politics/2010/05/18/tea-party-favorite-rand-paul-wins-senate-gop-primary-kentucky.html

4 This would continue while in office, as Rand Paul remained an outspoken opponent of the minimum wage. See https://www.courier-journal.com/story/news/politics/rand-paul/2014/04/28/rand-paul-west-end-knocks-

minimum-wage-hike/8421717/

5 https://www.cbsnews.com/news/rand-paul-under-fire-for-comments-on-race/

6 http://www.motherjones.com/politics/2010/10/rand-paul-kentucky-media/#

7 *Ibid.*

8 https://www.thedailybeast.com/rand-pauls-civil-rights-controversy

9 *Ibid.*

10 http://www.nbcnews.com/id/37358634/ns/politics-decision_2010/t/rand-paul-shakes-staff-after-firestorm/

11 http://independentpoliticalreport.com/2010/05/ky-libertarians-rand-paul-is-not-one-of-us-but-we-wont-run-a-candidate-against-him/

12 https://www.gq.com/story/gq-exclusive-rand-pauls-crazy-college-days-hint-theres-a-secret-society-involved

13 https://www.huffingtonpost.com/2010/08/09/rand-paul-abducted-female_n_675766.html

14 http://www.politifact.com/truth-o-meter/statements/2010/sep/27/jack-conway/jack-conway-campaign-ad-accuses-rand-paul-being-so/

15 https://www.politico.com/story/2010/10/aqua-buddha-ad-backfires-044222

16 http://thehill.com/blogs/blog-briefing-room/news/130545-menendez-aqua-buddha-ad-a-killer-for-conway

17 https://www.politico.com/story/2010/06/conway-will-miss-biden-louisville-event-039042

18 http://www.kentucky.com/news/local/education/article44053263.html

19 http://www.nytimes.com/2010/01/10/magazine/10florida-t.html

20 https://newrepublic.com/article/73299/the-republican-obama

21 http://www.washingtonpost.com/wp-dyn/content/article/2010/04/29/AR2010042904884.html

22 http://talkingpointsmemo.com/dc/marco-rubio-s-tea-party-problem

23 https://www.politico.com/story/2009/06/senator-endorses-crist-opponent-023754

24 http://thehill.com/blogs/ballot-box/other-races/92529-tea-party-express-announces-2010-targets-endorses-democrat

25 http://www.nytimes.com/2010/10/29/us/politics/29florida.html

26 http://stubbornfacts1776.com/tea-party-hijack-by-gop-and-afp-in-progress-in-lincoln-nebraska/

27 http://monoblogue.us/2009/12/09/message-to-tpx3-dont-forget-delmarva/ Unfortunately, they did forget us.

28 http://www.teapartyexpress.org/161/tour-schedule-tea-party-express-i

29 http://www.teapartyexpress.org/164/tour-schedule-tea-party-express-ii

30 http://www.teapartyexpress.org/169/tour-schedule-tea-party-express-iii

31 Notes from telephone interview with Joan Fabiano, February 25, 2018.

32 http://thehill.com/blogs/ballot-box/other-races/92529-tea-party-express-announces-2010-targets-endorses-democrat

33 http://www.teapartyexpress.org/171/tour-schedule-tea-party-express-iv#more-171

34 https://getliberty.org/2009/09/american-liberty-tour-launches-91009-in-sacramento-ca-to-take-back-america/

35 https://roadtorepeal.org/ This is a good example of how AFP markets its efforts.

36 http://www.washingtonpost.com/wp-dyn/content/article/2009/08/30/AR2009083002654.html

37 http://www.nytimes.com/2009/09/03/health/policy/03bus.html

38 https://www.afscme.org/news/press-room/press-releases/2009/afscme-highway-to-health-care-tour

39 https://www.sba-list.org/suzy-b-blog/votes-have-consequences-bus-tour

40 http://thehill.com/blogs/blog-briefing-room/news/113503-house-dem-swipes-at-obama-and-pelosi-in-campaign-ad

41 Michael Patrick Leahy: *Covenant of Liberty: The Ideological Origins of the Tea Party Movement* (New York: Broadside Books, 2012) p. 261.

42 Mark Meckler and Jenny Beth Martin: *Tea Party Patriots: The Second American*

*Revolution* (New York: Henry Holt and Company, 2012) p. 64.

43 Meckler and Martin, p. 75.

44 http://www.foxnews.com/politics/2010/07/13/tea-party-preempts-racist-resolution-condemns-bigoted-naacp.html

45 http://thehill.com/blogs/ballot-box/other-races/92529-tea-party-express-announces-2010-targets-endorses-democrat

46 http://idahofreedom.org/minnick-rejects-support-of-tea-party-express-over-racial-letter/

47 http://thehill.com/blogs/ballot-box/other-races/110647-embattled-activist-resigns-from-tea-party-express/

48 https://www.politico.com/story/2010/07/minnick-rejects-tea-party-endorsement-039929

49 http://www.foxnews.com/politics/2010/10/22/tea-party-express-rescinds-minnick-endorsement-because-wont-work-to-repeal.html

50 http://thehill.com/blogs/ballot-box/house-races/125381-tea-party-express-backs-idaho-republican-after-rep-minnick-rejects-endorsement

51 https://www.realclearpolitics.com/epolls/2010/house/id/idaho_1st_district _labrador_ vs_minnick-1266.html

52 http://abc13.com/archive/7704738/

53 http://politicalticker.blogs.cnn.com/2010/08/04/palin-endorses-murphy/

54 http://monoblogue.us/2012/08/20/bongino-gets-key-endorsement/ Little-known fact: the aforementioned Brian Murphy is the one who sprang nationally-known politico Dan Bongino on the political landscape as his initial supporter.

55 David Brody: *The Teavangelicals: The Inside Story of How The Evangelicals and The Tea Party are Taking Back America* (Grand Rapids, MI: Zondervan, 2012) p. 139.

56 http://www.nytimes.com/2009/07/04/us/politics/04ptext.html

57 https://www.washingtonpost.com/blogs/the-fix/post/sarah-palin-not-running-for-president/2011/10/05/gIQAzr9MOL_blog.html

# MANAGING THE DECLINE

1 Notes from telephone conversation with Gary Aminoff. January 28, 2018.

2 E-mail exchange with Ralph Reagan, January 1, 2018.

3 https://www.politico.com/story/2010/08/town-hall-rage-subsides-041490?o=0

4 Notes from telephone conversation with Joan Fabiano, February 25, 2018.

5 https://www.politico.com/story/2010/04/gop-operatives-crash-the-tea-party-035785

6 http://www.rollcall.com/news/Tea-Party-Turning-Pro-With-Paid-Jobs-205421-1.html

7 http://www.washingtonpost.com/wp-srv/politics/campaign/2010/spending/Our-Country-Deserves-Better-teapartyexpressorg.html

8 http://politicalticker.blogs.cnn.com/2010/12/17/cnn-and-tea-party-express-to-host-first-of-its-kind-tea-party-presidential-primary-debate/

9 https://web.archive.org/web/20110912102137/http://www.cnn.com/2011/POLITICS/ 09/11/debate.teaparty/index.html

10 *Ibid.*

11 http://transcripts.cnn.com/TRANSCRIPTS/1109/12/se.06.html

12 http://politicalticker.blogs.cnn.com/2011/07/29/who-is-the-tea-party-caucus-in-the-house/

13 https://www.youtube.com/watch?v=1fRxO_Yx99I It's not a long statement but the fact Bachmann is always looking toward her teleprompter and not at the camera is a little disconcerting.

14 http://www.teapartyexpress.org/2443/first-ever-tea-party-town-hall-announced

15 http://www.foxnews.com/politics/2011/02/17/teachers-march-wisconsin-capitol-senate-moves-curtail-union-rights.html

16 http://host.madison.com/wsj/news/local/govt-and-politics/anatomy-of-a-protest-from-a-simple-march-to-a/article_3c7f9cd2-4274-11e0-8f25-001cc4c002e0.html It should be noted there was a smaller counter-protest led by TEA Party groups and Americans for Prosperity, but it was basically Big Labor's caterwauling that was

the story.

17 http://www.teapartyexpress.org/182/tea-party-express-v-reclaiming-america-presidential-tour#more-182

18 http://www.teapartyexpress.org/2425/tea-party-express-launching-fifth-national-tour-this-summer They described the stops as “a rolling 4th of July show,” too.

19 http://www.teapartyexpress.org/2381/conservative-groups-join-tea-party-express-restoring-common-sense-wisconsin-tour

20 http://www.teapartyexpress.org/2404/tea-party-express-launches-4-city-campaign-throughout-iowa

21 http://www.teapartyexpress.org/2367/tea-party-express-holds-huge-rally-in-avon-oh-on-saturday While McCotter wasn't given top billing, this particular example is also good to describe their standard lineup of speakers featured at the rally in Avon, Ohio, just outside Cleveland.

22 http://www.teapartyexpress.org/2398/national-tea-party-express-holding-rallies-today-in-albany-and-concord

23 http://www.teapartyexpress.org/2352/national-tea-party-express-continues-with-star-studded-rallies-in-new-hampshire

24 http://www.teapartyexpress.org/2389/tea-party-express-holds-tea-party-rallies-in-south-carolina-friday

25 http://www.teapartyexpress.org/2467/statement-from-tea-party-express-on-freedomworks

26 http://www.freedomworks.org/content/freedomworks-and-new-hampshire-tea-party-groups-protest-mitt-romney-speech-concord-new

27 https://thecaucus.blogs.nytimes.com/2011/09/04/romney-speaks-at-tea-party-event-drawing-sparse-protest

28 http://www.teapartyexpress.org/2334/tea-party-express-launches-weekly-radio-show

29 http://www.motherjones.com/politics/2011/11/tea-party-goes-trial/

30 https://www.teapartypatriots.org/content/pawlenty-to-address-tea-party-patriots-at-1st-annual-policy-summit/

31 https://www.teapartypatriots.org/content/tea-party-patriots-presidential-straw-poll-shows-activists-looking-for-leadership/ Even Barack Obama got a total of four

votes – but Donald Trump (!) had 19 votes among the attendees.

32 https://www.teapartypatriots.org/content/tea-party-rally-to-turn-screws-on-congress-over-budget/

33 https://www.washingtontimes.com/news/2011/mar/30/tea-party-to-storm-capitol-for-gut-check/

34 http://www.motherjones.com/politics/2011/03/tea-party-rally-washout/

35 https://www.teapartypatriots.org/content/local-tea-parties-to-deal-in-the-district-on-debt-limit-tax-increases/

36 https://www.teapartypatriots.org/content/deal-in-the-district-lets-make-a-real-deal-for-once/

37 https://www.teapartypatriots.org/content/tea-party-patriots-and-leadership-institute-launch-state-grassroots-training-initiative/

38 https://www.teapartypatriots.org/content/tea-party-groups-reject-arizona-tea-party-license-plates/ The boilerplate press release was the funniest part.

39 https://www.teapartypatriots.org/content/tea-party-not-beholden-to-any-party/

40 *Ibid.*

41 https://www.foxnews.com/politics/tea-party-group-to-back-any-gop-nominee-including-romney

42 http://news.gallup.com/poll/186338/support-tea-party-drops-new-low.aspx This article is actually from what appears to be the final survey taken on the subject, in 2015. By that point, TEA Party support had dwindled to 17%, although opposition was also down to 24%. The big winner by then was "neutral" with 54%.

43 https://www.reuters.com/article/us-usa-politics-libertarians/most-u-s-libertarians-do-not-identify-with-tea-party-survey-idUSBRE99S03Q20131029

44 https://www.washingtontimes.com/news/2013/oct/29/libertarians-dont-call-us-tea-partyers-survey-find/ While the survey was taken in 2013 – a point where the TEA Party was already falling on hard times – it's interesting to note that the Libertarian breakup with the TEA Party may have cost Ken Cuccinelli, a staunch conservative, the governor's race in Virginia. Democrat Terry McAuliffe won with only 47.8% of the vote, a 56,435 vote margin over Cuccinelli easily eclipsed by Libertarian Party candidate Robert Sarvis and his 146,084 votes.

45 https://philrusso.wordpress.com/2010/07/28/the-problem-with-the-tea-party/

46 https://www.voanews.com/a/republicans-credit-tea-party-for-gains-in-midterm-election-106803248/129910.html

47 http://thehill.com/blogs/blog-briefing-room/news/173463-gingrich-says-he-regrets-2008-climate-ad-with-pelosi

# FRUSTRATION AND FRAGMENTATION

1 http://www.nytimes.com/2009/07/04/us/politics/04ptext.html

2 https://www.theguardian.com/world/blog/2010/oct/12/sarah-palin-tea-party-2012 It's interesting to read the foreign press reporting on the TEA Party, whatever the subject.

3 http://www.nj.com/politics/index.ssf/2015/04/christie_on_embracing_obama_after_hurricane_sandy_i_was_doing_my_job.html

4 https://www.teapartypatriots.org/content/tea-party-patriots-presidential-straw-poll-shows-activists-looking-for-leadership/

5 http://www.washingtonpost.com/wp-srv/politics/polls/postabcpoll_100211.html That poll had Mitt Romney at 21%, Herman Cain and Rick Perry at 14% apiece, and Chris Christie at 10% - all ahead of Palin and already on the trail.

6 *Ibid.*

7 https://web.archive.org/web/20110630233245/http://www.cnn.com/2011/POLITICS/ 06/30/bachmann.palin/index.html

8 https://www.theguardian.com/world/2010/oct/12/tea-party-guns-palin-washington

9 http://www.washingtonpost.com/wp-dyn/content/article/2011/02/02/AR2011020203272_pf.html Eight years later, the centrist Republican Fred Karger would also have to remind the media that he was the first openly gay Presidential candidate, not Democrat Pete Buttigieg.

10 https://www.politico.com/story/2011/09/flight-of-fancy-may-hurt-mccotter-064577

11 http://www.cnn.com/2011/10/31/opinion/frum-republican-tea-party-scenarios/index.html. This op-ed by centrist Republican columnist David Frum is a perfect example. He believed at the time a “Tea Party” nominee would be selected and lose the election.

12 https://www.politico.com/story/2011/10/exclusive-2-women-accused-cain-of-

inappropriate-behavior-067194

13 https://www.washingtonpost.com/politics/ginger-white-accuses-herman-cain-of-long-affair/2011/11/28/gIQA6H6T6N_story.html

14 http://swampland.time.com/2011/10/31/how-tea-party-indecision-is-boosting-mitt-romney/

15 http://www.telegraph.co.uk/news/worldnews/us-election/8993026/US-Election-2012-Michele-Bachmann-withdraws-after-Iowa-defeat.html

16 https://www.reuters.com/article/us-usa-campaign-roemer/inside-buddy-roemers-unlikely-white-house-run-idUSTRE7946K620111005

17 http://www.cnn.com/2012/05/14/opinion/zelizer-romney-tea-party-relationship/index.html The writer believed Romney would have to use the Nixon/Reagan/Bush approach of having a couple "broader themes" to appeal to the electorate.

18 http://live.nydailynews.com/Event/Election_2012_Florida_Primary_Coverage/22245472

19 https://web.archive.org/web/20120117053156/http://blogs.ajc.com/jay-bookman-blog/2011/12/06/a-gingrichromney-race-represents-failure-of-tea-party/

20 https://www.teapartypatriots.org/content/gingrichromney-race-not-a-failure-of-tea-party/

21 https://www.teapartypatriots.org/content/gop-gains-from-principles-and-tea-party/

22 David Brody: *The Teavangelicals: The Inside Story of How The Evangelicals and The Tea Party are Taking Back America* (Grand Rapids, MI: Zondervan, 2012) p. 135.

23 http://www.cnn.com/election/2012/primaries/state/va/

24 https://www.teapartypatriots.org/content/gingrich-leads-tea-party-patriots-florida-straw-poll/

25 Because of this, the Presidential campaign came to my sleepy little adopted hometown of Salisbury, Maryland. Newt liked our zoo, but I liked being able to cover the speech (purportedly for the local college students only) as a blogger/journalist. http://monoblogue.us/2012/03/27/2012-campaign-comes-to-salisbury-as-gingrich-gives-a-different-speech/

26 https://www.salon.com/2012/08/31/mitt_romney_tea_party_puppet/

27 https://www.theatlantic.com/politics/archive/2012/04/the-tea-partys-mitt-romney-crisis/256008/

28 *Ibid.*

29 https://www.washingtonpost.com/opinions/mitt-romney-the-stealth-tea-party-candidate/2012/01/31/gIQAy0BZnQ_story.html

30 https://www.washingtontimes.com/news/2012/mar/20/romney-gets-tepid-tea-party-support/

31 https://www.teapartypatriots.org/content/tea-party-success-highlighted-at-rnc/

32 http://www.foxnews.com/politics/2012/08/25/tea-party-movement-role-republican-convention.html

33 https://hotair.com/archives/2012/08/30/not-a-single-mention-of-the-tea-party-in-primetime-at-the-convention-so-far/

34 https://hotair.com/archives/2012/08/26/romney-rule-change-fight-on-convention-floor/

35 https://www.teapartypatriots.org/content/exclusive-interview-with-dave-nalle-national-chairman-of-the-republican-liberty-caucus/

36 https://www.forbes.com/sites/rickungar/2014/04/07/dramatic-little-known-gop-rule-change-takes-choice-of-presidential-candidate-away-from-rank-and-file-republicans-and-hands-it-to-party-elite/#57642c446c7a

37 https://jaretglenn.wordpress.com/2012/07/31/how-the-republican-party-stole-the-nomination-from-ron-paul/

38 https://www.theunion.com/news/meckler-resigns-from-national-tea-party-patriots/

39 https://www.teapartypatriots.org/content/statement-from-tea-party-patriots-on-recent-resignations/

40 http://www.motherjones.com/politics/2011/02/tea-party-patriots-investigated/

41 http://www.motherjones.com/politics/2011/02/tea-party-patriots-investigated-part-two/

42 http://www.motherjones.com/politics/2011/02/tea-party-patriots-investigated-part-3/

43 https://www.teapartypatriots.org/issues/tea-party-patriots-reacts-to-settlement-of-lawsuit-against-irs-for-targeting-of-tea-party-groups/

44 https://www.teapartypatriots.org/content/herman-cain-va-attorney-general-to-highlight-road-to-repeal-rally-in-washington/

45 http://www.teapartyexpress.org/4109/tea-party-express-vi-restoring-the-american-dream

46 http://www.teapartyexpress.org/4473/reclaiming-our-future

47 http://www.teapartyexpress.org/5229/tea-party-express-viii-winning-for-america

48 http://www.teapartyexpress.org/3273/tea-party-express-bus-is-rolling-through-florida

49 http://www.teapartyexpress.org/4947/support-mark-neumann-bus-tour

50 http://www.teapartyexpress.org/5169/tea-party-express-launches-mobile-phone-bank-bus-for-81-day-gotv-campaign#more-5169

51 http://www.teapartyexpress.org/5197/tea-party-express-mobile-phone-bank-bus-successfully-embarks-on-81-day-gotv-campaign#more-5197

52 http://www.teapartyexpress.org/5928/tea-party-movement-driving-gop-gotv-effort

53 http://www.teapartyexpress.org/5236/tea-party-express-celebrates-at-the-republican-national-convention#more-5236

54 https://thecaucus.blogs.nytimes.com/2012/03/09/tea-party-movement-takes-the-long-view

55 http://www.breitbart.com/big-government/2012/05/09/jenny-beth-martin-tea-party/

56 http://www.breitbart.com/big-government/2012/06/03/fewer-than-thousand-attend-clinton-rally/

57 http://www.theinvestigativefund.org/investigation/2012/09/26/kochs-ground-game/

58 https://www.teapartypatriots.org/content/in-wisconsin-a-partnership-for-liberty/

59 https://www.teapartypatriots.org/content/wisconsin-tea-party-patriots-defeat-washington-special-interests-again/

60 https://www.teapartypatriots.org/content/cruz-win-a-tea-party-values-victory/

61 http://articles.latimes.com/2010/feb/23/nation/la-na-scott-brown24-2010feb24

62 http://independentpoliticalreport.com/2010/01/carla-howell-and-michael-cloud-endorsement-of-joe-kennedy-warning-to-tea-party-activists-supporting-scott-

brown/

63 https://spectator.org/scott-browns-balancing-act/

64 http://archive.boston.com/news/nation/washington/articles/2010/12/24/brown_draws_ire_on_the_right/

65 https://www.salon.com/2010/12/27/scott_brown_tea_party

66 http://www.bostonmagazine.com/news/2012/10/08/endorsing-brown-tea-party-sounds-kind-warren/

67 http://www.stltoday.com/news/local/govt-and-politics/sarah-backs-sarah-steelman-wins-palin-endorsement-for-u-s/article_e0fbfc62-d05b-11e1-85be-001a4bcf6878.html

68 http://www.teapartyexpress.org/4043/sarah-steelman-us-senate-endorsement

69 http://www.stltoday.com/mike-huckabee-featured-in-todd-akin-for-u-s-senate/article_c4aefb66-c6b7-11e1-b8ca-0019bb30f31a.html

70 http://www.stltoday.com/news/local/govt-and-politics/akin-snares-michele-bachmann-support-in-senate-bid/article_7abea094-84c5-11e1-883d-001a4bcf6878.html

71 https://www.politico.com/magazine/story/2015/08/todd-akin-missouri-claire-mccaskill-2012-121262

72 https://www.huffingtonpost.com/2012/08/19/todd-akin-abortion-legitimate-rape_n_1807381.html

73 http://abcnews.go.com/Politics/OTUS/akins-rape-remark-draws-tea-party-pressure-quit/story?id=17041857

74 https://www.latimes.com/archives/la-xpm-2012-aug-20-la-pn-tea-party-rogue-todd-akin-defies-gop-bosses-by-staying-in-race-20120820-story.html

75 http://politicalticker.blogs.cnn.com/2012/08/20/tea-party-express-calls-on-akin-to-step-down/

76 https://www.theguardian.com/world/2012/aug/21/tea-party-republicans-todd-akin

77 https://www.csmonitor.com/USA/Latest-News-Wires/2012/0824/Why-Missouri-conservatives-are-rallying-around-Todd-Akin

78 https://www.realclearpolitics.com/epolls/2012/senate/mo/missouri_senate_akin_vs_mccaskill-2079.html#polls

79 https://www.washingtonpost.com/blogs/the-fix/post/sen-richard-lugar-loses-primary-to-richard-mourdock/2012/05/08/gIQAOcHXBU_blog.html is a typical take.

80 https://www.teapartypatriots.org/content/tea-party-ousts-indiana-senator-lugar/

81 http://abcnews.go.com/Politics/OTUS/meet-gop-establishment-tea-party/story?id=16314836

82 *Ibid.*

83 https://www.huffingtonpost.com/2012/05/08/dick-lugar-richard-mourdock-lugar-loses-indiana-republican-senate-primary_n_1501416.html

84 https://www.realclearpolitics.com/epolls/2012/senate/in/indiana_senate_mourdock_vs_donnelly-3166.html

85 The full debate is available, but this link is set to the time of the question: https://youtu.be/dyhTQJFEE_o?t=2648 There is also a transcript.

## THE TEA PARTY IS DEAD

1 http://www.breitbart.com/big-government/2012/11/05/tea-party-independents/

2 https://www.teapartypatriots.org/content/tea-party-vows-to-continue-the-fight-after-the-establishments-hand-picked-candidate-loses/

3 https://www.teapartypatriots.org/content/omaha-nebraska-where-americans-are-taking-a-stand/

4 http://www.teapartyexpress.org/5907/the-pony-in-obama-winning-a-second-term#more-5907

5 http://www.anncoulter.com/columns/2012-11-21.html

6 https://www.realclearpolitics.com/video/2016/05/04/flashback_june_2015_bill_maher__his_audience_laugh_at_ann_coulter_for_saying_trump_could_win.html

7 https://www.vanityfair.com/news/2016/09/ann-coulter-donald-trump

8 https://www.nytimes.com/2012/12/04/opinion/where-have-you-gone-bill-buckley.html

9 http://www.motherjones.com/kevin-drum/2012/09/how-tea-party-killed-mitt-romney/#

10 http://www.tampabay.com/news/politics/national/mitt-romney-is-republican-partys-nominee-but-not-the-standard-bearer/1248507

11 https://www.nytimes.com/2007/09/19/us/politics/19romney.html

12 One example: http://www.thegatewaypundit.com/2014/01/making-the-rounds-barry-soetoros-columbia-university-school-id/ Perhaps this is “fake news” but look at how much mileage the “fake but accurate” George W. Bush Air National Guard story received. As I have noted in previous chapters, the Left does its best and most dogged investigation on the Right and never shines a light on its own.

13 https://www.teapartypatriots.org/content/how-easy-is-it-to-save-your-country-watch-this/

14 https://www.teapartypatriots.org/content/the-tea-pot-is-boiling/

15 https://www.mediaite.com/tv/mitt-romney-number-of-things-i-like-in-obamacare-that-im-going-to-put-in-place/

16 http://www.nejm.org/doi/full/10.1056/NEJMp1211516

17 https://www.forbes.com/sites/theapothecary/2012/06/20/mitt-romney-outlines-his-plan-to-replace-obamacare/#555617e35494

18 http://abcnews.go.com/Politics/boehner-exclusive-raising-tax-rates-unacceptable-revenue-table/story?id=17672947

19 http://www.breitbart.com/big-government/2012/11/09/boehner-mocks-tea-party/

20 https://www.teapartypatriots.org/content/john-boehner-just-denied-you-exist/

21 http://www.breitbart.com/big-government/2012/11/11/bill-kristol-should-write-a-check-and-the-gop-should-ignore-him-again/

22 https://www.teapartypatriots.org/content/the-difference-between-the-republican-party-establishment-and-the-tea-party/

23 https://www.teapartypatriots.org/content/war/

24 http://www.mlive.com/lansing-news/index.ssf/2012/12/lansing_business_owner_alleges.html

25 http://dailycaller.com/2012/12/05/why-dick-armey-resigned-from-his-tea-party-organization/

26 https://www.buzzfeed.com/rosiegray/freedomworks-also-lost-their-director-of-campaigns

27 https://www.buzzfeed.com/rosiegray/inside-the-tea-party-factory

28 http://www.cnn.com/interactive/2012/12/us/sandy-hook-timeline/index.html

29 Contrary to popular belief on the Left, the "AR" in AR-15 does not stand for "assault rifle." It stands for ArmaLite, the company that developed it.

30 https://obamawhitehouse.archives.gov/the-press-office/2012/12/14/statement-president-school-shooting-newtown-ct

31 http://nymag.com/daily/intelligencer/2016/09/the-sandy-hook-hoax.html

32 http://www.chronicle.com/blognetwork/tenuredradical/2013/01/sandy-hook-massacre-a-left-wing-hoax/

33 https://www.huffingtonpost.com/2012/12/17/tea-party-nation-sandy-hook-school-shooting-teachers-unions-sex-bureaucracy-_n_2317135.html

34 http://www.cleveland.com/nation/index.ssf/2013/02/gun_control_is_new_focus_for_t.html

35 https://gop.com/growth-and-opportunity-project/

36 *Ibid.* Pages 76 and 22, respectively.

37 https://www.washingtonpost.com/blogs/right-turn/wp/2013/03/18/gop-autopsy-report-goes-bold

38 http://archive.azcentral.com/arizonarepublic/news/articles/2010/04/25/20100425immigration-bill-jan-brewer-arizona.html

39 David Brody: *The Teavangelicals: The Inside Story of How The Evangelicals and The Tea Party are Taking Back America* (Grand Rapids, MI: Zondervan, 2012) p. 19.

40 https://thegrio.com/2013/04/09/tea-party-is-over-ex-activist-says-racism-hypocrisy-killed-the-movement/

41 A longer discussion of this point comes at Brody, p. 63.

42 E-mail exchange with Ralph Reagan, January 1 and 9, 2018.

43 https://www.huffingtonpost.com/2014/06/25/dave-brat-tea-party_n_5531531.html

44 http://www.truth-out.org/news/item/18108-launch-of-green-tea-coalition-drives-a-wedge-through-georgias-tea-party

45 http://www.foxnews.com/politics/2015/01/16/green-tea-coalition-strange-bedfellows-fight-for-solar-power-in-sunshine-state.html

46 https://www.newyorker.com/tech/elements/green-tea-party-solar

47 https://www.yahoo.com/news/tea-party-plans-abandon-gop-stars-083902786.html

48 http://www.bridgemi.com/public-sector/kitchen-table-politics-tea-party-leverages-social-media-advance-causes Joan Fabiano was an early leader who revealed some of her tricks of the trade in this article. She was also kind enough to contribute elsewhere to this book in a separate interview, for which I am thankful.

49 https://www.washingtonpost.com/opinions/eugene-robinson-republicans-hollow-defeat/2013/10/17/ec54eb1c-375e-11e3-ae46-e4248e75c8ea_story.html

50 https://www.usnews.com/opinion/blogs/nicole-hemmer/2014/04/15/on-tax-day-the-tea-party-is-withering

51 http://politicalticker.blogs.cnn.com/2014/02/27/top-tea-party-group-celebrates-five-years/

52 http://www.cnn.com/interactive/2014/politics/hamby-midterms/

53 https://fivethirtyeight.com/features/tea-party-has-outlived-its-usefulness/

54 http://www.washingtonexaminer.com/word-to-the-wise-tea-party-voters-favor-smart-educated-candidates/article/2548642

55 Brody, p. 185.

56 https://www.theatlantic.com/politics/archive/2013/12/why-the-tea-party-isnt-going-anywhere/282591/ Emphasis in original. She added that "at least three successive national election defeats" would be necessary to kill off the TEA Party.

57 http://politicalticker.blogs.cnn.com/2014/04/18/first-on-cnn-amy-kremer-to-resign-from-tea-party-express/

58 http://dailycaller.com/2014/11/05/tea-party-values-and-enthusiasm-pave-the-way-for-gop-victory/

59 https://www.politico.com/magazine/story/2016/08/tea-party-pacs-ideas-death-214164

60 https://www.redstate.com/erick/2014/12/22/the-latest-tea-party-scam-called-from-

202-750-2399/

61 https://www.politico.com/story/2015/01/super-pac-scams-114581?o=0

62 https://www.teapartypatriots.org/2015-annual-report/

63 Notes from telephone conversation with Joan Fabiano, February 25, 2018.

64 https://www.politico.com/magazine/story/2016/08/tea-party-pacs-ideas-death-214164 Overall, this was a very instructive piece by Paul H. Jossey because fiscal issues were always there for local TEA Party units.

65 http://www.teapartytribune.com/2016/01/30/the-tea-party-then-and-now/

66 Notes from telephone conversation with Joan Fabiano, February 25, 2018.

67 http://news.gallup.com/poll/186338/support-tea-party-drops-new-low.aspx

68 https://www.teapartypatriots.org/news/statement-on-keli-carenders-resignation/

69 *Ibid.*

## OF GOD AND MAN IN THE TEA PARTY

1 David Brody: The Teavangelicals: The Inside Story of How The Evangelicals and The Tea Party are Taking Back America (Grand Rapids, MI: Zondervan, 2012) p. 15-16.

2 Theda Skocpol and Vanessa Williamson: The Tea Party and the Remaking of Republican Conservatism (Oxford: Oxford University Press, 2011) p. 35-37.

3 Michael Patrick Leahy: Covenant of Liberty: The Ideological Origins of the Tea Party Movement (New York: Broadside Books, 2012) p. 230-231.

4 Mark Meckler and Jenny Beth Martin: Tea Party Patriots: The Second American Revolution (New York: Henry Holt and Company, 2012) p. 23.

5 https://www.huffingtonpost.com/jim-wallis/how-christian-is-tea-part_b_592170.html

6 https://www.americanthinker.com/articles/2012/08/the_progressive_lefts_secular_theocracy.html As you'll see, Jonathan Wakefield is an author I will cite frequently in this chapter as a prominent example of a Christian TEA Party leader.

7 Brody, p. 20-21.

8 https://www.theatlantic.com/politics/archive/2010/10/is-the-tea-party-simply-a-division-of-the-religious-right/343918/

9 http://www.slate.com/blogs/weigel/2010/10/08/ virginia_tea_party_patriots_convention_lou_dobbs_and_the_next_tea_party_convention.html

10 http://www.pewforum.org/2011/02/23/tea-party-and-religion/ TEA Party regulars were also more hardline conservative on immigration and gun control than their registered voter counterparts overall.

11 https://www.thedailybeast.com/tea-party-is-it-the-christian-right-in-disguise

12 https://newrepublic.com/article/91661/tea-party-christian-right-michele-bachmann

13 https://www.americanthinker.com/articles/2012/08/the_progressive_lefts_secular_theocracy.html

14 https://www.thedailybeast.com/tea-party-is-it-the-christian-right-in-disguise For example, as of the date this was published, "more than 80 anti-abortion laws" and an "unprecedented blitz of measures aimed at getting creationism into public schools" were introduced.

15 Jonathan Wakefield: Saving America: A Christian Perspective Of The Tea Party Movement (Houston: Crossover Publications, 2012), p. 148.

16 Wakefield, p. 86.

17 https://www.thedailybeast.com/the-tea-party-isnt-a-political-movement-its-a-religious-one

18 Ibid.

19 http://www.myajc.com/business/chick-fil-keeps-growing-despite-uproar/9Qtv5hIeJUc59lFUfxZQ3L/

20 https://www.teapartypatriots.org/content/freedom-never-tasted-so-good/

21 http://monoblogue.us/2012/08/01/a-show-of-support/. Years later, Chick-Fil-A still gets a steady stream of business (and employees) from our church and its youth group.

22 Brody, p. 52.

23 Wakefield, p. xxvi.

24 Brody, p. 87-88.

## THE SINCEREST FORM OF FLATTERY

1 This isn't from the transcript. I wrote Levin's statement on my phone as I was listening to the program because I knew it would go somewhere in this book.

2 https://www.politico.com/magazine/story/2018/01/15/the-full-transcript-ben-rhodes-and-samantha-power-216322 Yes, Power admitted “I've had a lot of bad ideas in my life, but none as immortalized as this one.”

3 Hence, the National Popular Vote movement and compact: https://www.nationalpopularvote.com/

4 https://www.dailyprogress.com/news/local/city/charlottesville-city-council-changes-the-names-of-two-renamed-parks/article_9ac64d52-8963-11e8-853a-a3864982745e.html

5 http://www.washingtonexaminer.com/apparently-social-justice-vandals-are-decapitating-revolutionary-war-statues-now/article/2632612

6 https://www.bucyrustelegraphforum.com/story/news/2018/04/26/colonel-crawford-returns-his-perch-outside-courthouse/554693002/

7 http://monoblogue.us/2009/07/28/widespread-panic-about-our-freedom/ As I wrote at the time, “Let me say straight away that I wouldn’t have recommended the noose and effigy of Frank Kratovil.”

8 http://www.thegatewaypundit.com/2017/01/liberal-women-march-trump-leave-trash-heaps-someone-else-clean/

9 https://web.archive.org/web/20100323083209/http://www.cnn.com/2010/OPINION/03/ 18/park.coffee.party/

10 http://www.newsweek.com/what-founder-coffee-party-wants-70529 Given the description of the timing of events in the CNN opinion piece as creating the Facebook page on January 26, Park snapped in the immediate aftermath of the Scott Brown election, described in detail earlier herein.

11 https://web.archive.org/web/20100322192934/http://www.usnews.com/blogs/linda-killian/2010/03/15/meet-the-coffee-party-a-kinder-gentler-more-liberal-tea-party.html

12 https://web.archive.org/web/20100323083209/http://www.cnn.com/2010

/OPINION/03/ 18/park.coffee.party/

13 Their current list of partners is at the bottom of the Coffee Party website, a long scroll down. Here is a handy list from late 2017, before they redid the website: https://web.archive.org/web/20171228045834/http://www.coffeepartyusa.com/our_partners

14 http://www.coffeepartyusa.com/ When this chapter was originally written in 2017 the blog had been untouched since January of that year – while its podcasts remained active – but since then the Coffee Party site has been totally revamped and is current.

15 http://coffeepartyusa.com/2018/10/16/something-special-for-you-for-keeping-us-strong-for-10-years/ Accessed December 1, 2018. That is unless they are counting themselves as part of the Organizing for America crew as that was active in 2008.

16 http://nypost.com/2011/11/13/occupy-wall-street-costs-local-businesses-479400/

17 http://www.telegraph.co.uk/news/worldnews/northamerica/usa/8896636/Occupy-Wall-Street-eviction-as-it-happened-15-November.html

18 https://www.theatlantic.com/politics/archive/2015/06/the-triumph-of-occupy-wall-street/395408/

19 https://www.teapartypatriots.org/content/occupy-wall-street-theyre-no-tea-partiers-2/

20 https://www.teapartypatriots.org/content/ows-vs-the-tea-party/

21 https://www.teapartypatriots.org/misc/tea-party-is-nothing-like-occupy-movement/ This is apparently a reprint of a guest column McClendon penned for the *News-Sentinel* newspaper in Fort Wayne, Indiana. (McClendon still occasionally contributes there.)

## LOOKING FROM ACROSS THE AISLE

1 http://www.rollingstone.com/politics/news/matt-taibbi-on-the-tea-party-20100928

2 *Ibid.*

3 http://nymag.com/daily/intelligencer/2016/05/donald-trump-is-the-tea-party.html

4 http://www.washingtonpost.com/wp-dyn/content/article/2007/02/17/AR2007021701172.html The former VA facility closed in 2011.

5 Mark Meckler and Jenny Beth Martin: *Tea Party Patriots: The Second American Revolution* (New York: Henry Holt and Company, 2012) p. 61-62.

6 https://www.counterpunch.org/2011/03/08/who-are-the-tea-party-patriots/

7 https://www.freep.com/story/opinion/columnists/brian-dickerson/2015/01/18/tea-party-republicans-michigan/21898395/

8 Theda Skocpol and Vanessa Williamson: *The Tea Party and the Remaking of Republican Conservatism* (Oxford: Oxford University Press, 2011), p. 50.

9 Michael Patrick Leahy: *Covenant of Liberty: The Ideological Origins of the Tea Party Movement* (New York: Broadside Books, 2012) p. 216.

10 Meckler and Martin, p. 65.

11 Meckler and Martin, p. 5.

12 Skocpol and Williamson, p. 27.

13 Skocpol and Williamson, p. 28-29.

14 Meckler and Martin, p. 32.

15 Skocpol and Williamson, p.11.

16 http://www.irehr.org/2015/09/15/the-tea-party-movement-in-2015/

17 http://michellemalkin.com/2010/03/26/andrew-breitbart-offers-10000-to-united-negro-college-fund/

18 https://www.mediaite.com/online/video-protesters-in-confrontation-with-black-man-right-in-front-of-confederate-flag/

19 https://www.washingtonpost.com/news/post-politics/wp/2013/10/11/ben-carson-obamacare-worst-thing-since-slavery/

20 https://web.archive.org/web/20100715032843/http://www.cnn.com/2010/POLITICS/07 /14/naacp.tea.party/index.html

21 David Brody: *The Teavangelicals: The Inside Story of How The Evangelicals and The Tea Party are Taking Back America* (Grand Rapids, MI: Zondervan, 2012) p. 97.

# ONBOARD THE TRUMP TRAIN

1 http://www.cnn.com/TRANSCRIPTS/0904/15/lkl.01.html

2 http://www.businessinsider.com/donald-trump-to-oprah-in-1988-win-president-2015-9

3 http://thehill.com/blogs/pundits-blog/presidential-campaign/256159-a-look-back-at-trumps-first-run

4 https://www.thedailybeast.com/the-last-time-trump-wrecked-a-party

5 https://www.politico.com/story/2011/03/donald-trump-birther-051473

6 https://web.archive.org/web/20160413052151/ http://www.cnn.com/2011/OPINION/04/19/byron.trump.president/index.html

7 https://abcnews.go.com/Politics/poll-donald-trump-catapults-place-2012-gop-field/story?id=13318814

8 https://www.politico.com/story/2011/03/donald-trump-birther-051473

9 One example of the entertainment media giving Trump free pixels: https://www.insideedition.com/headlines/2132-is-donald-trump-a-birther

10 And again: https://ew.com/article/2011/04/19/donald-trump-good-morning-america/

11 https://www.cbsnews.com/news/trump-oreilly-spar-over-birther-issue/

12 https://www.c-span.org/video/?299058-1/donald-trump-remarks

13 http://politicalticker.blogs.cnn.com/2011/04/05/trump-to-address-tea-party-rally-in-florida/

14 https://web.archive.org/web/20110421032713/http://blogs.abcnews.com/george/2011/ 04/donald-trump-on-possible-presidential-run-i-might-win-as-an-independent.html

15 https://www.washingtonpost.com/politics/donald-trump-says-he-wont-run-for-president-in-2012/2011/05/16/AFU1FD5G_story.html

16 https://web.archive.org/web/20110518143514/http://www.cnn.com/2011/

POLITICS/05/16/trump.again/index.html

17 *Ibid.*

18 https://www.washingtonpost.com/news/post-politics/wp/2015/08/06/annotated-transcript-the-aug-6-gop-debate/ “They asked me a question as to pro-life or choice. And I said if you let it run, that I hate the concept of abortion. I hate the concept of abortion. And then since then, I've very much evolved. And what happened is friends of mine years ago were going to have a child, and it was going to be aborted. And it wasn't aborted. And that child today is a total superstar, a great, great child. And I saw that. And I saw other instances. And I am very, very proud to say that I am pro-life.”

19 http://www.ontheissues.org/celeb/Donald_Trump_Gun_Control.htm “I generally oppose gun control, but I support the ban on assault weapons and I support a slightly longer waiting period to purchase a gun. With today’s Internet technology we should be able to tell within 72-hours if a potential gun owner has a record.” Cited by site as coming from Trump's 2000 book *The America We Deserve*.

20 http://washington.cbslocal.com/2015/03/19/trump-says-his-business-experience-makes-him-the-best-candidate-to-reform-washington/ “I would make this country so rich that you wouldn’t have to cut it.”

21 https://www.washingtonpost.com/news/post-politics/wp/2015/08/06/annotated-transcript-the-aug-6-gop-debate/ Moderator Bret Baier: “Mr. Trump, it's not just your past support for single- payer health care. You've also supported a host of other liberal policies… you've also donated to several Democratic candidates, Hillary Clinton included, Nancy Pelosi. You explained away those donations saying you did that to get business-related favors.”

22 http://www.mcclatchydc.com/opinion/article88823407.html

23 https://www.thedailybeast.com/how-the-tea-party-got-hijacked-by-trumps-troll-party

24 https://money.cnn.com/2015/06/16/media/donald-trump-apprentice-nbc/

25 http://www.pewresearch.org/fact-tank/2014/11/20/those-from-mexico-will-benefit-most-from-obamas-executive-action/

26 https://money.cnn.com/2015/06/29/media/donald-trump-nbc-ends-relationship/

27 https://money.cnn.com/2015/06/29/media/donald-trump-statement-nbc-brian-williams/index.html

28 https://www.politico.com/story/2016/03/jesse-benton-pro-trump-super-pac-220596

29 https://www.vox.com/2016/6/9/11893300/women-vote-trump-super-pac-donald-trump

30 https://www.teapartypatriots.org/news/tea-party-patriots-ceo-jenny-beth-martins-remarks-from-cpac/ It should be noted that the TEA Party Patriots Citizens Fund endorsed Cruz earlier that month.

31 https://www.politico.com/magazine/story/2016/05/the-trump-sanders-two-step-213903

32 http://www.nationalreview.com/article/438651/fox-news-conservative-media-echo-chamber-hurts-conservatives

33 This is a nice "who's who" of Trump TEA Party supporters, at least at the point I chose to take the archive from – shortly before the election. https://web.archive.org/web/20161022091851/http://teapartyfortrump.org/

34 https://www.thedailybeast.com/tea-partiers-rage-against-rubio-2016

35 https://www.thedailybeast.com/the-tea-party-created-marco-rubio-now-they-can-take-him-out

36 https://www.reuters.com/article/us-usa-election-trump-teaparty-idUSKCN0WH133

37 https://www.youtube.com/watch?v=PFb6NU1giRA

38 http://www.breitbart.com/big-government/2015/09/23/tea-party-activists-say-graham-misses-carsons-point-islamists-pose-threat-to-constitution/

39 https://www.theatlantic.com/politics/archive/2016/05/did-the-tea-party-create-donald-trump/482004/

40 http://www.washingtonexaminer.com/tea-party-sours-on-donald-trump/article/2568552

41 https://www.vox.com/2015/8/7/9115493/tea-party-donald-trump

42 https://www.npr.org/2016/03/04/469149275/tea-party-patriots-stand-behind-sen-ted-cruz-for-president A bit of a misnomer, since TEA Party support was also there for Trump.

43 https://www.thedailybeast.com/how-the-tea-party-got-hijacked-by-trumps-troll-party

44 https://www.themaven.net/theresurgent/erick-erickson/the-tea-party-is-dead-good-riddance-lFhW0bFYnEer12Nn_OXOUQ

45 http://www.latimes.com/politics/la-na-trump-tea-party-divide-20160318-story.html

46 Notes from telephone conversation with Joan Fabiano, February 25, 2018.

47 https://www.politico.com/story/2015/11/donald-trump-katrina-pierson-216005

48 The snowflakes were offended that a TEA Party person would deign to speak at their university – so much so that the event had to become a private event lest the sponsor be stuck with a $2,000 tab for security against what turned out to be 15 protestors – a foreshadow of my final chapter. http://cornellsun.com/2017/02/15/students-protest-private-lecture-calling-it-a-safe-space-for-white-supremacy/

49 http://cornellsun.com/2017/02/15/valentines-dinner-with-a-tea-party-leader-michael-johns-defends-trump/

50 http://www.latimes.com/politics/la-na-trump-tea-party-divide-20160318-story.html

51 http://www.otheringandbelonging.org/trump-the-tea-party-the-republicans-and-the-other/ The quotes within are purportedly from Tea Party Nation's Judson Phillips, but the original links are dead.

52 https://www.thedailybeast.com/how-the-tea-party-got-hijacked-by-trumps-troll-party

53 http://www.breitbart.com/video/2015/09/15/glenn-beck-tea-partiers-who-support-donald-trump-are-racist/

54 http://www.breitbart.com/big-government/2015/09/16/tea-party-activists-blast-beck-over-racism-charges/

55 http://www.renewamerica.com/article/160624

56 https://www.redstate.com/leon_h_wolf/2016/06/11/wont-believe-much-less-money-trump-raised-hillary

57 http://www.wnd.com/2016/05/see-list-of-98-top-republicans-who-refuse-to-back-trump/

58 Such as the TEA Party in the city of my birth. http://toledoteaparty.com/toledo-tea-party-volunteers-make-3000-calls-for-trump/

59 https://web.archive.org/web/20161012024851/ https://www.teapartypatriotscitizensfund.com/trump-endorsement/

60 http://www.foxnews.com/opinion/2016/11/12/how-tea-party-helped-trump-win-election.html

61 http://www.nationalreview.com/article/438651/fox-news-conservative-media-echo-chamber-hurts-conservatives

62 http://www.cnn.com/2007/POLITICS/01/31/biden.obama/

63 https://www.huffingtonpost.com/entry/donald-trump-2-billion-free-media_us_56e83410e4b065e2e3d75935

64 https://www.thestreet.com/story/13896916/1/donald-trump-rode-5-billion-in-free-media-to-the-white-house.html

65 https://www.salon.com/2016/12/02/jill-stein-spoiled-the-2016-election-for-hillary-clinton/

66 http://www.irehr.org/2015/09/15/the-tea-party-movement-in-2015/

67 Theda Skocpol and Vanessa Williamson: *The Tea Party and the Remaking of Republican Conservatism* (Oxford: Oxford University Press, 2011) p. 203.

68 Skocpol and Williamson, p. 215.

69 https://www.redstate.com/diary/davenj1/2016/10/27/bastardization-tea-party/

70 https://www.washingtonpost.com/news/monkey-cage/wp/2016/12/01/how-the-tea-party-learned-to-love-donald-trump/

71 https://www.wsj.com/articles/trumps-style-is-his-substance-1518652786

## OBAMACARE ENTRENCHED

1 Social media conversation with Mark Williams, January 26, 2018. I lightly edited this for clarity.

2 https://www.healthaffairs.org/doi/full/10.1377/hlthaff.2010.0363

3 https://www.teapartypatriots.org/content/supreme-court-rules-against-american-people/

4 http://www.washingtonpost.com/wp-srv/politics/documents/supreme-court-health-care-decision-text.html

5 https://www.teapartypatriots.org/content/cornyn-on-obamacare-repeal-and-replace/

6 https://www.teapartypatriots.org/content/will-the-presidents-health-care-law-

survive-under-a-president-romney/

7 http://www.nytimes.com/2006/04/13/us/13health.html

8 http://www.modernhealthcare.com/article/20171114/NEWS/171119935

9 https://www.theatlantic.com/politics/archive/2017/02/resistance-tea-party/516105/

10 http://d35brb9zkkbdsd.cloudfront.net/wp-content/uploads/2009/07/townhallactionmemo.pdf This was a “leaked memo” alluded to in a separate story – see https://www.freep.com/story/opinion/columnists/nancy-kaffer/2016/12/22/donald-trump-tea-party/95757610/. “When a quiet town hall turns feisty, well, it's a good story.”

11 http://www.motherjones.com/politics/2016/12/progressives-tea-party-tactics-stop-trump/ This is actually a very in-depth playbook of how the Left was going to stop Trump.

12 *Ibid.*

13 https://www.theatlantic.com/technology/archive/2017/01/womens-march-protest-count/514166/

14 https://www.nytimes.com/2017/01/21/us/womens-march.html

15 An example from my adopted hometown: https://www.facebook.com/events/266508697103490/permalink/266811363739890/ I covered the event for readers of my website: http://monoblogue.us/2017/02/18/point-and-counterpoint-in-salisbury-some-observations/

16 Here's a local example of my Congressman's meeting gone national: http://www.cnn.com/2017/03/31/politics/maryland-town-hall-harris/index.html

17 https://qz.com/1065652/the-american-left-has-its-own-tea-party-and-its-coming-for-donald-trump/

18 *Ibid.*

19 https://www.mercurynews.com/2017/05/13/anti-trump-indivisible-tea-party/ Bear in mind this story was written about five months after Klein and Greenberg began.

20 https://www.nytimes.com/2017/10/07/us/politics/democrats-resistance-fundraising.html

21 https://capitalresearch.org/article/indivisibly-divided-faux-insurgents-for-the-

professional-left/ This was almost literally hot off the press as I began this chapter.

22 https://www.redstate.com/joshkimbrell/2017/10/01/socialists-democratic-tea-partiers/

23 This is a great "Cliff's Notes" version of outside-the-box thinking: https://www.conservativereview.com/articles/20-ideas-to-crush-obamacare-and-cure-americas-health-care-crisis/

24 http://www.foxnews.com/politics/2017/07/26/obamacare-straight-repeal-fails-on-senate-vote.html

25 http://cfif.org/v/index.php/commentary/56-health-care/3770-republicans-should-reject-bipartisan-solution-for-obamacare

26 https://twitter.com/RandPaul/status/909776871411392512

27 http://www.breitbart.com/big-government/2017/08/09/women-trump-pac-disappointed-trumps-luther-strange-endorsement-al-senate-race/

28 https://patriotpost.us/articles/51630

29 https://spectator.org/the-establishment-gops-meaningless-majority/

30 https://www.washingtonpost.com/investigations/woman-says-roy-moore-initiated-sexual-encounter-when-she-was-14-he-was-32/2017/11/09/1f495878-c293-11e7-afe9-4f60b5a6c4a0_story.html

31 *Ibid.*

32 http://www.newsweek.com/these-republicans-demand-roy-moore-withdraws-alabama-senate-race-710461

33 https://spectator.org/a-crazy-week-of-moore-reasons-to-vote-for-roy-moore/

34 http://www.cnn.com/2017/12/07/politics/al-franken-resignation-decision/index.html

35 https://www.politico.com/story/2017/12/10/democrats-alabama-roy-moore-doug-jones-288631

36 https://www.redstate.com/joesquire/2017/12/08/conservative-media-honesty-problem/

37 https://www.washingtonpost.com/news/powerpost/wp/2017/12/28/roy-moore-asks-alabama-court-for-a-new-election/

38 https://www.redstate.com/brandon_morse/2017/12/29/left-looks-back-resistance-accomplished-finds...nothing/

39 https://capitalresearch.org/article/socialism-the-tea-party-of-the-left/

40 http://thehill.com/homenews/house/360856-hoyer-heads-to-the-heartland-on-a-listening-tour

41 https://cohen.house.gov/media-center/press-releases/members-introduce-articles-impeachment

42 http://thehill.com/homenews/house/360856-hoyer-heads-to-the-heartland-on-a-listening-tour

43 https://www.politico.com/magazine/story/2018/03/14/pennsylvania-election-results-2018-analysis-217360

44 http://michaeljohnsonfreedomandprosperity.blogspot.com/2017/02/trumpism-can-make-america-great-again_82.html This speech before the Cornell Political Union drew 75 spectators and 15 protestors – who got most of the press. As noted when I cited Johns earlier, the event was made private when the university decreed the CPU pay for security to the tune of $2,000.

45 https://www.politico.com/magazine/story/2018/06/15/raul-labrador-profile-tea-party-congress-2018-218822

## ENDGAME: THE 2018 MIDTERM ELECTIONS

1 https://www.usatoday.com/story/news/nation/2018/01/04/drawing-today-decide-virginia-state-house-race-majority-party/1002910001/

2 https://www.washingtonpost.com/local/virginia-politics/danica-roem-will-be-vas-first-openly-transgender-elected-official-after-unseating-conservative-robert-g-marshall-in-house-race/2017/11/07/d534bdde-c0af-11e7-959c-fe2b598d8c00_story.html

3 Given subsequent alleged election shenanigans by the Harris camp, the question of whether Pittenger really lost is a valid one.

4 https://www.rollcall.com/news/lets_get_along_house_freshmen_embrace_bipartisan_comity-222476-1.html

5 https://www.politicsnc.com/nc-09-the-tea-party-challenges-pittenger/

6 https://www.charlotteobserver.com/news/politics-government/article9114665.html

7 http://www.teapartyexpress.org/9377/tea-party-express-endorses-mark-harris-for-u-s-congress-in-north-carolina

8 https://www.teapartypatriots.org/news/citizens-fund-endorses-mark-harris-for-congress-in-nc-09/

9 https://www.charlotteobserver.com/news/politics-government/election/article211815314.html

10 https://ballotpedia.org/North_Carolina%27s_9th_Congressional_District_election,_2018

11 https://www.newsobserver.com/news/politics-government/article222436915.html

12 http://www.wect.com/2019/03/15/nc-special-election-final-list-candidates-determined/

13 https://www.teapartypatriots.org/news/citizens-fund-endorses-mark-sanford-in-sc-01/

14 From the 2013 special election to fill the SC-1 seat: http://www.teapartyexpress.org/6637/tea-party-express-endorses-mark-sanford-in-sc-01

15 https://twitter.com/realDonaldTrump/status/1006630395067039744 Polls closed at 7 p.m. that evening, so Trump's Tweet was put out just before the end-of-work voting rush.

16 https://www.nbcnews.com/politics/politics-news/stunned-grateful-katie-arrington-republican-who-beat-sanford-credits-trump-n882796

17 https://www.redstate.com/streiff/2018/06/13/mark-sanfords-loss-last-night-shows-dangers-underestimating-president-trump-touch-rank-file-gop/

18 http://www.teapartyexpress.org/9402/tea-party-express-endorses-katie-arrington-for-u-s-congress-in-south-carolina The endorsement was made October 12.

19 https://www.nytimes.com/elections/results/south-carolina-house-district-1

20 https://www.cnn.com/2018/06/26/politics/alexandria-ocasio-cortez-joe-crowley-new-york-14-primary/index.html

21 https://www.nytimes.com/2018/06/26/nyregion/joseph-crowley-ocasio-cortez-democratic-primary.html

22 https://www.cnn.com/2018/07/25/politics/joe-crowley-working-families-party-democratic-house-caucus-race/index.html Remember back when I talked about New York's arcane ballot rules? Here's the example.

23 https://twitter.com/JoeCrowleyNY/status/1017408740855693314 In a Tweet, Crowley stated the issue: "I don't plan on moving out of New York, have a clean record, hope God's will is that I don't die, and won't commit what I honestly believe to be election fraud."

24 https://www.nytimes.com/elections/results/new-york-house-district-14

25 Jealous defeated his closest competitor, Prince George's County Executive Rushern Baker, by 10 points. Another county executive (and early favorite), Kevin Kamenetz of Baltimore County, suddenly died just weeks before the primary, too late to remove his name from the ballot. Besides the perennial candidates, Jealous also defeated a sitting state senator, former advisers to both Michelle Obama and Hillary Clinton, and the top attorney of the state's largest law firm. He even outpolled Republican Governor Larry Hogan by 21,000 votes, although that's simply a product of lopsided partisan voter registration numbers. https://elections.maryland.gov/elections/2018/results/primary/gen_results_2018_1_003-.html

26 https://www.usnews.com/news/politics/articles/2018-09-03/incumbents-fresh-faces-facing-off-in-massachusetts-primary

27 https://www.cnn.com/2018/09/04/politics/massachusetts-primary-democratic-direction/index.html

28 *Ibid.* Like Ocasio-Cortez, Pressley won in a majority-minority district. Unlike Ocasio-Cortez, Pressley had a walkover November election – one of four such contests out of nine Congressional districts in deep-blue Massachusetts.

29 https://www.usnews.com/news/articles/2016-12-27/trump-victory-shoots-consumer-confidence-to-15-year-high

30 https://news.gallup.com/poll/197474/economic-confidence-surges-election.aspx As one may expect, Republicans were suddenly bullish on the economy while Democrats were more apprehensive. The difference was that far more Republicans were dismayed with Obama's policies than Democrats were fearful of Trump's.

31 https://www.cnbc.com/2018/06/05/there-are-more-jobs-than-people-out-of-work.html While some of this was a product of what's described as a "skills mismatch," the sheer fact we have this situation is a testament to revived economic growth.

32 Just one of many examples, written days after passage: https://thinkprogress.org/trump-tax-buybacks-5f9f78cf6e27/

33 https://www.atr.org/sites/default/files/assets/NationalListofTaxReformGoodNews_2.pdf As of October 19, 2018, this was a 244-page list of companies that had announced new capital investments or passed on their tax savings to employees as raises, bonuses, or in additional benefits.

34 https://cei.org/blog/trump-regulations-federal-register-page-count-lowest-quarter-century As of the end of 2017 it was down to the 53,000 page range – territory unseen since the Bush 41 administration.

35 I say "proposed" because, as of publication, Congress has not voted on USMCA. https://www.agprofessional.com/article/usmca-ratification-around-corner

36 https://observer.com/2018/07/liberal-activist-groups-protest-trump-scotus-pick/

37 https://www.washingtontimes.com/news/2018/jul/9/womens-march-mocked-press-release-opposing-supreme/ I don't care who you are: proofreading is your friend.

38 Said Biden: "It is my view that if a Supreme Court justice resigns tomorrow or within the next several weeks, or resigns at the end of the summer, President Bush should consider following the practice of a majority of his predecessors and not… name a nominee until after the November election is completed." https://www.nytimes.com/2016/02/23/us/politics/joe-biden-speech-from-1992-gives-gop-fodder-in-court-fight.html

39 https://www.washingtonpost.com/opinions/trump-gets-to-fill-kennedys-seat--and-its-all-thanks-to-harry-reid/2018/06/29/048da3f4-7ba7-11e8-93cc-6d3beccdd7a3_story.html

40 https://www.judiciary.senate.gov/imo/media/doc/09-27-18%20Ford%20Testimony.pdf

41 https://poll.qu.edu/national/release-detail?ReleaseID=2574

42 All Democrats except Sen. Joe Manchin of West Virginia voted to retain cloture, while all Republicans except for Alaska's Sen. Lisa Murkowski voted yes on ending debate. "I can see 2022 from my house," teased Sarah Palin in a Tweet.

43 Because Montana Sen. Steve Daines (a yes vote for confirmation) was to be away at his daughter's (obviously planned well in advance) wedding, Sen. Lisa Murkowski of Alaska – who was against confirmation – made an agreement with Daines to forgo the final vote so as to not change the result and allow Daines to attend. Thus, the final vote reflected the 51-49 vote for cloture made two days earlier.

44 https://www.foxnews.com/politics/kavanaugh-abandons-script-to-deliver-blistering-opening-statement-on-assault-accusation

45 Regarding the Kavanaugh questioning: “In less than five minutes, Graham appeared to absolve years of shortcomings in the eyes of right-wing purists. Republican foes old and new sang his praises.” https://www.postandcourier.com/politics/sc-conservatives-say-lindsey-graham-rebuilt-reputation-in-kavanaugh-hearing/article_f5c09fe8-c327-11e8-9e09-6bc68ccc06f1.html

46 https://www.lgraham.senate.gov/public/index.cfm/2018/9/transcript-of-graham-s-remarks-on-kavanaugh-nomination

47 https://www.youtube.com/watch?v=IRnmnxVtDqg

48 https://www.weeklystandard.com/jim-swift/bomb-scare-shows-that-alex-joness-legacy-is-more-conspiracy-theorists

49 https://twitter.com/DineshDSouza/status/1055494477748551683

50 https://www.wired.com/story/how-feds-tracked-mail-bomb-suspect-cesar-sayoc/

51 https://www.usatoday.com/story/news/nation/2018/11/09/pipe-bomb-suspect-cesar-sayoc-indicted-weapon-mass-destruction/1924095002/

52 https://nypost.com/2019/03/21/maga-bomber-cesar-sayoc-breaks-down-as-he-pleads-guilty-faces-life-in-prison/

53 https://www.rushlimbaugh.com/daily/2018/10/26/drive-bys-call-arrested-suspect-maga-bomber/

54 https://www.weeklystandard.com/andrew-egger/the-arrest-of-bomber-cesar-sayoc-and-the-false-flag-conservatives

55 https://www.foxnews.com/us/pittsburgh-synagogue-shooting-leaves-11-dead-and-6-wounded-suspect-hit-with-multiple-charges

56 https://pittsburgh.cbslocal.com/2018/10/30/squirrel-hill-protests-president-trump-tree-of-life-synagogue/

57 https://patriotpost.us/articles/59135-the-caravasion-is-a-sideshow

58 https://www.themaven.net/theresurgent/contributors/breaking-pentagon-to-deploy-5-000-soldiers-to-mexico-border-Tiztd6gbkkah93Re6KpxjQ/

59 https://www.aljazeera.com/news/2018/10/hate-critics-slam-trump-anti-caravan-troop-surge-181029233810416.html

60 https://www.dailystar.co.uk/news/world-news/739010/migrant-caravan-refuse-mexico-housing-jobs-donald-trump

61 https://www.wkyc.com/article/news/nation-now/while-kemps-campaign-says-election-is-over-abrams-campaign-claims-major-victory-following-federal-judges-ruling/465-af53b8ca-027b-4320-81cf-f71dc0b91397

62 https://www.cnn.com/2018/11/11/politics/florida-recount-palm-beach-county/index.html

63 https://www.miamiherald.com/news/politics-government/election/article221709545.html

64 https://www.miamiherald.com/news/politics-government/state-politics/article221862885.html

65 https://www.fresnobee.com/news/politics-government/election/local-election/article222033525.html

66 http://www.rollcall.com/news/politics/5-house-races-still-uncalled-nearly-2-weeks-midterms

67 https://www.cnn.com/2018/11/12/politics/2018-election-what-changed/index.html

68 https://www.14news.com/2018/11/30/democratic-sweep-california-raises-gop-suspicion/

69 http://articles.latimes.com/1985-05-02/news/mn-20101_1_house-votes

70 Would Florida in 2000 have turned out the way it did if Republican Katherine Harris wasn't the state's Secretary of State? She eventually parlayed her notoriety into a Congressional seat, serving two terms there before losing a Senate bid.

71 Some moderate Democrats already believe so: https://thehill.com/opinion/campaign/ 413951-democrats-beware-we-are-leaning-left-too-far

72 One instant analysis: https://www.washingtonpost.com/politics/for-democrats-a-midterm-election-that-keeps-on-giving/2018/11/09/b4075ef2-e456-11e8-ab2c-b31dcd53ca6b_story.html

## EPILOGUE: SO WHAT COMES NEXT?

1 Social media conversation with Mark Williams, January 26, 2018. I lightly edited this for clarity.

2 http://www.history.com/topics/american-revolution/boston-tea-party

3 http://www.boston-tea-party.org/essays/essay6.html

4 https://www.bostonteapartyship.com/the-aftermath

5 https://www.historyguy.com/americanrevolution/boston_tea_party.htm#.WnUwtainGM8

6 Social media conversation with Eric Eisenhammer, January 28, 2018.

7 Dick Armey and Matt Kibbe, *Give Us Liberty: A Tea Party Manifesto* (New York: William Morrow, 2010) p. 70.

8 Armey and Kibbe, p. 177.

9 Since my church uses the King James Version of the Bible, that's the version I use here.

10 http://www.washingtonexaminer.com/republicans-repeal-and-replace-the-tea-party/article/2629829

11 https://www.washingtontimes.com/news/2017/nov/4/majority-millennials-want-live-socialist-fascist-o/

12 http://variety.com/2018/music/awards/hillary-clinton-reads-fire-and-fury-at-the-grammys-watch-1202679822/

13 http://variety.com/2018/tv/awards/grammys-ratings-oscars-1202680720/

14 https://www.redstate.com/kiradavis/2018/03/02/dear-conservative-parents-stop-raising-politicians-pundits/

15 http://www.christianitytoday.com/news/2017/december/johnson-amendment-repeal-blocked-final-gop-tax-bill-byrd.html

16 https://billygraham.org/story/billy-graham-my-heart-aches-for-america/

www.ingramcontent.com/pod-product-compliance
Lightning Source LLC
Chambersburg PA
CBHW051343280526
45784CB00007B/2789